NOTES from the NORTH COUNTRY

To Mike —

Have a nice Birthday

Love

Mom + Dad

NOTES from the NORTH COUNTRY

by
O. B. Eustis

Ann Arbor
The University of Michigan Press

To Eve
for a wifetime
of muddy boots

Contents

January

The bricks and stone of the fireplace reach to wrap me in the warmth of their security blanket. I nod and maybe snore a bit, or waken hours later to see red eyes still watching patiently from among the ashes.

A fireplace has to be one of the truly great pleasures a home can enjoy. Surely an open fire has brought more comfort and security to mankind than all his other discoveries. Even the marvel of television comes out poor by comparison. I count myself lucky not to have missed the pleasure of fire.

In our cities there are whole generations that have never smelled clean wood smoke, or stood, back to a fire and steamed out the cold after a day in the snow, or felt the sheer delight of fire glow on red-frosted hands, or seen a loved one's face, light touched by the master brush of flickering flames. What a pity that they may never know.

We have a fire every winter evening at our house and a light wood fire any other season that cool gives an excuse. Usually we start with factory scraps for kindling because we have them. They are efficient starters, and I'm lazy. For real satisfaction in fire starting you need wild kindling.

Sometimes I walk through the conifers snapping off low dry branches. The pruning is good for the trees, and an armful gives a spectacular start for a fire. When the flames from crumpled paper licks up through the cedar and fir twigs there's an exhuberant rush of flames, snaps, and crackles. Keep the screen closed tightly. What a sense of accomplishment! We really laid a good fire this time!

Conifers aren't much good except for kindling. As fire logs they give little heat and spit sparks eternally. For a real fire, hardwood's the thing—the heavier the better. Oak, beech, and sugar maple lead the list. At our place all these are scarce. Disease-killed elm is almost as good. It seasons standing, and when hard frozen, sticks to twelve inches are splitable. Birch is good, clean, and looks pretty stacked by the chimney. Dry poplar is spring and fall wood—cheery and fast, and not too hot. It snaps when not plumb dry. Our pitted carpet bears witness to my penchant for watching its lively flames with the screen open.

But, any wood is better than no fire at all—and whatever kind, the flames of the last log at night gives peace and comfort that you just can't match another way. ✺

People who live in snow country have a library of wildlife stories denied our southern brethren. Everything that walks, crawls, or hops writes a continuous story of its life from first infant step to last dying twitch. Most of the stories are legible only to those species with a good sense of smell.

Men have trained dogs to do some reading for them, but the stories lose most of the important details in translation. Usually all we get is, "He went that-a-way" or "Here he is." With snow, suddenly every word is visible. All we have to do is learn to read. It's easy to see that each species leaves distinctive prints. The real expert recognizes individuals. Like fingerprints, each individual's trail is different, both in appearance and odor.

I once had a deer hound bitch that could stick with a single trail through the confusing tracks of a whole herd. The dimness of years assures me she ran only bucks. Occasional recollection makes them never less than four pointers—a real canine philologist. You don't have to be that good to read most of the stories.

This winter has been good for tracking. Warm January weather kept snow depths down. Light fresh snow on the hard crust held every toe print etched in finest detail. Red squirrel tracks are everywhere. A half-dozen fox squirrels trace the larger script of their courting activity. How could so few make so many tracks?

The fascinating thing about tracking is that it tells of wildlife in its normal activities. Wild animals are shy. They usually see us first. Usually we see only their efforts to escape. Some of the most interesting are out only at night.

Mild weather has kept the river open and most animals active. The other morning I picked up two otter tracks above the house—across the floodplain ice, through the swamp to a hillside pasture—two hops and "whee," a belly whop slide away down the slope. Then a zigzag game of tag to the fish pond outlet—a mud-splashing race downstream, and one last slide into the river. No hunting, just play.

The warm weather aroused the sleeping skunks. Two came muddy footed from under a stump pile. No games for them; a sedate shuffling constitutional on a mild winter evening. They enter an old woodchuck hole and don't come out. Now, why did they change midwinter quarters?

A fox dragged something here, ten inches across, and limp, for the drag is deepest at the ends. I search for telltale hairs on the brush—nothing. The track leads downstream more than a mile. Darkness stops the reading. Fresh snow erases the record.

Now, I'll not know what he had, or where he went, or why. A mystery story! Next episode—continued. I'll find another chapter soon and get to know more about the author. 🐾

We run a trapline at our house. A half-dozen traps catch two to four mice per week. When I first discovered mice in the garage I thought we had moved some house mice in the packages from our old home. Not so—the mice we catch are deer mice, one of the many species of white-footed mice which inhabit our woodlands.

There are some 250 kinds of mice in North America. About 15 species are white-footed mice. The deer mouse is the most common. Anyone who has maintained a deer camp knows them. They nest in mattresses, shirt pockets, or any other sheltered corner.

Deer mice don't get their name from inhabiting deer camps. It derives from their color which is similar to our favorite big game. Their bellies and the undersides of their tails are white the same as our deer. House mice are gray, top and bottom, with scaly tails. The mice I catch are gray on top and white underneath, all the way to their tail tips. Their scientific name *Peromyscus maniculatus* means "slender mouse with little gloves." It suits their dapper appearance.

Just about all our woodlands have some kind of white-footed mice. They live mainly on seeds and berries, but eat lots of insects, snails, or any kind of meat lying about. They are not the mice that girdle our freshly planted trees. This crime is the work of their cousins, the meadow mice, a short-tailed vole that loves bark and prefers to spend the winter under the snow in open country.

Deer mice do most of their winter traveling on top of the snow. You can tell their tracks by a series of little paired holes. Usually the hind feet land in the prints of their front paws. In mud or very shallow snow, you can see the five toes of their hind feet and four toes of their front feet whenever the two pairs don't coincide.

Deer mice are careful about their appearance. They spend a lot of time cleaning their faces and whiskers, just like a cat. They also groom the fur over their whole body, sometimes spending fifteen or twenty minutes at it. They are, however, messy housekeepers. They go to the toilet right in their nests, which is one reason they aren't welcome in our homes and camps. When the nests get too foul, they just move, like the Texan who trades his car because of dirty ashtrays.

Deer mice have whiskers worthy of a hippie. They are born with them. Our dachshund once dug out a nest of newborn deer mice. They were naked, pink, and crinkly, but each had a fine set of whiskers.

If we were born with whiskers, I wonder if we would ever shave them off. ✹

Hairy and downy woodpeckers look like big and little brothers of the same family. They are almost identical in color, but different in size. They live in harmony side by side in our woods. In nature this is known as a sympatric pair of species. Coopers and sharp-shinned hawks are another sympatric pair of American birds.

Downys are our smallest woodpeckers. They are usually more abundant than the hairys, and more tolerant of man's presence. I have been studying both species this winter. The elm cutting where I watch is well back in the woods. Here both species seem about equal in number. There are piles of elm slash lying about, and a few sick elms totter over the river. The bark of most of the elm branches is riddled by bark beetles. These beetles live in the bark. It is not necessary for the woodpeckers to dig through to the wood to get them. They knock off the outer flakes, run their tongues into the exposed galleries and harpoon the insects. A woodpecker's tongue has a barbed point. He can thrust it out at least twice the length of his beak. It saves a lot of digging.

Downys and hairys don't compete, though they seek the same prey. The downys concentrate on the down slash and smaller limbs. Hairys go after the big wood. As they search they color the branches by exposing unweathered bark. Wood that has been thoroughly worked stands out bright tan against the gray winter landscape.

Occasionally the two species search the same wood, but never at the same time. Hairy woodpeckers would occasionally move to a limb just vacated by a downy. Their longer tongue reach, almost two inches, makes it profitable to follow the smaller birds. I did not see the downy woodpeckers ever follow the hairys.

Woodpeckers don't make much noise when feeding. Their steady tapping is as subdued as possible. More noise would simply invite predators. They can make a real fuss when they want to, and do so in spring. Then a loud tattoo on a dry limb establishes their territories and calls a mate. You can call them to you by tapping the same rhythm on a bare log.

Both these woodpeckers roost in cavities, some use old nests, and others dig winter roosts. They work efficiently, striking first to one side then to the other to remove sizable chips. Man may have learned to use an axe by watching woodpeckers.

I marvel at their ability. Their courtship drumming echoes over the forest, yet yields no chips. A slight change in angle, and a quiet tapping makes the chips and bark fly. Hairys and downys, big and little woodsmen, experts at their trade. 🦅

Nature has subtle ways of disclosing her secrets. The other day she used intense cold to show me some of my neighbors' winter homes. A subzero sunrise disclosed a plume of steam rising from a brush-covered hollow stump. The opening through the snow was embroidered with inch-long frost crystals.

The hard crust showed no tracks. I suspected skunks. The size of the steam plume indicated several animals. Female skunks like community winter dens. They don't hibernate, but stay inside in cold weather.

Further search for steam plumes found a wisp of vapor coming from high in the crotch of a half-dead poplar. A hole at the bottom contained bean-shaped droppings—porcupine.

My three-year battle with these rodents has finally gotten them under control on our place. In reasonable numbers I can view them objectively. They are almost as much fun as "Pogo Possum's" comic strip colleague.

Porcupines have the noisiest courtship of any mammal in our woods. The male has a falsetto voice, and the female squalls. Last fall a friend tape-recorded the action. It sounded like a Chinese Tiny Tim mooning over a reluctant contralto.

The young are born in spring after seven months gestation. Almost always there is only one baby. He is well developed at birth—eyes open, about ten inches long, and with a full set of quills. The quills harden within a half hour.

Last spring I found a little porcupine on a cedar branch about six feet up. He could only have been a few days old, and was one of the cutest wild babies I have ever seen—but very solemn. My close examination caused erect bristles and vigorous lashing of his miniature tail—embattled infancy.

Little porcupines develop fast. They can walk in a few hours, climb in a day or two, and start eating green food within a week. They are weaned a few days later.

Except at mating, porcupines are solitary animals. I visited my little porcupine occasionally, and one day found him on the ground. Unaware of my presence he would curl in a ball, erect his quills, and lash his tail. Sometimes he would rush backward a few steps—a lone little wild baby playing war games by himself.

Porcupines are strict vegetarians. In summer they like green herbs and vegetables, particularly sweet corn. In spring it's fresh tree buds and flowers. Winter diet is evergreen twigs or the inner bark of almost any kind of tree. They spit out the corky outer bark and eat the phloem and cambium layers. That is where the tree stores sugars and starch.

Porkys dearly love salt. That's why my steaming neighbor is not welcome so close to the house. I'm afraid he'll sample the snow shovel handle or the salt-stained tires of my car. In his hollow he is home free. I hope I won't have to catch him off base.

To really appreciate the beauty of a mink coat you should see one against the winter snow—on its original owner. Yesterday I watched one along our river. The mink loped along the streamside ice, detouring occasionally to explore brush piles and stumps. Finally she disappeared through a crack in the ice.

This was a small animal. A big male would be half again as large. Through the binoculars I could see the wind ripple her rich brown coat just as I once saw a furrier blow on a prize pelt to show off its texture. Hers was given added beauty by the animation of her hump-backed gait and the intensity of her streamside search.

All members of the weasel family have similar gaits—an inch worm sort of gallop. The hind feet land just about in the front footprints, giving a two-by-two track in the snow. I can't tell a small mink track from a large weasel's, except that the mink usually ends up in water.

This little mink lives here year round. She moves nightly along both sides of our river. In the fresh deep snow she sometimes tunnels through like a weasel. I have never seen a mink walk, but from her tracks I find she sometimes pushes a belly-down trough through the snow. Once I found a slide mark on the ice like her big cousins, the otters, make in play.

Varying water levels in our river often leaves a bankside passage under the ice. This is used for travel by all sorts of wildlife. I think sometimes the ducks, which dive for food in open water, come up in this ice tunnel for air. This morning I watched three whistlers feeding upstream from where I throw corn. Every so often one emerged flying from a dive. I put it down to just skittishness, for they always returned to the baited area.

A big fox squirrel came out to get corn. He drank at the waters edge, then dug under last night's snow. Suddenly a brown streak flashed across the ice. A scrambled mixture of brown, gray, and orange fur—a mad dash to the shore, and the squirrel made it up a tree. Our little mink scrambled up a few feet, then returned to the ice. She had missed a squirrel dinner by inches.

Later I examined the story in the snow. A big crack gave access to the underice passage. The mink had hunted there, frightened the whistlers, and finally used it as a cover to get as close as possible to the squirrel. A few rusty hairs on the ice showed how close the kill had been. 🐾

We males have our moments of foolishness around females. When I was young, it was whistling, showing off, and general horsing around when girls strolled by the corner drugstore. Now it's more apt to be horn blowing, tire squealing, or gunning of a snowmobile motor—modernization of our courtship display.

The other day I watched some goldeneye drakes behaving the same way. Five of them have been inseparable this winter. Their favorite hangout is the point where we spread corn. There they dive in one, two, three order until well fed, then swim in close rank, simply enjoying the company.

One day three hens appeared. The drakes fluffed their head feathers to twice the normal size. Necks stretched, bills pointed far forward. One threw his head back to his rump, bill pointed straight up. The others imitated in order. Orange feet flashed out as the males showed how far they could kick water behind—tire squealing on a January river.

Male foolishness. January is no time for duck courtship. The hens play out the charade by completely ignoring the show. Maybe they giggle a little—it happens. Serious courting must await the warming of spring.

What prompted this unseasonable show-off? One of the hens has a yellow-tipped bill. Normally goldeneye hens reserve this for spring and summer. Their bills turn black in fall. The yellow bill tip is courting-time dress. Who can blame the drakes for acting up?

Most females advertise the approach of courtship time by color, or odor, or shape. I remember the first time I noticed it. I must have been about fourteen years old. It makes males act kind of foolish long before there is any serious intention of mating. Those drake goldeneyes were just doing what comes naturally.

Today the yellow-billed female didn't show. All the hens have black winter bills. The five bachelors ignore them. Small fry too young to create interest? Or is it just winter dress that covers up their charms? Around town I see a lot more male courtship displays when the girls first shed their winter coats.

The spring courting of goldeneye ducks is one of our finest wildlife shows. When the first open water appears in lake ice, look for little flocks of these black and white divers in every open hole. Several drakes beseige one shyly interested hen. Time and again they repeat the courtship ritual. She finally chooses one and lies prone in the water beside him. Females of many duck species stretch on the water when ready to mate. The goldeneye carries it to an extreme. She drifts as if dead for many minutes, while her chosen mate swims around her. Finally mating takes place in and under the water. 🌾

Flying squirrels are cuddly. Everything about them seems to invite snuggling. If their nocturnal habits didn't make them so seldom seen, I think they would have made a much better model for a child's toy than Teddy Roosevelt's bear cub.

Recently I found one of these little fellows looking me over from the mouth of my favorite wood duck box. This box, in an isolated tree protected with a metal sleeve, seemed impregnable. It has produced five consecutive duck broods, never once disturbed by coons, squirrels, or mice. Now I find it usurped by these lovable little rodents. I must make a hard decision before spring—evict these delightful tenants, or make our most beautiful ducks find a new nest cavity.

Flying squirrels don't fly. They have folds of skin between wrists and ankles. When at rest this gives them the pudgy cuddly look that is so appealing. When they spread their limbs the membrane is stretched, converting them to an efficient, almost square glider. The tail is flat like a big, soft feather. From a tall tree they can easily glide thirty or forty yards, so had no trouble reaching my protected duck box.

Flying squirrels steer in the air by raising or lowering arms. This warps their flattened form like the ailerons on an airplane—prototype for the Wright brothers? At landing they bring hind legs forward, lift the tail, and land with a thump. Sit quietly at dusk, where they live, and these thumps may be the first indication of their activity.

For some reason they don't come to our feeders. One of our friends has them regularly. They quickly become tame and will sit feeding even when floodlighted. They enjoy seeds and suet. Ours seem to prefer the deciduous forest just upstream. Flying squirrels are great insect eaters. They will seek out wormy acorns to get the white grubs. Meat of any kind attracts them. Carrion, baby birds, and eggs are gobbled up. They are much more carnivorous than our other squirrels.

My first encounter with flying squirrels was in my childhood home. The family was aroused one night by a ruckus in my oldest brother's bedroom. He had made a dip net of a coat hanger and pajama pants and was trying to capture a very active soot-covered flying squirrel. The frightened little animal dashed madly around the picture molding. When cornered, it would sail across the room, scamper up the window drapes, and back to the molding.

Finally, amid the bedlam of five screaming kids, my parents ordered all doors thrown open, and the squirrel escaped into the night. I think that sooty night prompted installation of central heating. Shortly thereafter all the fireplace chimneys were sealed.

Yes, flying squirrels are cuddly, but don't frighten them, especially if they've come down the chimney. 🦌

One of our hairy woodpeckers is a real musician. Recent clear cold nights have finally tuned his sounding board to the proper pitch. This morning he gave his first winter concert. Just as the sun gilded the cross-river hardwoods, his clear tattoo pealed across the forest. What a joyous way to announce winter sunshine.

All woodpeckers drum in spring. Then it is a way to establish territories and advertise for mates. Only a few individuals drum in winter. A big maple across the river has several bone-white bare limbs. When hard frozen, one of these has a bell-like pitch. Our black and white drummer seems to know when conditions are just right. He is very particular.

He doesn't play on cloudy days. Dampness muffles the drum beats. As soon as the sun thaws the surface of his anvil the concert is over. Even when performing he keeps his flourishes short. It is as if he paused after each burst to savor the sound. He has no full musical scale. A single tone must do. Accents and echoes are his tools—a frozen sunrise forest his amphitheater.

I think ornithologists place too much emphasis on the instincts of their subjects. Birds deserve more credit for individuality. I cannot believe that our morning percussionist performs just from some mistimed instinct to claim territory. Art for art's sake is not reserved just for man.

We have a wealth of woodpeckers. Dying elms have encouraged a steady population increase. We watch them by the hour. They are a kaleidoscope of personalities.

Woodpeckers are naturally preoccupied with tree trunks. They dig homes in trunk hollows and find much of their food under the bark. The ones that visit us fly in at rooftop level. They stop high on the balsams, then dive headfirst down the trunks to feeder level. None of our other visitors are so adept at vertical flight. They put sky divers to shame. Both hairys and downys follow the same routes, but individuals vary greatly in performance.

Some dive with the dash and flourish of supreme confidence. Others flutter brakes long before landing. Most erupt like skyrockets when leaving. A few stay and try to stare me down. When they leave they seem to follow the tree trunks toward the sky. Probably instinct causes that, but how does one explain the individual differences?

I must believe that the hairy that beats his song at sunrise does so for the love of music. He rings his frozen one-note xylophone, then listens for the echoes through the trees. And I arise in zero cold to listen. ❄

Wildlings are remarkably tolerant. Daily we see seemingly competitive species living peacefully together. Yet there are limits. Except during nesting, these usually evolve around head-to-head competition for food.

We watched a mink fishing. She dived through a hole in the shore ice, bringing up crayfish. This animal has a well-established territory including most of our river frontage, our fish pond, and several acres around our home and in the floodplain across the river. She raises a family here each spring. This is her land.

She noticed something across the river, loped upstream, and stood watching intently from the edge of the ice. Suddenly the water erupted. An otter catapulted onto the ice. The chase led down the shore, up into the fluffy snow, back to the ice. It ended when the mink left the river to cross the ice of our boat slip. She has a den there under a stump.

The otter had stayed just one jump behind—stopped as soon as it was obvious the mink was leaving. I don't know if an otter can catch a mink in all-out chase, but he certainly didn't want to this time. Neither animal ran full speed. This was a charade to establish fishing rights. The mink ran slowly enough to proclaim ownership. The otter ran just fast enough to usurp it.

A second otter surfaced. The two fished a few minutes, then disappeared downstream. They often travel while fishing. When cold ices most of the river, they may spend days at an open spot. The bend by our house is one of them. They will return for a longer stay in a month or so. Otters have the pick of fishing spots. The only animals on our river large enough to argue with them are beavers, and they don't fish.

Otters will vacate a fishing hole before a wading fisherman, but don't recognize a man in a boat as competition. I have had them dive right under my boat and hang around a good fishing spot for several minutes. If there are two or more they invariably spend some time floating head high to look me over. They comment with pleasant whickering voices—disconcerting. It makes me feel I'm on the wrong side of the bars at a zoo.

The mink gets much of her food from dry land. She has depleted the muskrat population, and now hunts regularly around our bird feeders. The red squirrels treat her with utmost respect. She is an excellent hunter and will help keep their numbers under control.

Fishing is not essential, but she has reclaimed her fishing rights. When the otters return she will relinquish again with dignity. After all, they outweigh her ten to one. Wild animals are realists. They accept what they cannot change and live with it. ₩

We don't get many bright moonlit winter nights. Last week we had one. I walked out to enjoy it. Someone had turned off the color. Everything was silver, and black, and gray, and white. Diamonds lay all over the snow crust. They scattered with my every movement.

Moonlight has a way of slipping around the edges of things and fuzzing up their outlines. Shadows close to the ground look sharp, black, foreboding. My back to the moon leaves a Neanderthal figure, hulking, long armed, and broad with wrappings against the cold.

The hardwoods stand stark naked against the sky. On the snow the moonlight wraps their shadows in modesty until the treetops dissolve in sheer negligee. I think the moon is feminine. She touches the landscape with gentleness unmatched by sunlight.

Back in Maine the woodmen called conifer forests black growth. Now I know why. The pines, firs, and spruces make black caves beside the path and stand in stern picketed ranks—black accents on a silver sky.

I venture into that black cavern—snow squeaking every hesitant footstep. The moon sends little probing beams to find each cranny through the roof. Here dappled gray exposes illness. Thin ailing quills of an aged fir lets frost through to the forest floor. It is not really dark in here. Half-light is everywhere. Every daytime trail is clear with the sharp shadows of footprints.

It is well that things close to the ground show clearly. It's easier to walk. No need to stumble or bump a tree trunk. All are clear and sharp. The deer trail meanders ahead like a sun-sparkled brook.

At the field edge goldenrod stalks scribble in the breeze. Grub galls make ink spots amid the writings. I must come here sometime to gather bait for ice fishing.

There might be deer in the winter wheat, pawing through crust for frozen greenery. Headless shadows made by gray ghost shapes. But not tonight. No owl flies over. No weasel or fox crosses the path before me. The snow creaks warning of my approach. I cannot wait for wildlife tonight. Cold hastens my footsteps.

Orion, mighty hunter of the sky, shows his star-studded belt above the tree line—Sirius trotting at heel. I listen, but even the pines murmur too softly. There is only the moon and the sky, and the snow and the trees.

It's good to be out sometime when no one else is—in the cold, and the quiet, and the silvery shadows. It's good that there is still a place to do so. 🌿

Feudin', fightin', and fussin' is what's going on in our front yard. The row between blue jays and red squirrels is one of the long-standing vendettas in wildlife. Right now around our feeders it is at a peak.

The severe cold weather has driven the red squirrels to our suet. Normally they prefer corn and sunflower seeds, sampling suet only occasionally. When it's very cold they hit the suet hard. The frozen fat, shattered by countless pecks from woodpeckers, blue jays, and smaller birds comes loose in big chunks. The squirrels carry these off to hide in crotches and among the fir boughs. Inveterate hoarders, they return repeatedly for another load.

The jays watch from hiding. At first chance they snatch the squirrel's stored goodies and carry them to their own hiding place, often only a few trees away. As soon as a squirrel finds one of his caches emptied, he begins a tirade against the world in general and jays in particular. Let him catch a blue-feathered thief in the act and mayhem threatens. His fruitless chase almost denudes the trees. The jays seem to enjoy the ruckus. Let the squirrel return to the main suet, and the jays will berate him for stealing their suet.

Of course, both species are hardened thieves, deserving the worst that either can deal out. The feud may stem originally from the squirrels dining on eggs and nestlings, and both species liking for the same sorts of forest mast. Blue jays are one of the few birds smart enough to vie successfully with squirrels.

This winter we have few blue jays. I believe it is due to the acorn crop failure. When the meager wild food supply was exhausted, most jays migrated. The same shortage has brought hordes of red squirrels to our feeders. In self-defense I have shot two dozen, but the supply is endlessly replenished from the seed-poor forest. Another dozen are still with us.

In mild weather the squirrels and jays fed in relative peace. No jay was allowed on a squirrel-occupied feeder, but cracked corn spread on the ground was shared by all. Occasionally a squirrel would dash at a jay, but they do that to the grouse too. The grouse bounce straight into the air over the squirrels and quickly resume feeding. The jays usually fly to a perch and cuss a little. There is no real evidence of the deep simmering feud.

Zero weather threatens survival. Concentrated fat calories are insurance. Most of our suet eaters feed right at the holder. Squirrels and jays will haul off anything they can carry. Each recognizes the other as a threat to the supply.

So the feud is on in earnest. The chill air is split by shocked profanity. We chuckle endlessly at the display. The Hatfields and McCoys of the conifer forest. ❦

Just about every living thing has something good about them, but I had just about given up on the porcupine until today. The critters have chewed up almost everything useful ever carried into a camp—axe handles, canoe paddles, kitchen tables, and toilet seats. In their insatiable search for salt they'll tackle anything—even automobile tires. Gnawing on a greasy frying pan they can make enough noise to wake the dead. I've had to dequill every bird dog I've taken into the woods at least once, and some of them never learned. I've had a blood feud with porcupines for years.

Our woods was overrun with them, and last winter I decided to clean them out. I have a good-sized conifer swamp with big trees and no underbrush. The only rabbits there live across the road in a cutdown where the deer compete with them for what choice low food plants are available.

I was surprised to find a well-beaten rabbit trail right in the middle of the big tree swamp. Following it up, I found a room-sized area of packed snow liberally spotted with rabbit droppings and bits of cedar twigs. Overhead were several well-pruned cedar trees and a big poplar with a porcupine in the crotch. Obviously several rabbits had been regularly feeding on the spillage from the porcupine's table. He is a particularly messy eater when feeding on twigs.

My .22 rifle disposed of the porky and I continued through the swamp, shortly to encounter another rabbit trail which led to another porcupine. I shot this one too, and a few minutes later was dumbfounded to find the same scene repeated a third time. This porky was in a hollow tree, and by that time I was so impressed with the relationship between porcupines and rabbits that I didn't molest him.

Surely the porcupine was not consciously feeding the rabbits, but the rabbits must have been deliberately searching out the porky's spillage. This is an old swamp, and a shortage of rabbit food must have existed for years. Recent nearby timber cutting had solved the food shortage, but the rabbits still ventured into the big trees far from cover to get their traditional handout. In my woods this was made extra hazardous by a pair of great horned owls and an abundance of foxes and other predators. Maybe the tender treetop twigs are worth the risk.

At any rate it looks like some porcupines do some good, even if it's only for the rabbits.

A river is always a wildlife highway. This winter ours has become one for deer. For the first time in many years it is frozen hard. The ice came after much of the snow, so the river is easy walking compared to the two-foot-deep white stuff on land. The deer take advantage.

About a dozen deer come each day to the grain we spread for birds. They used to come through the woods. Now they come by ice. Unencumbered by trees and underbrush, their grace is almost breathtaking. I wish for an artist's talent to preserve the scene.

The ice has also added entrees to their salad bar. Cedar and hardwood sweepers, usually out of reach in the current, are now at perfect snacking height. As the deer head toward our dining room, they wander back and forth along the shore. It is a perfect chance to study their eating habits.

A nip of red maple, across to the current-tipped basswood, then back to sample the cedar in front of our house. Really hungry deer feed avidly on any available browse. I think we can judge their condition by how much they pick and choose. Our herd isn't hurting yet. The only food they are pushy about eating is our cracked corn. We scatter it widely to accommodate the birds and slow the deer. The deer act like kids around the Good Humor truck. They crowd out the doves and grouse. Big does sometimes drive fawns from choice bits. The big bucks come only after dark. That's one reason they are so big. They, and some of the does, have learned to stand on hind legs and lick out the feeder. It's expensive. Next year I'll raise it a foot higher.

Deer must have an instinctive ice understanding. Upstream there is a blanket-sized patch of open water. Turbulence must keep ice thin all around it, but snow hides the danger. We watched three deer wander near. The fawns' necks stretched in peering, legs tilted to retreat. Then, carefully, they backed away. Instinct warned them—experience could not. One crash through that ice is death, for the current would quickly sweep anything downstream.

Ours is a dangerous river in winter. It used to freeze hard every year. Old-timers tell of harvesting eighteen-inch-thick, clear blue ice. Now discharge from the power storage reservoirs keeps the temperature higher. Usually we only have ice all across at isolated log jams. We have seen previous freeze-ups disappear in hours.

Probably not one deer in ten of our herd has ever seen this stream frozen before. But they take its blessings in stride and their instincts keep them safe. ❈

If I ignore the snow and half-frozen river, I can imagine our bird feeder is in Mississippi. Thirty doves and three cardinals peck busily at cracked corn, ground spread for the grouse. Four fox squirrels, two of them black as midnight, reinforce my nostalgia. Here are childhood friends from the sunny South keeping me company in midwinter Michigan.

I'm sure none of these individuals ever saw my home state, yet all three species live mostly in the South. The doves seem particularly out of place. I recall hoards of doves that flushed before our dogs on midwinter quail hunts. Why should these stay north when such bounty awaits them below the snow line?

There is much we don't know about migration. Banding records indicate that those doves which nest far north, winter far south, leapfrogging over their shorter-traveling brothers. Yet we really don't know if the birds at our feeder were hatched locally or are newcomers from more northerly nestings.

There are always exceptions to prove the rule. The migratory instinct must be a very powerful one, for it guides migrating species to their destinations, sometimes under unbelievable conditions. In each species there are some individuals that seem to completely lack the instinct to migrate. If they survive and breed I do not think they could pass to their offspring an instinct they never had. So, whole flocks of nonmigrants could be built up.

Each winter Audubonists report more and more north-wintering doves at feeders. Some theorists say the earth is getting warmer, causing more southern species to gradually expand their ranges north. This might explain the presence of such southerners as opossums, cardinals, and more and more fox squirrels. It may explain why more doves nest here each summer, but it doesn't tell why some stay all winter. To find out if our winter birds hatched here, we would have to band many of our dove nestlings and also band those that winter with us. It would be a long difficult job, for doves are as hard to catch as they are to shoot.

Those that visit us feed in a flock. They arrive from every direction, yet all within a few minutes, two or three times daily. We are well back in the woods, certainly not dove habitat. On a bitter cold weekend, with the ground half-bare from a January thaw, doves flushed from under tag alders as we hunted rabbits. I think doves have no business in such a place, but they were there anyway.

I like the theory that nonmigrating parents raise nonmigrating flocks. It gives us bird feeders a sense of responsibility. Now, if we do not feed them, they may perish, for they do not know how to go south—an excuse to pay the high price for birdseed. And how important we feel—or it just may be because of this mild winter, but we're glad they are here anyway. ❧

I guess everyone who spends much time in the outdoors gets to associate certain sounds with the seasons. In spring it might be the cheery notes of the first robin or the babble of a stream as it frees itself from the ice.

For the hunter it's more apt to be a partridge drumming, or the first flock of geese returning. The geese—ah, there's a sound that breaks the grip of winter—not the high lonesome calls as they pass overhead, but the gabble and conversation as they search out some black water cracks and settle on the rotten ice of the river. Then I know, even though the world is still half-frozen, spring is really coming one more time.

Summer is a noisy, lazy time, with a dozen birds singing, a rustle of leaves in the breeze, and way off a crow complaining. But for me, the real summer sound is a big old bumblebee at work. I had forgotten how good it was till I took up lazy fishing again last summer, and lay one day on a grassy bank, not paying too much attention to my fish line and bobber.

His muted bass fiddle interrupted my study of the sun patterns through the cap over my eyes, and I rolled over to watch him sorting out the dandelion petals, all dusty yellow with pollen—just the same as he was so many years ago on the bank of a bar pit by the levee where I first fished for bullhead catfish.

Fall is getting ready time, and the sounds are hurried and restless. The flush of partridge and the chuckle of mallards as they invite some new arrivals to the pond. Now the geese call high and away, and they are going—going. The wood ducks squeal up and down the river, but best of all is the whistle of a woodcock's wings, as he gets up, half-seen, before the dog. That's really what all the rest of the year is for.

Winter is the silent time with even footsteps muffled to keep the peace. And, because sounds are so few, the best is saved for winter. Nature gave the goldeneye duck a special whistle for his wings, and told him to stay where the snow is deep and only the rapids gives him water to live by.

Each day the whistlers fly over on some unknown mission, and the whistle of their wings is like tiny bells in the sky, rising and fading until it is felt more than heard. And the silence is good, because you couldn't have heard it if there were any other sounds.

Henry Beston said that in the old magic, the first fire on a new hearth must always be lit by the woman of the house—ours was. It is also wise to lay the new fire on a few ashes from an old hearth, best of all from one which has had humanity and fulfillment about it, and at whose flames friends have warmed their hands.

It takes cold weather to make a good fire. When a northeaster flails spumes of snow about the eaves and huffs and chuffles at the chimney, little shivery skin prickles run up my spine. I inch closer to the fire, not to get warmer, but because it just feels so good to have a private little island of comfort in winter's howling maelstrom.

Fireplaces are fine, but stoves are more efficient. When I was a kid we had one in the living room. Every winter it was brought in and setup on a tin-covered pad all decorated with squiggly designs from Sears Roebuck. The smoke pipe went through a hole in the chimney that had a tin cover with a picture in summer.

It was a wonderful stove with big nickel-plated corners and a steeple on top that you could slide aside to heat a kettle. The rest of the furniture sort of gathered around it, friendlylike. There were mica windows in the door. With the lights out they winked at you and made secret signals against the walls.

Right now my favorite fires are ones that are hours old, a thick bed of coals that you can feed one stick at a time. This year our wood is split birch and round maple. The birch dried fast. It is fine for getting started. The maple is just dry enough to hold a slow hot fire. We never take out all the ashes. Leave enough to keep the heat close to the wood. New fires and big fires roar. Old fires mutter from among the coals—make slow and friendly conversation. They tell of being carried in a firepot to the next camp, or as smouldering punk packed in a buffalo horn; of torchlight against a painted cave wall; of a bond with man, so ageless, that many of our words about friends are also words about fire.

We used to have a fireplace in each bedroom. Every morning there were some hot coals. A few pokes, some kindling, then back to snuggle in bed and listen to the snap-crackles as the wood caught. Oh, the delight of getting dressed by the hearth, shivery on one side, toasty behind, and hurrying to warm the other side.

We got central heating—a big ribby radiator in each room—very impressive. I guess the house was warmer, but sitting on a radiator was never as good as snuggling up close to that open fire. ❧

February

Every month has her bragging days. This year February started right off with hers—a handful of jewels to mark her place in the calendar. I could hardly wait to greet each one.

My late night sleep is restless. I wander about the house, check moonlit snow from every window. Westerly shadows stretch ever longer to tell the hours. Sometimes there are deer back for a final check beneath the feeders. I shiver, creep back beneath the covers to lie half-dozing in the sensuous joy of warmth. Finally the first hint of gold alloying the night light fondles me full awake.

The moon is silver, sun is gold. On those mornings when the moon lingers in the west to greet the sun, there is a subtle amalgam of light, gradually enriched, that beautifies all it embraces. I would not miss it.

Winter moonlight lies across the landscape, cold and keen as a Toledo blade. The sun's first light is molten, but gentle, tentative. It pushes its advance, molecule by molecule. Only when full rays brush the treetops is the moon suddenly unarmed. Pale in the west, she stands empty handed, her cutting edge of light dissolved and washed away.

I hurry with workaday chores—poke up the fire, start coffee, bundle in down jacket and ear-lapped cap, and arouse the dog. We must be about to watch the sun march up earth's eastern foothills, peer over the horizon, then stand and claim the field. Only clear days let us see this triumph. Clouds move the advance to their peaks, sometimes giving us glimpses of the blood and flames of combat. On clear mornings day's conquest of darkness is peaceful. Such are these bragging days of February.

A flurry of doves shatters the silence. They are the earliest of birds, come at first daylight to glean grain crumbs from the river path. Slim pickings left by the deer. I scatter glovefuls of fresh eatables. The doves watch from across the river. They'll be back almost before we leave.

East is the way to go at daylight. Silhouettes are sharper. Colors first show their tones. The bleached sky tints blue, then yellow and golden. Right at the edge a hint of orange, but no garish waves of flames. Today's light is a gentle tide, creeping into the small places, turning blacks to green, grays to brown, until finally it floods the unsuspecting landscape.

The air stands breathless for a while. No breeze to carry scent announcements. We see no wildlife, though cold has made it active. Fresh tracks all about, but subzero snow squeaks our every movement. Stop to wait and watch; cold creeps up pant legs, down coat collars, inside cuffs. Memory of coffee perking melts my determination.

I whistle the dog to kennel, bare my hand to ruffle behind his ears. Inside, hands huddle around a steaming mug. I watch sunrise wash gilt and diamonds down the bare maples. February has brought another fine day, one for bragging. ❦

Who's gonna be first? Every day we see that game played at our feeders. It's not just a fun game. It may be a matter of life or death.

Doves come in flocks. They light in the trees and trickle across the yard toward the ground-spread corn. Then they sit and sit. Finally one dove flutters down to eat, then another, and suddenly there is a stream, a torrent of doves fluttering to the buffet.

Evening grosbeaks behave the same way. Scores come each day to our upstairs feeder. There they are safe from any except winged predators, yet they sit talking endlessly in the trees, till one scout dares to be first for breakfast.

Wild things don't elect who's going to be first. The first are the young, the foolish, and the hungriest. Every day deer come to get spillings from our feeders. A fawn is always first, sometimes two, head and tail up, almost drooling in anticipation. Young, foolish, and of course, very hungry. When the whole herd arrives, the fawns are crowded out. In late February I noticed one of the most subordinate fawns browsing spruce twigs. This is bad. Deer can starve to death eating spruce. This little fellow hadn't been first that day, but he was near the head of the line and got a few grains of corn before being run off. We seldom see very large deer at our feeders. They can reach browse the others can't and are truly man shy. They aren't hungry enough to be first. We see their tracks in the mornings.

Duck flocks sometimes seem to alight all at once, but really one bird is first. Over decoys, some species circle and circle. That's when to watch for number one. One duck, often back in the flock, will deviate from the line of flight. If it's toward you, they are coming in. If it's away, give them the old come back call. Goose families stick together. The old ones lead in migration. When coming to feed or to decoys, the youngsters rush ahead. If there is no obvious danger, the oldsters follow or circle one more time.

Nature's system is a good one. It protects the best of the species. If a fox lies in the thicket by the corn, if a hawk hides above the feeder, let the ones they catch be the foolish or the weak. Some must die, so let it be them. Save the proven breeders, the strongest, the smartest. In all life there is a struggle for existence, not just against predators, but for the limited supply of food, or water, or even air where it is in short supply.

Every living thing varies. In life's struggle, the fittest survive and pass their fitness to other generations. Thus, inch by inch, all species change. It's called evolution. I watch it at work as I see who's gonna be first at our feeders. ❧

Upside down is heads-up hunting for a nuthatch. It's one of the most sensible things these little birds do, and believe me, nuthatches are sensible birds.

This winter I have fallen in love with the red-breasted nuthatches. Our home is in a grove of fir and spruce. About two dozen red-breasts come to our feeders. They far outnumber the white-breasted nuthatches, so common at urban bird feeders. Red-breasts just won't go far from their beloved conifer swamps. White-breasted nuthatches prefer deciduous trees.

We have a mesh bag of suet hanging about six feet from our breakfast room windows. Woodpeckers, jays, and chickadees visit it, but it really belongs to the red-breasted nuthatches. One of them almost always occupies it. One of these nuthatches will feed peacefully with a chickadee, a woodpecker, or even another nuthatch. Two more is too much.

Nuthatches are broad-shouldered little birds. From above they look like blue gray pumpkin seeds. When crowded, they thrust out their shoulders like cocky young boxers. A few threatening wing flutters, and the intruders invariably retreat. I have seen no nuthatch fights. Their threats work too well.

I figure each bird needs about six inches of work space. At a large suet holder three red-breasts occasionally feed, but the six-inch margin is never crossed. They demand and respect privacy.

At our house red-breasts are meat eaters. They stick mostly to suet or meat shreds picked from the occasional bone we put out. The white-breasted nuthatches spend much time hauling off sunflower seeds to eat or to hide. The red-breasts seem to like conifer seeds. I see them occasionally probing the cones at branch tips.

Eighty percent of the nuthatch time on our suet bags is upside down. I examined them closely to find out why. From the top, the suet chunks are pecked full of holes. All the loose fat has been pulled out by the woodpeckers and jays. The pecking of these larger birds loosens the undersides, a treasure trove for our topsy-turvy hatches. It just makes sense for them to look upside down from the bottom. That's where the goodies are that everyone else missed. Upside down on the tree trunks must find the same treasures.

Red-breasted nuthatches are our smallest bird visitor. Each is an individual in coloration as well as style. The females have gray caps, the males black. Males are more rusty underneath. Some have almost sky blue backs. They are the most adept flyers of our winter birds. They can hover momentarily like a hummingbird. In summer they catch insects on the wing.

In my studies of the suet bags, I approached one little male very closely. He regarded me with beady-eyed intensity until I was inches away. Then he swelled his chest, threw out his shoulders, and quivered his wing warning. I sat back on my heels and retreated inside.

Some of our neighbors hoard dead mice. One of them has a cache under our straw pile. I uncovered it by accident. It held nine deer mice and three voles (meadow mice). Needless to say I carefully re-covered this treasure. Wouldn't want to do anything to discourage this fellow's collecting. The owner was a weasel, probably our most beneficial mammal.

We may have three or four weasels on our place. As weasel population goes, this is high density. We need them. Since we came to this woods, the rodent population has boomed. Deer mice come nightly to our bird feeder spillings. They invade the garage to nest and get seed from our stores. We run a constant trapline there. Meadow voles live in the thick grass around our fishpond. Next to insects, they are the only serious threat to our garden. A fence keeps out deer and rabbits. The voles get about one-fourth of our bean crop and probably more of our beets than we do. Without predators we'd really be in trouble. For our particular problem the weasels are specialists.

The weasel population has gradually built over the years. We estimate their numbers by tracks in the snow; now we find them all over the place. A weasel may have a home range of twenty to thirty acres and travels even wider on occasion. An abundance of food means smaller territories. In fresh snow I often track the one that lives by our garden. He sticks pretty close to the five acres right around the homestead. Away from the house, territories are larger, for there our activities have given less stimulus to the rodents.

I think the weasels on our place are shorttails. The ones I have seen look to be a foot long or less. In winter they are white with black tail tips. Longtail weasels are larger. I can't tell them apart. In summer the longtails' feet are brown. Summer shorttails have white feet. Neither species stays still long enough for a sure identification study.

Weasels don't eat just mice. One cache I found contained an evening grosbeak. The bird was partly plucked. I suspect the weasel took it from our resident sharp-shinned hawk. A larger hawk would not have lost.

Owls and hawks sometimes eat weasels. I once saw a red-tailed hawk flying with a live weasel. The weasel, a big one, wriggled like a barrelful of snakes and finally sank its teeth into the hawk's leg. It was promptly released. I reached the weasel just as it died—could hardly believe it could still fight so badly wounded.

Weasels are killers. They must kill to eat, and they'll try to kill until they die. Their life-style is truly bloodthirsty. I'm all in favor of these fierce little friends. They won't admit my friendship, but if they want to store dead mice in my backyard I'll let 'em.

No wonder the Indians never invented the wheel. They had snowshoes. For the chores of living outdoors in snow country you can't beat 'em.

Just for fun I spent a day of this winter's first thaw at make-believe survival in the wilds. With snowshoes you can get around in any kind of snow. Some kinds are easier. If you can't wait until the whole snowpack has settled, start early in the morning before the crust gets soft. That's what I did; easy walking except when the crust breaks enough to catch a shoe tip.

Survival outdoors requires food and shelter. That's what my exercise was about. Since it was early morning, food was the first order of business. An acre of small fir trees was paved with rabbit tracks. A trek around the thicket located a dozen well-packed exit trails, choice sites for snares. Snaring rabbits is not legal, but it is a legitimate survival technique. I crisscrossed twigs in each runway, then crashed about in the brush for ten minutes. Knocked-down twigs on three trails showed where I might have snared dinner. Without snowshoes that project would have been exhausting if not impossible. Skis would have been worse than useless.

To me, shelter means a roof and a bed. Balsam fir or spruce will provide both. A spruce with limbs to the ground made a nice hut. Inside, dry limbs were handy to start a fire. Limbs that break easily above snow level are always dry enough to burn.

To gather bed boughs, cut a pole about five feet long. Leave a few inches of one limb near the butt. Break off green boughs and push the pole between the twigs near the stem ends. Push the boughs down the pole, around and around to make it symmetrical like an old-fashioned haystack. The boughs will stay on. You can carry a big load.

To make a bed, lay the balsam fronds like shingles, tips up. The boughs should tilt a little, but the straighter you stand them the softer the bed. Pack the snow underneath first. Since I wasn't going to sleep out, I just made a pad to sit on. Extra boughs covered gaps in the spruce limbs. A small fire at the entrance made everything cozy.

My last-ditch emergency kit includes matches, tea bags, jerky, (in case the snares don't work), twenty feet of monofilament, fishhooks, salt and pepper, and a handful of waxed paper, all stuffed in an empty soup can. I always carry a knife or belt axe. If I can't find birch bark, the paper starts a fire. To make tea water, put little snowballs in the soup can. Warm slowly, or you get steam and no water.

A survival day is good practice and fun, but, you know, I was sound asleep that night before my feet got rid of those snowshoes.

❧

Doves are different. They don't look like most other birds. They don't act like most other birds. The true extent of their differences gradually dawned on me as I watched a flock at our feeder. About thirty mourning doves have wintered with us. Their appearance and behavior contrast so greatly with those of our other boarders, it is easy to see they are only distantly related.

When doves come to the ground they flutter all the way, letting themselves down feet first, one wing hold at a time. Blue jays close their wings and dive headfirst, braking just at ground level with a few quick wing beats. Most of the other feeder birds light the same way. Most small birds fly with a series of flaps and closed wing swoops. Woodpeckers and finches are the most obvious. Doves don't fly anywhere with closed wings. Their wings beat all the time except when sailing. They don't even sail much except during courtship. Doves walk, the other feeder birds hop except grouse and ducks. To drink, doves stick their beaks in and suck up water like a horse. Other birds have to raise their heads to swallow.

Doves and pigeons belong to the order of columbiforms. Most of the other feeder birds belong to the order of passeriformes. These are the perching birds. There are about 5,100 species, roughly three-fifths of the known living birds. The passerines are the latest development in birddom with the most rapid evolution and diversification occurring in the last ten million years. Doves and pigeons date back some 40 million years; possibly earlier. No wonder they are different.

The names, doves and pigeons, have no technical significance. Generally we call the larger chunkier birds pigeons and the smaller more graceful species doves. However, the pigeons we feed popcorn to in the park are rock doves when the Audubonists count them. These birds are descended from the European rock dove which is a member of the wood pigeon subfamily.

Columbidae vary in size from the little six-inch-long ground dove of southeastern United States to the giant three-foot-long crowned pigeons of New Guinea, yet there is no mistaking them. They are all stout-bodied birds with short necks and small heads. They have short, slender, rounded bills. Their feathers are dense and loosely attached to their thin skin.

Feathers of our mourning doves are particularly loose. Hunting them down south, sometimes a shot will shake loose a pillow full of feathers. Goshawks regularly catch doves at our place. Each kill is a regular feather storm. Even grouse caught in midair don't explode so.

Yes, doves are different. It is good to have them at our feeders. Their contrast livens the show and sends me to the ornithology books to find out why. I know they are birds because they have feathers, but they sure aren't like the others. ✠

We don't eat dinner in the bedroom, but it would be better if deer could. When our deeryards were in good condition that's exactly what they did. Now there is almost nothing to eat in the conifer swamps. The deer just sleep there. They go outside to eat.

Recently I spent a weekend checking deeryards. It was the usual windy subzero weather. Packed deer trails leading into the conifers let me shed my snowshoes. Inside it was still and almost warm. The trees held the north wind high over my head where it scratched and whined to get in. Up ahead there were flickers of movement as the deer moved out ahead of me. Slowly, slowly—this is no time to chase deer, they need every bit of energy just to live, don't make them waste it in running.

The trail I followed became a crisscross of tracks; intersections from every direction. Under wind-tilted trees the snow was tight packed. Cedar twigs were stripped bare, balsam untouched. Count the fresh beds, two, five, a dozen. Older snow-covered beds pockmarked a quarter acre. I think deer choose a new bed each day because the snow keeps them off the cold ground, or maybe it's just softer.

I followed a main trail across a hardwood run to more evergreens. Packed snow and ice hollows marked another bedroom community. The deer sleep in family groups. Usually there are two or three beds close together. A porcupine had served tidbits from his treetop. I shook down some of his limb-hung spillings.

The trees in our swamp are mature, limbs dead or pruned twenty feet up. What shrubs once grew in their shade have long since gone. I remember my first visit to a deeryard forty years ago. Ground hemlock (Canadian yew) stood waist-high under the tall conifers. Bedded deer peeked from among the straggly branches. These deer were yarded tight by two feet of heavy snow, but they could almost dine in bed. *Taxus canadensis* is choice deer fodder.

Old-timers tell me that once ground hemlock was everywhere in our swamp. It didn't die, too many deer just ate it. For all practical purposes this plant has been eliminated from the ecology of our swamp. Now the deer must find a new winter way of life.

They travel daily to young cuttings for sprouts, or to the river for sweeper twigs. Some visit our bird feeder for snacks. Light snow has let them keep the trails open. A big storm could change that— lock the bedroom door. That's O.K. if there is something to eat, but with a bare bedside cupboard it's disaster. ❦

A brown creeper looks like a nutmeg with a surgeon's needle on one end and a tail on the other. Come to think of it, maybe nowadays some folks may not know that nutmegs are little brown oval-shaped nuts that have to be grated to deliver their delightful flavor and aroma. Every kitchen used to have a nutmeg grater. I remember my mother putting the finishing touch on Christmas eggnog by a light grating of nutmeg powder over the brimming bowl.

Nowadays nutmeg comes in cans, and it's not as good. Besides, whole nutmegs could be hung around the neck on a string to ward off various ailments as well as hexes and all sorts of evil spirits. For a long time I didn't trust Yankees because one of my grandmother's old friends claimed a Yankee trader sold her wooden nutmegs.

I expect lots of people also don't know what a brown creeper is. It's a tiny little bird, brown streaked on top and white underneath, that is hatched and lives its entire life in close association with tree bark. Creepers' nests are always on dead tree trunks under a loosened slab of bark. They feed entirely on bark insects and their eggs, or spiders, etc., that hibernate in bark crannies. Their curved awllike beaks are marvelously adapted for probing. They get tidbits that chickadees can't reach and woodpeckers have to dig for. Their tail feathers are pointed and stiff. They use them for propping like woodpeckers, but they never hitch downward. When a creeper descends, he flies, then hitches methodically upward.

A brown creeper wintering with us proves that never and always is usually wrong. He likes suet. He began appearing daily in our front yard balsams. No way could he find food in the trunks, overscoured by our chickadees, nuthatches, and woodpeckers. He was so inconspicuous we missed his actual feeding. Finally, we discovered him at the foot of the trees below our suet holders. There the snow and root flares were littered with infinitesimal bits of spilled suet. The pieces were just bite size for him, though almost invisible to my feeble eyes.

We watched him do things creepers never do. He lit on the ground, turned halfway or even head down on the root flares, and once even shouldered a chickadee out of the way. Truly, here was finally an individual in a species so meek and monotonous in behavior, that even ornithologists seldom study them.

Brown creeper's calls are thin and high pitched. In mating, they have a beautiful four-note song almost above human hearing frequency. They seem absolutely silent to me. Those whose ears are attuned to hear their pitch say creepers are noisy little birds—but noisy so high and softly that they retain their privacy—common in our woods, but as rare to our modern society as . . . whole nutmegs.

Two goshawks at a bird feeder is one too many. Birds of their eating size just won't tolerate it.

Each winter we have had a goshawk living in our woods. As usual, with the first permanent snow, one arrived: this year, a male, noticeably smaller than last winter's big hen bird. He caught an occasional dove, made passes at the few grosbeaks we had, and generally kept things alert around the feeders.

In nature predation is a fact of life. Everything is eaten by something. Wild things learn to live with this hazard. If they don't learn, they don't live. Feeding stations create artificial concentrations of birds. These attract predators, but also have built-in protection. Everyone watches everyone else. There are hundreds of eyes on the lookout. Let one bird give an alarm—all freeze or fly. There are lots of false alarms, but it works. Most of the hawks' swoops at our feeders are unsuccessful.

Except when feeding young, most avian predators make a kill about every other day. No more than five or six a year occur in our front yard. The birds there are like kids on city streets. They learn to watch for and avoid the hazards.

Mourning doves seem to be an ideal size for goshawks. We started the winter with about forty doves coming daily. The flock held above thirty despite the male goshawks activities. Of course, he took other prey. I found remains of blue jays, grosbeaks, and red squirrels which were probably his work. He seldom bothered the smaller birds. They almost ignored him.

In mid-January a female goshawk arrived. The male hawk plucked a goldfinch from our balcony as casually as I might take an olive from a buffet. This was unusual enough to bring us to the window just in time for our first sight of the big female as she caught a flushing dove over the river. Feathers flew almost like a shotgun kill.

From then on it has been all downhill. The grosbeaks left. The dove flock is down to a dozen. They are as spooky as low water trout. Even a movement inside the house scares them. Little patches of dove feathers are all through the woods. Goshawks take their prey to ground. They pluck off most of the feathers, then tear the kill to pieces. Everything goes down the hatch—on doves, even the beaks and feet.

The hawks will probably be leaving soon. The surviving veterans will be too tough to catch. We see nature teaching survival of the fittest, but with two such teachers, the lessons are almost too much to bear. ᴪ

"Out of the night that was fifty below and into the din and glare." It wasn't as cold as Robert W. Service's Yukon, but it sure hasn't been warm around here. The cold spell has afforded a good chance to see the effect of low temperatures on the wilds.

The coldest nights are the prettiest times of winter. Earth kicks off her blanket of clouds and lies shivering while she enjoys the moon- and starlight. Then I grasp the real majesty of nature. Storms and earthquakes can be more deadly, but to feel the insignificance of man, there is nothing quite like standing alone in the forest on a really cold winter night.

The trees, brittle with ice crystals in their veins, snap in protest. The river ice groans and cracks. Even the springlet creek is silenced, its infant gurgle frozen quiet for the first time this winter. I think nature holds the wind still on her coldest days, so all her creatures can hear the weight of that towering mountain of cold air piled on her land.

The deer are more tame and feed in full daylight. They look me over and then stand on hind feet to reach the cedar. Cold has given a full stomach priority over a whole skin. Birds at the feeders are bold with the urgency to stoke their inner fires. A barred owl crosses my path, hunting in daytime. The hunger moon rests deadly on the land.

The law of survival hangs on the wall of winter. The weak will not see its tapestry tomorrow. The one-legged grosbeak did not appear today. One sisken sat huddled by the window, gathering what warmth seeped out. Two days he huddled so, or were they different birds? Now only three come to feed. Where are the rest?

The fox squirrels stay home, riding out the deep freeze in insulated hollows. Red squirrels spend less time eating and more time toting food to hoard. For the first time this winter they dip into the suet and carry off chunks of cold insurance.

There aren't as many chickadees. These days are why they need such a birthrate. More woodpeckers come to our suet. Even the shy ones leave their endless tapping at the giant elms across the river. They take my handout of fat to fight the cold.

I am an alien to this northern land. A naked tropical animal surviving, wrapped in synthetic insulation, warmed by the sunlight from a million million days ago. I hurry inside and turn up the thermostat. I wonder if I really am above the law of survival—or do those fossil fuels that keep the cold outside provide only a reprieve.

The other day we lost a distinguished visitor to our town. A voice from the cement quarry phone announced, "We electrocuted Al's owl." The big snowy that has patrolled our lakefront all winter was dead; brought down by a way of life that she neither recognized nor understood. It takes a big bird to span between two high voltage wires. A snowy owl is big enough.

She was Al's owl because Al spent an hour searching the quarry to include her in Audubon's Christmas bird count. He finally found her sitting solemnly on a rock pile regarding his explorations. She was Mike's owl because she caught a rat from the shore behind Mike, waist-deep in ice water after steelhead. She was Jack's owl because she brought a duck to the ice to dine before his front door. She was white and speckly gray, and those who saw her were amazed and thrilled, and glad she was in our town.

Snowy owls may live and die and never see a man. Those that visit us accept us as another animal in their world; too big to eat, too slow and earthbound to fear. They find us in a peculiar square-blocked, straight-lined terrain, full of unusual noises and hazes. This one had learned to live with us.

She was fat and healthy: Five pounds fourteen ounces, twenty-three inches long, fifty-five-inch wingspread. Barring the hazards of civilization, she might have returned to her arctic birthplace to breed and, someday, send offspring to excite our lakefront in other winters. This was her first year of life. There is no reason she mightn't have had many. Most raptors (hawks and owls) die their first year. Her excellent condition shows she had passed the critical point. She lived well, and in a strange and hostile land.

Owls are particularly adapted for their way of life. Their tremendous eyes are far larger than mans' in relation to body size. For night sight they have great light-gathering power. In tests, one specie captured prey in light equivalent to a single candle almost half a mile away. To gather light they sacrifice color detection. Owls see only black, and white, and gray—but who needs color at night. Even in summer, snowy owls live in a gray and white landscape except for flowers, and they don't eat them anyway.

Everything about owls is remarkable. Most birds blink eyelids from bottom to top. Owls blink from top to bottom like us. Their eyelids are softly feathered; seductive as a come-hither look. I'll never forget a wink from the big yellow eyes of our distinguished guest. She sat calmly on a light pole, and her wink said, "Hello, brother." ✹

Yesterday's snowstorm was big, and wet, and beautiful, and deadly. We saw death stalking when some of the chickadees began to show up with a sort of fuzzy, finger-combed look to their feathers. Some of the siskins had balls of snow frozen to their belly feathers. The wind increased and grew colder.

For small birds the cardinal rules for winter survival are: Stay dry—stay out of the wind. These birds were wet. Unless they found a windproof roost they would not live the night. This morning we waited anxiously.

The first dim shadow is a junco. We only have one. He sleeps in the brush pile. Then two nuthatches—some siskins—no chickadees. These little bundles of enthusiasm are usually first to breakfast and last to bed. But not today.

I think those early and late chicks have drafty roosting places. They need every ounce of food to warm them through night's chill. Yesterday's wet sped the clock up for them. Time ran out before light to see. They will not show today.

We wait, we wait. Finally, almost at sunup, the first chickadee arrives. Tiny, exhuberant, and hungry as ever. Then another—a trickle all day, but only a trickle. How many are gone?—a third? —half? We'll never know. There must have been a hundred here before.

Two years ago we banded seventy chickadees, and that was less than half. No banding since. Last year about two dozen banded chicks wintered with us. Yesterday there were four. Today just one. The chick with the broken wing feather is back. He's a tough little rascal. But there are so few.

Our woods are ideal chickadee habitat. Plenty of conifers mixed with hardwoods—hollow trees and nest boxes. Chickadees stay out of windy places in winter. Across the river is all hardwoods, a treasure trove of insects in dying elms and drift. In winter wind the chickadees will not cross the river, yet spring finds them swarming all across the flats.

I think our chicks that survived last night must have slept inside. We've seen them entering the empty wood duck boxes and the sapsucker's nest by the garden. Snug and warm, no wonder they were late from bed.

Roost holes may be the limiting factor on our winter bird threesome. Woodpeckers and nuthatches roost inside too when they can. Downys and hairys dig roost cavities. Nuthatches are bigger than chickadees. The chicks get what's left over, and there's never enough to go around. Most winters these mighty mites drop off one by one. They are too small to have many enemies. Only weather is impersonal enough to kill a chickadee. Yesterday she did it very badly. 🦋

Yesterday we had a visitor from the taiga, that somber forest of spruce and fir that extends entirely around the northern hemisphere. Our visitor was a white-winged crossbill, a bird that could not have evolved anywhere except in that great cone-bearing forest.

These little birds and their close relatives, the red crossbills, have the tips of their bills crossed, just as you might cross your fingers. The top mandible has a particularly sharp bend, almost like a parrot's beak. This is an adaptation for opening cones.

I once watched a red crossbill opening spruce cones. It snipped the cone from the tree and held it base up between its feet. The bird then slipped his closed bill under a scale and opened it slightly. The crossed mandibles neatly pried the scale up, and the bird's tongue scooped out the seed. In rapid succession the operation was repeated round and round the cone until all the seeds were removed. I've not seen such a display of dexterity by any other bird.

No other bird species have beaks like crossbills. These specialists are found all around the northern hemisphere in the great coniferous forests. White-wings nest north to timberline. Red crossbills are slightly more southern in range. Both species are erratic wanderers. They may not migrate at all when there is a good cone crop.

Our visitor was a rosy red adult male with black wings and tail, and two broad white bars on each wing. Females and young are olive gray. Juvenile males gradually acquire their red feathers after the second year. A flock may contain birds of all color gradients, but the drab females and young generally predominate. Red crossbill males are brick red with no white on their black wings.

Both species are very tame. Our visitor fed calmly on seeds spilled from the feeder while we approached to within four feet. In their native habitat they may never encounter man. This one certainly didn't consider us dangerous.

At our place we had a flock of red crossbills five years ago, then no more until our lone white-winged guest yesterday. He was with us for two days.

Lone birds are vulnerable to predation, particularly strays from species that usually travel in flocks. Without the protection of multiple friends watching for enemies our visitor was living on borrowed time. It was a short life.

Our resident goshawk got him this morning. As my wife watched in anguish the hawk swept our prize visitor to the snowy path, mantled over him for a moment, then flew off to dine.

Nature insists on conformity. She has harsh ways of enforcing her rules. Of all species, only man feels pity for the victims. ❧

The Chinese didn't invent paper. They were just the first men to make it. Since that small beginning paper has become one of our most useful products. In the United States we use about 300 pounds per person per year, everything from boxes to books, newsprint to napkins. Most of it is made from wood pulp.

To make paper you take wood to pieces right down to the fibers, discard some unwanted components, add a bit of different chemicals, and put the wood back together in a thin flat sheet. Hornets and wasps have been doing this for millions of years. This winter I decided to check the quality of their product.

Last summer bald-faced hornets built an immense nest high in one of our maples. When building in trees these wasps usually suspend their football-size nest from slender twigs. This nest was about half a bushel, attached to a two-inch-diameter branch. After killing frosts, a red squirrel dug into the nest. A hairy woodpecker tore off great chunks of the covering. Neither forager found anything edible, but the structure was so weakened that winter winds brought it down.

Each fall a few mated queen hornets hibernate in sheltered spots. All the rest die at the first severe frost. In spring each surviving queen starts a new nest—a few paper cells in a paper cover. She lays an egg in each cell and feeds the larvae on bits of captured insects until they develop into mature workers. These take over nest building and carry back plunder to feed the next generation. The queen just lays eggs. Adult hornets eat nectar, fruit juice, and sap, but they are active predators and scavengers. They chew up insects, spiders, and dead animals to feed the larvae.

Our big nest contained four brood tiers, the largest eight inches in diameter, about 2,000 cells. The tiers hung facedown, fastened one above the other by ribbons of paper. Each cell had a light-colored fine paper lining which was extended and sealed during pupation. A two-inch multilayer maze of paper housed the brood cell tiers. Entrance was at the bottom.

Hornets make paper by chewing up weathered or rotten wood, plant stems, and even man-made paper. This fiber is mixed with salivary secretions. This pulpy mass becomes a firm paper when dry. Color is usually gray, but varies with the source of fiber. Our nest contained some pink stripes that looked suspiciously like an old carton dumped by our shed.

Hornet nest paper resembles the nine point corrugating medium used to make the wiggly inside part of corrugated paperboard. The nest cover sheets, calipered nine one-thousandth of an inch, had good water resistance and stiffness. The cover shield was built up in sealed sections to form windproof, crush-resistant protection. Its insulation value was at least as good as a sixteen-inch brick wall. The brood cell tiers easily supported a ten pound weight without crushing.

I have always respected paper wasps for their potent stings, and predation of harmful insects. After testing their paper, I respect them even more. They qualify as experts in the paper trade. 🐝

Last night we had a rare and welcome visitor. He circled the house, checked every snowy footprint, the ridges the snowplow left, the mailbox, and the shrubbery. Only a weasel would have done such a thorough job of hunting and the characteristic twin print track definitely identified him. The very small size of the track showed that our nocturnal hunter was a least weasel, the smallest living carnivore, and generally quite rare in these parts.

Of course we did not see our visitor, but even if we had been awake, it is doubtful that the bright moonlight would have shown us more than a shadow. Only about six inches long and weighing less than two ounces, he is snow white, without even a black tail tip like his larger cousins, the ermine and the longtail weasel.

This little terror, for that is exactly what he is to his selected prey, is probably the world's most efficient mouser. About the size and shape of a hotdog, he can follow a mouse anywhere and makes them, and similar-sized rodents, almost his entire diet.

A friend of mine had one of these little weasels that visited his cottage on a Canadian island about once a week, and did an excellent job of keeping it completely free from mice, a major accomplishment as any owner of a wilderness cottage knows. One evening he suddenly appeared under the Franklin stove and gave us a fine demonstration of his hunting tactics. As we sat quietly, he eagerly explored every cranny of the living room, including the furniture, in no more than three minutes. Never have I seen such intensity of purpose in a wild animal. In his brown and white summer coat he seemed to flow over the floor in little wavelets, occasionally making a surprising leap of two feet or more. He disappeared into the kitchen and we saw him no more.

I tracked our last night's visitor to the tall weeds at the rear of our lot. There I found a colony of meadow voles last fall, which I expected would give me trouble with the garden I planned for this spring.

I'll have no trouble now. The weasel's tracks disappeared into a nest hole in the snow, and did not reappear. I expect he has appropriated the meadow voles' nest and long since disposed of all its occupants.

With that kind of service, he can have the run of our place as long as he wants to stay. 🐾

Once I watched one I loved die. It was slow. It was ugly. Now I watch the elm trees die.

Across the river half the trees are elm. They rise in stately Corinthian form, ever opening, reaching for the sun. One by one their slender tips collapse. Snags, reaching skyward, ever breaking back, cut down by disease in their lifelong search for sun.

The Dutch elm disease is one of the great catastrophes of American nature. Only the chestnut blight so altered our land. The chestnut was a tree of the highlands. Elms dominate our flats. With ash and red maple they patrol the floodplains of our rivers, binding up the banks, casting limber shade on the ripples. Soon they will all die. Our lowland forests will not be the same.

Trees suck up water and breathe it out to cool the air. A big elm, like those across the way, will transpire seven tons of water in a summer day, enough for twenty air-conditioned rooms. Woods are not cool just because of shade. Without trees the water table will gain inch by inch in its rise to surface. With too few living roots to suck it to the sky, water will drown the lesser plants. Marsh grasses and cattails will tangle midst the fallen giants. How many bone white elms have I seen rotting knee-deep in green-scummed sloughs: desolation from the failure of nature's water pumps.

Two Aprils ago I watched fat fox squirrels gorging on elm buds, stoking up with vitamin-ladened spring tonic. This spring they will not do so well.

In May the elm tops used to flash with goldfinches harvesting the mighty crop of seeds. Where will these golden mites go next year? I'll miss their beauty against the spangled green.

Even the catfish will miss our stately friends. I once caught a bullhead stuffed so round and fat I opened him out of curiosity. His stomach was packed tight with elm seeds. These flat little seeds surrounded with their horizontal parachutes must be full of nourishment. They are eaten so much it's a wonder any grow. Yet, light as feathers, 68,000 to a pound, how could they be so big in our ecology?

The woodpeckers are working hard to save the elms. The beetle disease carriers are wintering beneath the bark. Hairys and downys keep a constant tapping. Flaking off the crust to reach their prey, they tint the forest tan as they scale each dead limb. Some elms still live, gray barked, across the way, but not for long. Each year the gray turns tan to the woodpecker's search, then peels to bone bare wood. Twigs fall, then limbs and trunks. No leaves to grace next summer's sky.

There are more black fox squirrels than there are black gray squirrels. You would never believe it from some of the literature about them. Those writers should spend more time watching the squirrels. They must have learned their squirrel by reading what each other wrote.

Melanism (excess of dark pigment) is more common in both gray and fox squirrels than in other North American mammals. When Europeans first reached America, gray squirrels were undoubtedly the most common tree squirrel specie. In the great deciduous forests they were so numerous that massive migrations occurred, probably due to failure of mast crops. The great number of black individuals impressed the observers and has been firmly fixed in all squirrel writings ever since. Opening up of the forests for farming favored the fox squirrels. They have steadily extended their range and are now the most numerous squirrel throughout the eastern United States, with the exception of the Appalachian Mountains.

In the South fox squirrels vary widely in color. Besides being black or foxy they may have black heads, white noses, black, white, orange, or gray bellies. Blacks may be jet black or sprinkled with gray or orange hairs. Gray squirrels are either gray or black with some of the blacks showing a few gray hairs.

Melanism varies widely geographically. Some populations of both species have almost no blacks, others may be predominately black. There are more black squirrels in the South. Northern populations seldom show the duke's mixture of colors found in some southern fox squirrel litters.

As I write this a black and a foxy fox squirrel feed together on the river ice. I think they get more corn than the ducks. Blacks used to make up about 10 percent of our local squirrel population. They disappeared completely in a 1975 mange epidemic. Blacks are not more susceptible to mange. All of them just happened to be among the 90 percent of the population that died from the disease. The one with us now is the first we have seen in two years. We hope its color shows up in this year's litters; adds variety to the outdoor show.

Until I learned wing shooting, squirrel hunting was my forte. I spent every free fall day in the woods. A few hides were removed flat and cured for dollhouse rugs. My sister prized the black ones. There was a small but constant demand, as my curing was faulty. The rugs developed a certain aroma necessitating frequent replacement.

Times change and little girls no longer have bearskin rugs in their dollhouses. If they ever do again, they may not know whether they came from gray or fox squirrels. But the brother who supplies them will know. To a squirrel hunter, that's important. ⚜

In the war of the seasons there comes a time each year when I know our side has won. Oh, there will be some more battles. In March winter brings out some of her heaviest artillery, but by the end of February she's licked. Some of the wild things know it. They tell me.

The horned larks are usually first. These hardy little birds show up about as soon as the snowplows get enough ahead to wing back the drifts. Let a few spots of bare ground show along the highway and horned larks will find them. That's where I first see them each year. It never fails to give me a lift.

Then I notice weed heads poking above the snow and combs of wheat stubble in the windswept fields. We're going to make it to spring one more time. This winter I sometimes had my doubts. It's been a doozy.

Around here we really haven't had all that much snow. The cold just fixed its teeth in the landscape and hung on, driving the frost ever deeper. The wind, winter's second deadliest weapon, gathered up what little snow there was and used it over and over, wearing and wearying the earth.

Horned larks are the most terrestrial of birds. I've never seen one perch on anything. Snow buntings will light on a weed stem and ride it down to get the seeds. Fluffy snow doesn't bother them. I think they roost in it. The horned larks don't arrive until there is something flat to walk on, crust or bare ground. They reach weed heads from standing on the snow crust. They must find something besides gravel on the roadsides, for they prefer the grassy spots.

Horned larks live all over North America. There are twenty-one subspecies. It takes an expert to tell them apart. I don't try. Prairie horned larks nest here, and some stay all winter in the southern lower peninsula. I don't know whether our early arrivals are prairie horned larks or northern horned larks headed for the arctic. The northern larks have a little more yellow around the face. In some of the weather they arrive in, we are lucky to see a bird, much less judge face color.

Horned larks close their wings tightly after each beat. Once learned, it is an easy means of identification. I pity people who don't know birds. They miss a lot. What a shame not to recognize the lark's flit-swoop flight. It carries the first promise of spring. How else can you get such an early lift of spirits. ✤

March

In March the dreary hand of winter weighs heavy on my shoulders. The lengthening days still plod at an old man's winter pace. Even that friendly trio—chickadee, downy, and nuthatch—the Our Gang of our winter woods, no longer can sustain me.

These faithful three are the reliables of our bird feeders and winter woods, the resident cohosts of our daily bird show. Around a crowded feeder they may bluff in fretful competition. It's in the woods that the companionship of the club really shows. All three, preoccupied with the bark of trees, communicate continuously in their different languages, livening the woods with their multilingual conversations. I remember a childhood pal, newly moved from southern Italy. We could not speak the same language, yet we understood each other. So nature finds a way for her creatures to live together in happiness, if they will.

If I had to pick a sound to tie my memories to the winter woods it would be the "yank yank" of our white-breasted nuthatch. The chickadee chatters with gay abandon. The nuthatch always speaks with purpose. Here is a bird that really cares. Sit quietly, where they feed, and by and by one will surely come hitching headfirst down a trunk to study you with beady-eyed concern. Earnest is the word for him, and he must find you all O.K. before he flits away.

One spring I watched a nuthatch cleaning a knothole nesting cavity. He paused each trip at the entrance with a leaf or bit of the former tenant's rubbish. Then he flew off a distance before dropping his burden. How many trips he made. He could have been done in half the time had he simply swept off the doorstep to the ground twenty feet below. But there was a right way to clean house, and he must do it so.

Nuthatch pairs stay together all year. In winter they are never far apart, yet there is no display of affection, and their nasal monotonous "yanks yanks" are most all their conversation. In spring a young man's fancy suddenly turns—and then he sings his love song. First, of all the birds, his simple lisping lightens the winters burden.

Thoreau said it best. "When only the snows had begun to melt, and no rill of song had broken loose, a note so dry and fettered still, so inarticulate and half thawed out—. As if the young nuthatch, in its hole, had listened only to the tapping of woodpeckers and learned that music—. Only a little clangor and liquidity added to the tapping of the woodpecker. It was the handle by which my thoughts took firmly hold on spring." 🦋

A red squirrel moves fast even when he goes slowly. His locomotion is a series of stops and goes. In slow travel the stops are longer than the goes. He speeds up by cutting down on the stops. The goes stay about the same speed.

Red squirrels can walk, but they almost never do. Their normal gait is a series of leaps. A red squirrel on the run gallops in two-to-three-foot bounds. Strolling, the leaps are only a few inches with pauses between.

All the coniferous forest of North America have red squirrels. In the West they are called pine squirrels or chickarees. A beautiful orange-bellied subspecies lives on the Pacific Coast. All have the same fits and starts life-style. Anything they can lift is theirs for the taking. The world is their oyster, and they boldly berate anyone who may dispute their claim. Strictly diurnal, they are the most obvious mammals in our forests.

When we moved into this stand of conifers, most of the animals moved away to give us living room. The red squirrels moved in with us. We eventually discovered them raising families and havoc in our rodent-proof attic. After paying an astonishing amount to replace the packed ceiling insulation, we started control operations. There is no way to count red squirrels. We estimated our resident population at twelve. After shooting forty-seven from our balcony, we still had five or six at the feeders each day. We try to keep them at that number.

Every so often we find them gaining on us, so I unlimber the .22. Red squirrels are as edible as the big tree squirrels, but because of their small size, we use most of them to bait the crayfish traps. Winterkills are saved in the freezer. If we can't catch crayfish we can always eat the bait. My wife says, "No way."

There are enough hardwood cavities in our woods to house all the red squirrels. The few outside nests are far back in the cedar swamp or used for summers only. I have seen squirrels moving babies to an outside nest. I think it is to escape nest parasites. Nest material is invariably cedar bark. Even when they take over one of the duck boxes they fill it with bark which they must carry at least 200 yards. I suspect their knowledge of home insulation is the reason they took over our attic.

We like red squirrels. If they just didn't push their claim to our universe so hard we would never harm them. Red squirrels are plain fun to watch. We do it for hours, but you know, after a while their hyperkinetic antics leave us exhausted. They just go, go, go, too much. 🐾

She was very old, very tired, very hungry. The old doe first came to our front yard at midday late in the winter. Her hipbones thrust out like a dairy cow's, ribs like rows of pickets. She came slowly. Stop, look, test the breeze. A bullet hole through one ear showed one reason for her caution. There was man smell, and dog smell, and the smell of cracked corn. It took desperate hunger to overcome the wariness that had served her so many years.

Thereafter she came each day, always alone, always in full daylight. If other deer came, she left. We spread a couple of pounds of cracked corn mornings and afternoons for the birds. Many deer come about sundown to clean up the leavings and spills from our bird feeders. A few come in midmorning. We took to driving these away so there was always some grain for the old doe. There was usually plenty of spillings under the feeder, but it was too close to the house. She would only feed in the river path. Once she arrived when a small herd was already eating. She stood on the river ice and watched for a long time. Then she went away. We never let that happen again.

Our deer herd has wintered well. The snow has been light. There are plenty of sprouts from recent logging. How could she starve? She has no teeth. We watch her closely with binoculars. Her chin and throat are old-crone creepy, cheeks loose and wrinkled. Tooth wear tells a deer's age, but few survive long enough to wear theirs completely out. She has.

How old is she? Maybe twelve or fifteen years. A captive doe lived twenty years and birthed fawns until she was fifteen. This old lady will have no more fawns. Even if she were pregnant her condition would make live delivery improbable. She is heavily infested with parasites. Saclike swellings along her nose suggest nose bots. These evil-looking grubs infest about 25 percent of our deer, usually without serious harm. She also probably has lungworms. During starvation, parasites can be killers. They may kill her.

The corn we feed seems to be helping. When she first came her walk was a plod. She will never regain the innate grace of younger deer, but her gait is a little lighter, her head higher. When thaw opened up the fields to grazing she was carrying her years a little better.

This old doe will not survive another winter. I know our corn for her is really wasted. We try not to get sentimental about wildlife. There is no place for sentiment in wildlife biology. In nature the very old seldom retain their dignity. But, the last time we saw the old doe leave the herd she did so with dignity. We think it was worth our help. 🌿

When I used to walk in the woods with my Lab I was often jealous of his ability to read with his nose the fascinating story of the woodland life, so completely hidden from me.

Occasionally this daily drama is revealed to us mere mortals by the winter's snow. The best-quality etchings occur when there is a light ground of new snow over the crusted plate of the forest floor.

For reading the fine print, about a quarter inch of new snow is best. If it falls in the afternoon or evening the full story of the night's adventures will be legible. There will be only one copy of this original etching, and our changeable weather can erase it in a few minutes. Those who would read nature's animal track stories must do so at her convenience.

Recently my wife and I spent a morning reading a page of this outdoor literature. The stirring of spring and open water in the river had made many animals more active. A tractor trail to a riverside logging show was the stage for our viewing.

The heart-shaped tracks of two large and one small deer lead us down the trail. Suddenly they have changed. Hoofs wide spread, dew claws showing; they have started to run. The tracks are very fresh. They must have left just ahead of us, but not very frightened, for the bounds are only six or eight feet long.

A muskrat came up from the river. See where his tail dragged. There were two of them. One of them wandered into the small fir thicket, the other stayed in the road. A fox used this road too, but not at the same time. Both tracks are walking. Suddenly danger—the rat tracks skid and twist, a few flakes of blood—but he escapes across the road in desperate bounds, into the big timber. No safety here—a twist, a turn—back across the road and down the steep bank to the water.

What caused this episode? Not the fox, his tracks go on. A little ahead a mink has come up from the river, but it wasn't him. A close study on hands and knees shows the feather marks of a wing tip on one side of the road rut; the crust blown bare on the other side. An owl missed his dinner here.

The fox track is joined by a smaller one, and the two go off together. A skunk comes in on a snowmobile trail. Probably a male going courting, for it plods steadily on. No time for hunting now.

And so it unfolds. One night in the life of a forest; melodrama, near tragedy, mystery, even a love interest. ❧

A male cardinal wintered with us. He fed each dawn and dusk, occasionally appeared at midday to brighten the landscape. Until the first drippy thaw of March he seemed perfectly content in his bachelorhood. On that prespring daybreak the bare woods fairly vibrated with his song. Head back, tail down, he leaned first right, then left as he rolled his "whit, whit, whit, cheer—cheer—cheer." Any red bird within miles had to hear him.

Usually we have one or more mated pairs of cardinals wintering with us. The males ignore the females most of the winter, even crowding them aside at the feeder. By March they start mending fences. He sticks close by as they feed, may even offer choice tidbits. Ardent attention and good manners are the order of the day. Finally, from the tip of a bare maple, he will burst into delicious song. From a nearby treetop she may join him. Her softer notes add a depth to the duet unequalled among bird sounds. In one moment, at daybreak, a cardinal duet can slash winter's bonds that seem to bind me almost to suffocation at this time of year.

But this spring there was no duet. Day after day our suitor rolled out his song; an invitation to the females, a warning to rivals. There was no answer. We listened as hard as he did, but in vain. Finally, one day he was gone.

Our cardinals usually start nesting about May 1. In late April we hear the male's territorial announcements near the fir thickets up-stream or down from the house. One year we had two pairs, one in each of the two preferred territories. The house was about halfway between, and both males visited us occasionally in peace. Cardinals are fiercely territorial. They will fight another male or their reflec-tion in anything shiny in their territories. Apparently our feeder was no-man's-land.

As soon as brooding starts the female disappears. The male feeds her on the nest and keeps his territory intact by song. When the young hatch, in about two weeks, both adults feed them. Insects are the major diet as they must have lots of protein. Bird feeder offerings are ignored. When the young are fledged they become the male's sole responsibility while she prepares for a second brood.

As she is setting, he will bring her food while he still feeds and teaches their teenagers. That is when they first show at our feeders. The young are brown with dull black beaks. They learn quickly. After having a few bits of cracked corn or shucked sunflower seeds stuffed in by the old man, they feed themselves.

Each still spring dawn I listened for the cardinals with fervent yearning. We long to hear their duet, his proud territorial melody, and see the new generation take their first free steps to independence.
ꖜ

A skunk is one animal whose encounter is guaranteed to cause a pause in any outdoor activity. Therefore, it was only natural that my return from the mailbox early the other morning was brought to a prompt halt when one of them came humping across the field between me and the house.

To meet a skunk in the middle of a twenty-acre snow-covered field is unusual, but this encounter was particularly uncommon because the skunk was a very large one; he was coal black except for a white tip on his tail; and he was in a hurry.

Skunks aren't built for hurrying. Their chemical warfare equipment makes it unnecessary. Their normal gait is a sedate shuffle, and when they must resort to the back-humping gallop of the weasel family, they really have to work at it. A skunk's portly figure cuts his speed so much, you can easily catch up to him if you are so inclined.

The amount of white in skunks' coats is highly variable. A solid black one is uncommon though not particularly rare. Solid black hides are said to be considerably more valuable in the fur trade than the more usual white-stripped ones.

Skunks are mainly nocturnal, but now is the mating season, and that is probably what kept my passing wayfarer out so late. It may also have accounted for his hurrying, though I suspect he was just running to find cover in the nearby woods.

Skunks are peaceable animals, and generally use their built-in Mace system only as a last resort defense. With care and no sudden movements, it is possible to herd one about with considerable success. When his patience wears thin he will stamp his front feet; first one, then the other, sometimes both. His final warning is a raised tail. Then it's prudent to be well upwind. His weapon is a highly volatile liquid with a range of about twelve feet. It's odor may carry a half mile or more, but it's defensive value is due to it's pungent acidity which, at close range, will burn the skin and cause temporary blindness if it gets in the eyes.

Skunks themselves don't smell bad, but the males fight during the mating season, and may spray each other. The odor lingers, and is particularly noticeable in damp weather. One reason they raise their tails before firing is to keep from getting themselves all scented up.

These animals are known to suffer from sinus trouble, though you'd think they possess plenty of remedy to clear up their nasal passages. In colonial days some asthma sufferers carried smelling bottles full of skunk scent glands. A deep sniff brought prompt relief from an asthmatic attack—it also helped assure the sufferers privacy. 💥

Every now and then it's good to have a snow day; one so bad you can't even get out to get the mail, and it probably wasn't delivered anyway. To be of maximum value the storm has to be big enough so you don't even consider going to town. That's the kind that proves most of what we do isn't really important. It sort of shakes down my self-importance to realize that if I do absolutely nothing for a whole day it really won't make much difference.

Bird feeders are more fun when you can't get out. Watching full time I see things I've been missing. One of our creepers has brown stains on the belly. The other is clean white underneath. Now we can keep track of them individually. The white outer tail feathers of most of the woodpeckers are brown stained too. It must be bark that makes the stains, but what kind and why?

In our fir trees the fox squirrels climb up the trunks and down the limbs. Fir limbs grow in spaced whorls. Even in dense stands they are slow to prune. Each fir trunk is a many-runged ladder. The fox squirrels gallop headfirst down the ladders releasing two feet at a time. In hardwoods they trot down the trunks. This gait releases one foot at a time. It's not as fast as the gallop.

What causes chickadees to lose toes? One of ours has no toes on one foot. Another has lost three toes from one foot and two from the other. Both birds seem healthy, but they have to hover to feed from the peanut butter holes. It seems hard enough just to be as tiny as a chickadee in winter—and then to lose half your toes. Chickadees are plucky little birds. Caught in a banding net they struggle and peck fiercely—never giving up. If they grew as big as blue jays, we'd have to stay indoors.

Doves would rather fly than walk. We scatter corn in handfuls. The doves alight exactly where they want to feed. They will walk among one handful, but fly to the next patch. They can't scratch in the snow. They flip it aside with their bills—not very effective. If the feed is buried too deep they just sit and wait. They will follow anything that scratches—squirrels, grouse, or even the little meadow vole that scurries about under the feeder.

Doves are extending their winter range north. Is their storm survival dependent on other species? For doves, at any rate, we know our feeders help. For today at least, that much we do *is* important. I'm glad most things aren't. I'd be fretting about the weather. 🔥

The first wood ducks returned two days before spring; two drakes and a hen. They appeared unannounced amid the blacks and mallards at our streamside feeder. Suddenly the world was beautiful all over again.

Nothing, but nothing, quite so decorates the drab prespring river bottoms like a pair of woodies. The drakes are certainly the most beautiful of our waterfowl, and they know it. The demure hens seem to enjoy basking in the reflected glory of their mates.

This first threesome was a mated pair and a still-questing bachelor. The odd drake was tolerated, but there was no question about the hen's allegiance. Her mate occasionally rushed his rival off just to keep him in place. The pair always exchanged reassuring touches after each of these forays. My wife reveled in the romance of the display. I marveled at the biology of mating behavior. Both of us enjoyed the show.

Enter the villian. Our goshawk almost ended the drama. He struck the mated drake as he rested on the shore. My wife saw the hawk start his stoop from across the river. The actual catch was out of sight around the bend. Later we discovered feathers and blood at the site. A handful of iridescent scapulas and purple chestnut chest feathers identified the victim, but where was the body? A goshawk would surely butcher a kill this size right where it fell.

Of all our wild neighbors, the goshawk most strains our tolerance. My wife threatens him with every form of retribution. Even my objective view of nature's balance is shaken. He has already taken most of our grouse and now this. The birds at our feeder are never safe. He's a marvelous killing machine. We hope maybe the woodie got away.

Next day the lone drake appeared in front of the house. All day we watched for the others or hoped, at least, for the hen. I put out the daily corn ration without any real enthusiasm. Still we checked the feeding flock frequently.

Glory of glory, the missing pair return. He is obviously lame. Both wing tips sit at an odd angle above his rump. He is agile as ever afoot, but can he fly? She sticks close to his side as they feed. Suddenly something flushes the flock of black ducks. Both woodies fly with them. He is going to be all right.

Today the threesome is back together. Nothing has changed. The missing feathers and cocked wings are a hero's wounds. My wife says that she actually admires them. Biologically it can't be so—but it's nice for a springtime flight of fancy. ❦

Wind is air running downhill. In March it runs fast and furious. Wild things try to avoid winds. On a cold sunny day I went to see how they do it. The hardwood flats are deserted. Boney limbs creaked against one another and rattled skeletons to add shivers of superstition to the chill. I did not linger.

The conifers are where to be today. They turn off the windchill like a closed door: nature's green barns, smelling of balsam, spruce gum, and cedar boughs. The black-green acoustical ceiling muffles Boreas's passage through treetops. Hunched shoulders relax. Mittened hands unclench. Comfort edges misery out of collars, cuffs, and leaks where the wind has probed deadly fingers. No wonder deer yard in conifers. The delight of being out of the wind is sheer luxury.

Nothing moves here. It's the siesta hour. "Mad dogs and Englishmen go out in the midday sun" and only a foolish naturalist walks about in a March gale. Sunglow leads me toward a southern edge, logged years ago, now cluttered with wind throws and hardwood sprouts.

A deer eyes me from her bed, reluctant to leave. I crowd a tree trunk to steady binoculars. Her head periscopes up infinitely slowly, yet suddenly perceivable. Deer carry magic with them. The woods are their blanket of invisibility. They can peek out from it or throw it off in a dash. Suddenly the swamp is full of white flags. I've interrupted a slumber party. Along the sunny edge are many deer beds, too comfortable to resist. I find one against a sun-warmed trunk. Why let such luxury go to waste? I'll sit a while.

In March the north wind fights a rearguard battle with the sun. Exaggerated temperature differences between the north polar region and the equator at the time of the vernal equinox, send chill winds rushing off to hold back the advance of spring. Air flows from high pressure to low according to logical meteorological laws. Earth spin swirls it about. It's all very scientifically explainable. But who can be objective about spring weather?

For me, the spring sun's fight with wind is personal. I sit with my back to our ally, the forest, on spruce quills thawed by a sunshine foray. Warmth pleasures my whole being, heavies my eyelids. I revel in the frustrated keening of the wind through spruce tops and its rattling passage amongst the saplings in the cutdown. The swamp lets just enough breeze to its floor to promise spring against my cheek.

Wild things know where the action isn't. There the trees hold off the enemy while the sun pacifies it with warmth. We all know who's going to win. So, we doze in comfort and root for our side. Spring is coming one more time, and the March wind can't stop it.

You can swim if you want to. If you don't want to, you can still swim if you have to. This seems to be true of all wildlife. I've never seen a wild animal or bird that couldn't swim when necessary. Some surprising ones do so by choice. Spring is a good time to see them.

The fox squirrels that cross the river to our feeders are reluctant swimmers. I watched one this morning. Three times he tested the water. Brr!—there must be a shorter crossing. Finally from the end of a log he carefully entered the water. His bushy tail floated high, hardly got wet. Soon he was up a tree drying off. He licked legs and forearms, then scratched off missed droplets. Finally he flirted his tail and combed it. Only then did he come down to eat.

Deer swim the river without hesitation, but seem to have favorite crossings just like their dry land runways. Whitetails are strong swimmers. While duck hunting I watched a doe swim a mile or more from a Lake Huron island. As she approached the mainland she knelt neck deep in the shallows. Finally, sure all was safe, she stood up and walked ashore. Deer shake like dogs to dry off. Their skin is remarkably loose, like a half-filled gunnysack.

Beavers are our second-best swimmers. Despite their pear shape they are faster than anything on the river except otters. I have heard tales of these animals teaching their young to swim. I doubt the details. Once I saw a very small beaver clinging to its mother. She simply pushed the kit away and it started to swim; splashy at first, but soon smoothly and confidently. She stuck close by, but it seemed strictly a case of sink or swim. She may have chuckled encouragement. I was too far to hear.

The little voles by our river are enthusiastic swimmers. They dive for corn I spread for ducks. I once hid for hours by the shore for a close identifying look. They did not show, but a star-nosed mole swam almost at my feet as if he owned the river. He disappeared into an underwater tunnel. It never occurred to me that moles swam.

I once watched a flock of turkeys fly across the Mississippi River. Several young ones didn't make it. They hit the water about 100 feet out and simply swam ashore. No casualties. I couldn't believe it.

Nature has a never-ending box of surprises. Porcupines sometimes probe for succulent water plants. They swim well. Their quills help them float high. Swimming chipmunks hold their tails up high above the water.

Once by a trout stream, I flushed a tiny animal. It ran across the surface of a quiet pool—didn't even get wet. Water shrews can walk on water! It isn't true—but my fishing partner was a priest. He saw it too. ✹

Nature has a way of foretelling each new season. A symphony promises spring. Long before the trees begin to blush in welcome, spring sends her music on ahead. I sat the first warm day of March to listen.

Melody is carried by the stream, laughing from its new freedom. Tinkling driplets add counterpoint from the shelf ice, sweet as wind chimes in a gentle breeze. Spring's first symphony is the song of little waters; tentative, tenuous, not ready yet for the crescendo of freshet.

The woodwind section echoes from the trees. Nuthatches sound their oboe love songs. All winter they have kept in tune with nasal conversation. Now their half-thawed tunes complement the streamlets. The chickadees play piccolos. They only know two notes as if just learning how. Their "fee-bees" make up in enthusiasm for what they lack in scope.

All winter the hairy and downy have been readying the drums. Now the woods reverberate. Their territorial poundings lend variety to the sonata. Each bird has found a limb to suit his ear—far and near—jazz musicians doing their thing at the year's first jam session.

A pair of pileateds rush on stage with the trumpets, boldly sounding, almost shouting, their duet holds center stage, then flies on black and white to send clarion harmony from the wings. Their departure almost leaves a silence. But no—the waters continue their pianissimo melody. Distant crows play bass. No spring symphony would be complete without their raspy obbligato.

I love this prespring music. Each year's rendition is different, molded by the snow depth, rain or fog, and the first south wind. In our snow country the musicians do not change. The same company is on hand each year to play new compositions.

The smell of flowers tells you summer is coming. Flocking birds write against the sky that fall is near. Leaves flutter down to warn of winter's touch. Each season foretells its coming long before it's here. Each chooses its most beautiful messengers—odors, flight patterns, fluttering colors. What can cold bare March produce to rival them?

Spring sends her small musicians. No tales of lazy sunshine days, harvest bounty, flights of fancy to far places. No flamboyant flashy colors telling tales of deeds accomplished. Her small trickles tell a story, echoed by her winter wild things, of the time for life's renewal. ❧

Ferocious is just a word in the dictionary most of the time. We don't see ferocious things in modern life. Yesterday I did.

A goshawk chased a screaming blue jay almost into my face. If ever I saw stark terror it was in that jay's face as it swept past me into the swamp. An instant behind, the hawk tore in pursuit. I got a fleeting glimpse of a blue gray shape, black and white face, and a red eye that made my neck hairs prickle. Here was death inevitable.

The drama disappeared into the conifers. Did the race end or just leave my hearing? Nothing, but nothing, could fly so through those picket thick trunks. The jay did, and marvel of marvels, the two-foot-long goshawk followed every twist and turn. She must have had almost a four-foot wingspread. A male would have been much smaller.

In that photo-clear glimpse I saw the marvel of accipiter adaptation. The rounded wings seemed never fully open. Short, quick, wing beats, built-in maneuverability—what better equipment to chase food in the forest.

I think this goshawk has been with us since January. Our grouse have gradually disappeared. We used to see three budding each evening. Then there were two. Now we see one's tracks in the snow. He doesn't feed high in the bare poplars. There are slim but safer pickings for him in the thickets. He'll survive to drum next spring and entice some hens to raise a new grouse population for our woods.

Last week I got a good clear look at our visiting predator. She dived at three jays sampling corn we spread. My arrival flushed the jays just in time to save a life. Her dive swept over the bank and into the woods beyond. Her wings were swept back, wrist bent. A falcon's stoop is swifter, more delta shaped. The goshawk held her wings cocked, ready to fly in pursuit. I think this relentless chase is what strikes terror in her prey. Much wild predation is quick and opportunistic. Initial escape is home free. Not so with goshawks. Intent on prey they will dive into brush and run on the ground until the victim is caught or scared to hopeless flight.

I could fight the goshawk for my grouse. Maybe I could win, but I would lose. I need her help. Snowshoe hares have overrun our woods. They are eating the autumn olive and other shrubs we plant. If we would have berries for the birds some day, we must save them from rabbits now. She is a better rabbit hunter than I and is at it every day.

The lost grouse are the price I pay for this alliance with a feathered Attila. The bonus is my glimpse of ferocity. ❦

Mankind has lived with wood for so long that it inevitably finds a special place in our hearts. Totally apart from endless utility, each tree species has its own little niche from which it endears itself—the smell of new sawn pine, the soft patina of hand-rubbed walnut, scarlet maples, a white cathedral of birches. The list is endless, but when I'm just ready to expire from the winter wearies, an unimpressive little tree tops all the rest.

I think the pussy willow's main role on earth is to lift the spirits. Its string of silver catkins is a rosary of thanks that winter is on the wane. I look for them at each winter thaw, but they are always a surprise. Suddenly little ranks of silky pussycats are marching skyward. It's as if they came from nowhere.

Each March impatience at winter obsesses me. At the first sound of running water I don hip boots and blunder about the landscape. Crotch-deep drifts are floundering soft. Wetlands ice supports only half my steps. Leg up, leg down, I wander on a fool's errand and find a treasure. A handful of silk-jeweled twigs brings a fortune of sunshine into our home.

The pussies of pussy willows are catkins of the male flowers. Willows are dioecious. Male and female flowers grow on different plants. Flowering time varies widely with individuals. Usually one or two precocious bushes rush the season. They are the ones that seem to appear by magic. All about, more cautious catkins are just beginning to creep from beneath their scales, or stay still locked tight in protective sheaths. Those early adventurers are the ones so dear to me.

If you want to play tricks, anyone can have pussy willows in midwinter. Mark one of the precocious plants. Next February put a few branches in water in a sunny place inside. Soon, instant springtime! Take them out of water before the pollen develops. Willows produce nectar to attract bees, but in case bees aren't available, there is a tremendous pollen crop for wind pollenation. It furnishes abundant bee bread for any bees early enough to find it.

Pussy willows are easy to plant. Cut a stick a half inch or thicker in diameter and about twenty inches long. Stick it in a damp place with two inches above ground. Be sure to get a male stick. Female flowers aren't very attractive. Their seeds have hairy covers for wind scattering. A big female willow in seed can blind window screens, roll white windrows into every corner, and make shrouds of spiderwebs.

Yes, the female pussy willow can be a nuisance in June, but in March the male makes it all worth while. ✺

The first geese are back. That small vanguard of six to eight that precedes the main flocks each spring just arrived.

The Canada geese are among the most fascinating residents of our wildfowl refuge. Mating for life, brave in protecting their nest and young, wary and wise in the face of danger, they are unequaled in character by any other bird. I have twice witnessed shows of their valor.

Some years ago I found one nesting on a muskrat house. Canada geese like to nest in an open spot where they can see about them. In spite of this, they are not easy to locate. This goose lay prone on the nest with her neck draped motionless down the side. At a distance her protective color gave the impression of simply a larger than average muskrat house. I fished in the area for several minutes before I realized what I was seeing.

Hoping to get a close-up picture, I worked my boat slowly into the shallows. Suddenly I noticed the gander standing at attention among the half-emergent cattails. At that moment, deciding I threatened his mate, he launched himself directly at me with a great clamor and hissing. I tumbled backward in the boat and barely avoided his wings. He landed in the water beyond the boat. Stretching his neck and opening his beak, he hissed loudly as he came forward to renew the attack. I backed the boat in a hasty retreat. As soon as he considered me safely routed, he swam to the nest and reassured his mate by running his neck alongside hers and over her body. She had remained motionless throughout the battle.

I once came upon a pair of these geese on the shore with their newly hatched brood huddled between them. Offshore a belligerent swan swam back and forth, obviously threatening the little family. My arrival presented a new threat, putting the family in untenable danger. Without hesitation, the gander charged full tilt at the swan. Half flying, half swimming, he swept past, just out of reach of his startled heavyweight adversary who turned in hot pursuit. The chase swept across to a reed-grown isthmus leading to a small bushy island. Here the gander gained ground and disappeared into the reeds. The swan, tall enough to see over the reeds, rushed across and plunged into the open water in search of his prey. While the swan vainly searched the bay ahead, the goose reappeared around the island out of sight from his enemy.

Meanwhile his mate had left the shore with her brood swimming close alongside, as soon as the chase was well underway. She disappeared on the shore of a large island just as her lord and master completed his elusive maneuvers.

Without a glance in my direction, also ignoring the swan who now swam in the distance still wondering what had happened, the gander went straight to the large island for a happy reunion.

Surely no knight in shining armor could have done better. Truly he deserves his title—grandest of all waterfowl. ❦

Once each year there comes a day which makes March worthwhile. Yesterday was it. A quartet of barred owls greeted me with a chorus of "who cooks, who cooks, who cooks for you all?" Back and forth it rolls, two near, two far, announcing territories and mating time. A mob of crows comes to harry the performers. The noisiest critters in the woods announce the day. It's going to be a good one.

There's a stirring in the air and a rustling in my being. I must be out to see winter's leftovers and who's arrived from south. Checking the hawk nests upriver is a good excuse if I need one.

A band of chickadees come tree skipping. I stop one skip away. A chick lights on my shoulder. Another hovers in front, checking my beard for bugs. A "dee dee" in my ear announces their departure. A few weeks hence they may tweak my hair for nest lining, but now it's breakfast time. No insects here.

The otters have a new playground a mile upstream. It used to be at our doorstep, but people and dogs are not to be tolerated. They move rather than accept integration. Their new ground is complete with icy slide from the high bank, a nice flat-rolled plot of snow and piles of signpost droppings. Two fresh tracks enter the river.

Here two deer swam the river. One slipped on the tilted shore ice—lost a patch of belly hair. Their muddy tracks lead inland. Now why did they pick last night for a swim?—Dogs? My glasses find no clues on the far bank.

Conifers provide cover to sneak a mob of crows. Such ruckus is always worth investigation. A red-shouldered hawk flushes, pursued by the screaming rabble. I check the nest nearby. The great horned owls, that hooted so last month, have not appropriated it. Maybe the red-shouldereds will nest there next month.

I glass every large tree hole. A few hairs show at the top of a shattered snag. Raps on the trunk brings a coon's disapproving bandit face. One glance, a couple of twists and turns, then back to bed. The hole will barely hold him. He half blocks the entry, but it's a southern exposure. The sun warms his back, solid comfort.

A network of tracks pinpoints a winter-killed deer. No starvation this year. Just a weakling fawn that didn't make it. Survival of the fittest, and food for the coon, and some mice, and a couple of stray dogs that shouldn't have been there.

A stone fly helicopters low over the river and stalls against a log. A chickadee snaps him up. More flys creep the sunlit snow. With the first hatch already, trout opener can't be long now.

Yes, one day can make a whole month worthwhile. For March that takes some doing. ❦

April

A fir tree points a finger toward heaven when it sprouts and keeps it there till it dies. Spruce trees point skyward too, but their cones dangle. Firs hold their cones upright as if in reverent offering.

No other trees point quite so emphatically. Destroy the leader of a fir tree, and one of its limbs will turn up to do the pointing. The roof of a spruce-fir forest looks like a carpet of spearheads. No other forest type has such a pickity profile.

There are forty different kinds of fir trees. Nine are native to the United States and Canada. Only one, balsam fir, is native to the lake states. As trees go, balsam fir doesn't grow very large or live very long. The ones in our yard are fifty feet tall and sixty years old. They've about had it. Heart rot has set in at the base of many.

Balsams are aggressive trees. They like moist sites, as does cedar. The saying is—"Cut a cedar, get a balsam back." This is not entirely the balsam fir's fault. Deer love cedar. It is a winter staple in the big snow country. When a little cedar sticks its tip above the snow a hungry deer nips it off. Not so with balsam firs. Deer can't digest them. If you find deer eating fir they are starving.

Balsam doesn't make very good lumber. For pulpwood it is second only to spruce, but light in weight so the yield is poor. For firewood it is awful. The only worse wood is spruce. Both will smoke up your cook pots beyond cleaning, pop sparks on everything burnable, and barely give enough heat to prevent freezing in July. Dry, it burns like gunpowder. Green, it smoulders like a wet blanket. Man would never have discovered fire had he evolved in the spruce-fir forests. Balsam fir has resisted mans' exploitation by being as useless as possible, truly a weed of the woods.

As I sit here wondering at all these negatives I ask, "Who am I to judge?" The tall slender trunks weave striped patterns against the westering sky. Sparrows scurry riverside through the young fir minithickets. Some will nest there soon. Last fall, hunted hard, deer found haven in the small firs. Rabbits prosper there. Woodcock find an easy place to dodge the shot. At blizzards blast, the fir thicket makes a refuge in the wilds; safe from wind and with the snowflakes held aloft upon the limbs. Suppose fir isn't good to eat, or build, or burn. Nature does not ask for man's judgment.

Fir thickets are nature's green barns. They point their hands to heaven and say, "Send me your cold and frightened. Send me the small and the meek. When the cold wind blows and death in its throes stalks a landscape drear and bleak, I'll keep them warm and midst the storm make a refuge for the weak." 🌿

One of our black squirrels is a gray squirrel. I probably couldn't prove it without counting her teeth, but the gray gray squirrel that visits us knows without tooth counting. He told us by his actions.

This year we are overrun with big squirrels. The buildup started in January when the river froze. Each day we watched the big rusty fox squirrels cross the ice. When the ice went out they swam. There is nothing wetter than a wet squirrel. I think it bothered us more than it did them.

The swimmers would comb water from neck and ears, flirt their tails, and have at the corn spillings. In very cold weather ice formed on hair tips. Then they would stop and comb out the crystals. Freeze-drying—very efficient.

By mid-March we could count up to twelve rusty fox squirrels and six blacks. Then the gray gray squirrel arrived. We were delighted. Ours is not good gray squirrel habitat. The extra species was a welcome addition to our outdoor show.

We gradually realized that the gray was paying more than casual attention to one of the blacks. This prompted close binocular study of each squirrel. Winter gray squirrels have ear tufts similar to red squirrels. There is also a little white behind the ears. The attractive black squirrel also had ear tufts. Both were about the same size; half as large as the biggest fox squirrel.

Fox squirrels don't have ear tufts. None of the big blacks had long ear hairs. There was considerable color variation. One was coal black, some had a scattering of gray hairs, one had a rusty tinge to his tail. One black had a gray face and a white nose! All had the sedate behavior of the rusty foxes. They were far more clumsy in the trees than the gray squirrels. When frightened, they fled on the ground. The grays took to the trees.

Last year we had few big squirrels. The ones that came were infected with mange. We shot several half-naked ones to try to curb the epidemic. We've seen no mange this year.

I think all our present squirrels were immigrants. They came from farm woodlots and the logged-over forest across the river. Snowless December made for early cleanup of the cornfields. January buried the few grains left under two feet of snow. By now the squirrels should be feasting on elm buds, but there are none. Hundreds of bleached snags show the larder bare as Mother Hubbard's.

So, the foxy fox squirrels and the gray gray squirrel, and the black fox, and black gray squirrels join the red squirrels and the birds at our feeders. To us it's a show of delightful confusion. But the squirrels don't get mixed-up. They know. ❧

When the windstorm blew down most of our trees, it damaged the maples left standing. Good sap weather that followed made icicles from broken twigs. I first noticed when a siskin hung head-down to drink from the tip of one of the icicles. Siskins are not very acrobatic little birds. One hanging upside down from a slender twig will surely get a birder's attention. A little later I watched an evening grosbeak. He wasn't satisfied to sip from the tip. He snipped off an inch, straightened up and crushed it just like a sunflower seed. Didn't spill a chip.

These birds may have been just getting a drink. They regularly eat snow in winter and prefer that snow lodged on the branches of trees. I think they ate the sap ice because of taste, or for vitamins, or some other spring tonic goodness. Sap was also seeping from the freshly scarred maple trunks. Red squirrels crept upward, licking as they went. They paused at every little cranny that held an extra sip. I have often seen squirrels, both red and fox, nibble through the bark on top of maple limbs, then lap the sap that collects in the depressions. They only do this in spring.

I first encountered sap ice in Maine. Our home had a big maple tree which, of course, we tapped. We drank more sap than we boiled, but we did make enough maple syrup to prove you shouldn't do it on an electric stove. One morning I found a slender icicle hanging from a broken twig. I popped it into my mouth. Not sweet, but delicious, just full of good spring taste, surely the most pollution-free thirst quencher on earth.

I couldn't understand how maple syrup could be so sweet and the sap not. Of course, it's a matter of dilution. My maple-wise Yankee wife boiled down a pail of sap to half and—presto—it was sweet. After that we made no more syrup. Sap was boiled to sweetness and chilled in the fridge. Maple flavored and better than Kool-Aid before Kool-Aid was invented. The kids loved it.

All kinds of maple tree sap will make syrup. Sugar maples are supposed to be the best, but sugar content varies with individual trees. A good red maple may produce more sweets than a poor sugar maple. Even box elder sap will make syrup. An old-timer told me the redder the leaves in fall, the sweeter the sap in spring. I've never proved it. My sap-boiling experience has been limited to what maples were handiest, regardless of leaf color.

In the outdoors I have never found anything new. Each delight I discover is old hat to some wildlings. I'll bet the first man that ever licked a maple sapcicle learned it from the birds. It was a delightful gift. I thank them every spring. ❦

"Along the cool sequestered vale they keep the noiseless tenor of their way." Even before the frogs and toads start their spring chorus, some salamanders gather in icy pools and streamlets to do their courting thing—in silence. Salamanders are mute. They have neither eardrums nor middle ears, yet each spring the males and females find their noiseless way to meet for mating. How do they communicate?

Biologists tell us that salamanders seem to depend on the forelimbs and special muscles to transmit ground vibrations to the inner ear. They also tell us salamanders gather in the shallow water of streams and pools for breeding.

I found a spotted salamander plodding his way down a snow-filled rut 200 yards from the nearest water. Experimenting, I carried him back a ways and headed him from where he had come. A few moments hesitation, then around he turned to resume his intended way. Three times, but he would not be diverted. Finally I carried him toward our pond outlet where, on some early spring nights, I have found dozens of these little amphibians. He confirmed my guess of his destination by heading straight for the water. No other salamanders were there. I hope I didn't mess up the party by helping him arrive too soon.

The common salamanders on our place are the spotted and blue-spotted. Spotted salamanders are black with large yellow or orange spots along each side of their back and tail. The blue-spotted have lots of light blue spots on back and sides. They look much like the old-fashioned blue-and-white-speckled enamel kitchenware. These two belong to the mole salamander, Ambystomidae, family. They spend most of their time underground, occasionally coming out on wet nights to forage for earthworms.

When I dug potatoes last fall, I turned up a big six-inch blue-spotted salamander. He was beautiful, and I promptly tucked him safely under some damp straw. I suspect he had been mining for the june bug grubs which infested my potato patch. They got more than their share of potatoes, so I need Spotty's help against them. Hope he doesn't return from courting until after my spring plowing. I doubt he could survive those whirling rototiller blades.

Salamanders have teeth, but the ones around here don't bite. A large salamander on the West Coast bites and also barks—the only ones with voices. Aquatic amphiums (we called them lamper eels in the South) are also vicious biters. Their poison is supposed to be deadly—but not so. The salamanders of Michigan are harmless and our friends. They also harbor some marvelous mysteries.

I still wonder how a male salamander can find a female 200 yards away on an icy spring night by feeling ground vibrations. 🌾

Lovely is the word for a hen wood duck. Exquisite fits her mate. A pair rests on an elm snag high above the river. April sun and the brush of breezes play gentle games with their colors. An invisible artist who can't make up his mind. Each time I look there is a change—more beautiful than before—yes—no—try again.

The drake's spectacular plumage camouflages his mate. She vanishes by comparison, a gray burl on the log. But, look close, blue and silver iridescence washes across her. Lovely, lovely, the most highly colored of all female ducks. She needs a brilliant mate to complete her disguise.

This year, for the first time in my memory, spring arrived right on time. March 20 dawned warm and bright. Just as sunrise lit our upstream point, a pair of woodies splashed the current. "Aix sponsa, waterfowl in wedding raiment." Spray scattered diamonds to celebrate. Black water and white snow replaced the wedding flowers.

Foul weather had held back migration. All the first arrivals were already mated. They promptly started house hunting. Alas, we missed the show. Overflow drowned all the floodplain. All our duck boxes, and most of the hollow trees, are in the lowlands. In dry years or in wadeable water, I spend spring mornings in the floodplains. Make like a stump and the ducks will ignore you. You can't watch from a boat—too obvious. They insist on privacy. Disturbance will drive them away for the season.

Wood ducks spend several days selecting a nest. The pair lights in trees, crane necks and peer about. When a cavity is found the female investigates. She can enter a hole four inches in diameter. Once I watched one at a pileated woodpecker's hole. Pileated nest holes are large enough, but oblong vertically. The duck grasped the lip of the hole, tail braced against the trunk. A look inside to inspect the premises, then she tipped sideways and entered—remarkably agile.

The drake doesn't enter the nest cavity. When the hen finds a hollow to her liking the drake may wait outside for an hour while she puts the place in order. Wood ducks must have some loose material in the cavity. I use sawdust in my boxes. The duck swishes around in it to make a hollow.

The hen lays an egg a day in early morning while the drake waits nearby. After about four days she starts plucking down (feathering her nest). By the time the clutch (about twelve eggs) is complete, there is enough down to cover them.

When brooding starts the drake deserts his mate. Why stick around if she's not coming out? But, until then, it's a honeymoon every day. He's adoringly attentive—chases all rivals. He makes her safe by being too gorgeous for any danger to overlook. 🦆

The tide of sparrows that swept south over us last fall started returning in mid-March. Bird migrations are very much like the ocean tides. Early individuals trickle into favored habitat, filling and crowding until suddenly they are everywhere. Just so does the salt tide push into the estuaries filling the little creeks, then flooding the flats, and rising, rising until only the reed tips show. Then tips become longer and longer until again only the creeks are full, rushing madly seaward. Suddenly the water is gone with just salty trickles and puddles in favored spots awaiting the tide's return.

Each species has its own tide table, stirring and mixing with others, pushed or held by the weather. The first arrivals were tree sparrows. By April 1 they were spreading out of the weed patches and brush piles. They build and build until finally the peak rolls past. By May 1 many are in their tundra nest grounds across Canada and Alaska.

At the first April snowstorm our front yard was almost paved with tree sparrows. With them was a good scattering of juncos and a handful of song and fox sparrows. Juncos usually tag close behind the tree sparrows. Some of them will go all the way to Alaska's north slope to nest among the oil rigs. Others will spread across Canada from the Pacific to Labrador. A few nest here.

Fox sparrows are our largest and one of the most handsome sparrows. Their heavily streaked, central-spotted breast suggests a song sparrow, but the bright orange-brown rear end makes them unmistakable. All sparrows are scratchers. With foxies it's compulsive. They will stand knee-deep in grain and scratch madly with both feet. On leafy ground they can make as much fuss as a turkey. Fox sparrows nest along the border between trees and tundra. They like low brush. When other sparrows fly to flee, the foxies vanish into the fir thicket with one hop and a flit.

Many song sparrows nest with us. Their nesting range extends all across the northern United States and Canada to the tree line. While the transient tree sparrow and foxies sing anticipatory spring songs, some song sparrows are already staking out nest territories and protecting them by singing.

As the first arctic sparrow tide passes another will arrive. White-throats peak about a month behind the tree sparrows. Many will nest with us. At our longitude their summer range coincides approximately with song sparrows. With them come a few white-crowned sparrows. These elegant sparrows nest on the tundra with the tree sparrows. I wonder why they don't travel together?

Then other tides, spring and neap: savannah and grasshopper sparrows, swamp and field, our beloved chippies and many others. Twice each year the tides of migration sweep their gust of life from the arctic to the gulf. The spring sparrow tides are first. We like them best. ✺

Seems like half the subdivisions along the Gulf Coast have a "Mockingbird Lane." This is not just indicative of the developers' lack of originality, it is a tribute to a very fine bird. That country is full of mockingbirds, and they deserve all the accolades we can bestow.

Mockingbirds are people lovers, or, at least, they like the same habitat people do. They are very partial to nest sites near houses; porch vines, foundation plantings, garden shrubs. My childhood home always had a mocker's nest in the privet hedge. A bedroom window was just above the highest bush. Any spring night wakening heard the male mocker pouring out his melody—cure for childish nightmares, serenade for lovers. In daytime he sang from the chimney top, occasionally bounding in the air, possibly from pure exuberance, or to show off his white wing patches as emphasis of territorial claims.

Mockingbirds are intensely territorial. Our March trip south struck the peak of site selection. Dog fights among mockers were common. Singing was almost continuous. One of our early morning stops was in a huge, almost vacant parking lot. A mocker poured forth his territorial claims from one of the light poles, a symphony of all the countries bird songs, plus original mockingbird compositions. He laid claim to five acres of concrete plus manicured lawns and tourist attractions, all the way to the bay-side shrubbery. It put the battleship *Alabama* and World War II airplanes in proper perspective. We listened for half an hour.

Mockers will imitate anything within their pitch range; spring peepers, crickets, squeaky swings. Expert composers, they simply incorporate any sounds that fit their song motif. Copied songs, or their own inventions, are usually repeated several times. Each bird's artistry is unique. Some copy half their notes, others less than 10 percent. In a day's singing they change arrangements endlessly.

During nesting, mockingbirds are fearless defenders. Cats, dogs, snakes, and people are tweaked or pecked till driven away. Our privet hedge was a great place for small child hiding games. In nest season, it was a no-no. My kid brother's long blond hair was a prime mocker target. Until the young were fledged he had to play elsewhere.

All mimic thrushes evolved in America. Like so many nonmigratory New World species, mockers are gradually pushing their range northward. They regularly nest in southern Michigan. Last summer a pair nested in one of our northeastern lower peninsula cities. At least one mocker spent the winter there. No immigrant could be more welcome. I dream of watching Michigan mockers tweak the neighborhood pets, and hearing those master singers in all our towns. Someday, if we are lucky, one of our developers may even name a Mockingbird Lane. ✤

You can't train dogs on wild game from April 15 to July 15. This is a good law to protect nesting wildlife. It probably should be more stringent. Dogs don't have to be in training to disturb wildlife. Any dog running loose in the open may do damage.

Aside from man himself, the most effective predators in Michigan are domestic, or once domestic, dogs and cats. In large wild tracts wild predator species may be more effective, but near human habitation, nothing equals dogs and cats for sheer volume of wildlife destroyed. Wild predator numbers are controlled by the population of prey species. Domesticated predator numbers are controlled by people. I am sure the dogs and cats in our little village far outnumber the total population of wild predators within reasonable hunting range. From the tracks in snow, far too many are allowed to range at large, some miles from their homes.

In the winter of 1978–79, dogs killed four deer on our place. The deer were in poor shape, so some might have died anyway. The tracks showed that these deer, all fawns, were actually pulled down, but in severe winters dogs don't have to catch deer to kill. A 110 pound deer at rest uses about 1,300 calories in twenty-four hours to stay alive: running, it consumes 900 calories per hour. Dogs just out for a frolic may double the energy consumption of deer they disturb. This may kill them before spring.

But dogs and deer are not the whole story of pet predation. Small game and nongame species probably suffer the most. Cats are particularly hard on ground-nesting birds and young rabbits. They also climb trees to raid nests. I have seen one sitting on top of one of my bird houses catching young swallows as they came to the opening. Cottontail rabbits build fur-lined nests for their young. Free roaming pets find them. I think house cats are the main controlling factor on cottontail population in our village.

Dogs break up nests too. My dog is kenneled except when I am out with him. Each year he kills a few woodchucks, occasionally he retrieves an infant snowshoe hare, and in spite of everything, he finds a few birds' nests. Last summer a robin nested on the center rail of our driveway fence. Working a few feet away, I turned my back, and slick as a whistle, the dog licked out the three blue eggs. Swallowed shells and all. I could have wrung his neck.

We who own pets own responsibility, not just for their welfare, but for their behavior. We can teach them to be well mannered at home, but we can't control age old instincts if they run loose and meet temptation. No dog or cat should be allowed to run uncontrolled. Those who do it abuse our wildlife as much as poachers. 🦌

I remember when bluebirds were better harbingers of spring than the robins. Always some robins stay north all winter and appear prematurely to announce spring's arrival. The bluebirds all winter south. When their liquid warble echoed across the melting snow you knew spring was here.

But now—when did you last see a bluebird in March, or April, or even May? So many are gone. I weep that somehow, some way, we have changed the world to have fewer bluebirds. No one would want fewer bluebirds. But, in our thoughtless bumbling round this old world, we humans have stumbled and trampled some species into oblivion. These little birds, with the warble of melting snow in their song and the sky on their backs, are some of the innocent victims.

The other day three crossed before my car. I stopped to watch. They searched a fall-mowed lawn for stirring insects. Surely no cutworm, grub, or beetle seeking the warming sun can miss their search. They pounce on movements unseen in my binoculars, whap the victims still, then down the hatch.

I grew up in the South with bluebirds year round. Each fall arrivals from the north swelled the crowd. Imagine a hundred bluebirds on a close-cropped pasture. They seldom sang, but lord, how those flickers of sunlit sky did cheer our winters.

I didn't learn that bluebirds announced spring until I came north. I'll never forget my first April in New England; crawling through tag alders in freezing rain, dropping a worm in a yard-wide brook for trout too cold to bite. My shivers drove thoughts to the green sunlit spring of Mississippi. What a miserable fool I was. Then one little bird changed all that. A gentle song curled between the sleet drops and married me to the North. Never again have I endured slow creepings around the calendar. Let seasons arrive with a crash and clangor and the new sound of almost forgotten friends.

Bluebirds are gentle. They will not fight to find a home, but retreat before the starlings and sparrows, hitchhikers on European man's migrations. Bluebirds like people. Orchards and shade trees and boxes with holes too small for starlings may yet bring them back to our lawns. They like close-mowed grass, not treated with too many pesticides. Give them a chance and they will be far more attractive bug getters than chemical powders and caution-labeled liquids.

Bluebirds favor cemeteries and golf courses. If you don't take par too seriously, they will brighten your day out of all proportion.

Wind is for hawks. One recent windy day I watched a pair of red-shouldered hawks in courtship flight. It was spectacular.

The show first included two males wheeling and diving high in the sky as they made the air fairly ring with their "kee-yar, kee-yars!" Lower, a large female soared with equal animation. With half-closed wings, a male came tearing down invisible ski slopes, then a change of wing angle and up he rode on the wind's shoulders, a wing over, then pendulum side swings to show off his russet shoulders. The other didn't wait his turn, but did his thing in his own piece of sky. There were no repetitive school figures. This was exuberant freestyle competition.

Occasionally the female swept higher. She seemed to favor one suitor, almost touching him each time. Finally she coasted down at escalator speed to alight on a lone tree in the marsh. Her favorite made one more wide swing, then sailed in dead slow just above her perch. Legs extended, his talons rested lightly on her back. His cupped wings controlled the wind lift. This master of the airways needed no wing beats—deadly talons with a velvet touch. Only the really strong can be so gentle. The other male disappeared.

Next day the couple returned. He still courted on high. She perched at treetop or swept through the forest pinnacles, probably house hunting. I watched them mate at the forest edge. Red-shouldered hawks pair for years, possibly for life. Yet, each spring he courts her anew and she responds.

Red-shouldereds usually nest in big hardwood trees. One pair I know has raised three young in the same nest for the last three years. Another pair lost one brood to a marauding coon, but returned next year to raise a family in the same tree. The birds add to the nest each year. They advertise each spring's occupancy with a green conifer twig. Many hawks use greenery for occupied signs.

I have been watching a big old hawk's nest upriver. In February a pair of great horned owls appropriated it. By April their incubation was well underway. I happened to check them the day the red-shouldereds returned. The hawks were outraged. Back and forth they flew, screaming curses and anything else appropriate. All in vain.

Through my glasses I watched the hen owl brood, unperturbed. She was bigger and stronger than the red-shouldereds and, besides, had the help of her mate who was surely hiding nearby. The big owls nest early and take any nest they want. Their claims always stick.

The red-shouldereds will build a new home, but not too close, for the owls accept no predator neighbors. There, on the first windy day, the beauty of their courtship will bring a new spring's zest to their old love. With such affection, even the loss of a home isn't really very important. 🦌

Buffleheads are just plain cute. Now, duck hunters don't think of ducks as cute. Years ago my little daughter thought teal were cute. She tucked some I brought home in her bed, like dolls. I thought she was cute, but not the ducks.

I quit shooting buffleheads ten years ago when my son and I discovered how really cute they were. It was one of those comfortable duck hunting days when the wind didn't blow and nothing flew. We were set up on a small woodland lake to try to decoy some blacks. Our blind was right at water's edge.

A young bufflehead swam into our spread. Those little ducks will come to anything that looks like a duck. This one was no exception. It talked softly to our wooden replicas with a voice like a baby's snore. My son snored back to our visitor. The little duck swam right to shore and peered mightily into the brush of our hide.

The snoring conversation continued a full quarter hour. The little fellow just couldn't screw up the courage to come ashore, but its curiosity wouldn't let it depart. Finally our visitor swam away, but not before checking every decoy to make sure it wasn't sociable. Ever since that day, when a flock of these little black and white butterballs swing into my decoys I remember our friendly little visitor and hold my fire.

A pair of these little ducks stop a while each spring on our river. Today, amid a late snowstorm, they brighten the black water highway. The drake's black and white dress puts even this snowy landscape to shame. He fairly sparkles.

Buffleheads are late migrants. The ones that stop here are always mated. Further south I have watched their courtship. The drakes fluff the glossy feathers of their black and white heads till they are twice normal size. This gives them their name "buffalo head," later shortened to "buffle." In courting they are as indecisive as a child at a candy counter. The males fight viciously, then strut first before one hen then another. He stretches his neck, puffs his head, then, drawing his bill against his swelling chest, he struts across the water on his tail. Finally mating is settled, but I think he changes partners just to prolong the fun.

Buffleheads nest in tree hollows. We urge them to stay with nest boxes and feed. As I write, the pair dozes slowly downstream, bills tucked amid back feathers, solid comfort in the storm. Their home is north and west. I expect soon they will travel on. We keep hoping that one day a fickle pair will decide to stay here for nesting.

These little divers would be a welcome treat to our summers. After all, if the adults are too cute to shoot, what must the babies be like? They've just got to be winners. 🦆

Spring is the time to see grebes. But, who wants to see grebes? And what are they anyway? If you wait till summer you won't know, for grebes seem to disappear as soon as migration is over.

When I was a kid I didn't know what a grebe was, but I knew that a hell-diver was a little water bird that could dive faster than gunshot or sink slowly like a submarine. When I finally did shoot one that wasn't looking, I found it had the softest, silkiest, springiest feathers of any bird. No tail at all, just a tuft. Legs way back with only the feet sticking out, and these with wide flat toes. Three spatulas, as good for swimming as webs. A flattened little handful so cushiony and different, I'll never forget holding it. I've liked grebes ever since and never shot another.

The bird I shot was a pied-billed grebe. It is the only one that commonly breeds in the eastern United States. It has a rounded chicken bill with a black ring around it in summer. Other grebes have a pointed unmarked bill.

On a recent bird-watching weekend we saw four different kinds of grebes. Horned grebes have bright buff-colored ear tufts or horns, and rufous necks and flanks. Almost any Great Lakes lee shore may hold them in spring. Red-necked grebes are twice as big—long red necks and white cheeks, uncommon. They frequent the same waters as the horneds.

One Audubonist found an eared grebe, very rare in the Great Lakes, but common in the West. This handsome little bird was riding out a north gale in a small boat harbor, harvesting smelt around the keels of anchored boats. It had the same buff, black, and rufous coloring as the horned grebe, but arranged differently.

Grebes lose their bright colors in winter. The pied-billed even loses its bill ring. All are gray, white, and black, easily overlooked. When they are noticed, they are often a funny little duck that dives and never comes up.

Grebes aren't even closely related to ducks. They are primitive birds that are poor fliers but exceptional swimmers. Their eggs, in floating nests, are often wet all during incubation. The pied-billeds that nest in Michigan prefer quiet reedy ponds with lots of aquatic insects and small fish. The young can swim as soon as they are dry from hatching, but prefer to ride on mom or pop's back. When the adult dives, they sometimes shake loose and pop, cork light, to the surface.

I watched a pied-billed gagging down a three-inch sunfish. It resembled a man trying to swallow a spade. Shake and bobble, stretch and gurgle, the hand-shaped fingerling stretched its way down the hatch. It was a remarkable demonstration, but then, most everything about grebes is remarkable. ❧

On the way home from the environmental Teach-In I saw two of nature's most diligent pollution control workers soaring over the woods north of town. Next day I saw one of them cleaning up a mess of unwanted smelt that some pollution-unconscious person had dumped beside the road.

The turkey vulture probably qualifies as one of our most beautiful creatures in the air and ugliest on the ground. It is a case of the closer you are the nicer you *don't* look.

With binoculars I've watched soaring buzzards by the hour. Their wings tilt up to form a dihedral angle. The long tip feathers seem to feel the air like sensitive fingers, bending and spreading to constantly take the pulse of the thermal that supports them. I watched them a long time before I realized that they were constantly gliding downhill, banking, and turning to follow the vertical breezes that kept pushing their invisible toboggan slide higher and higher. They are marvels of grace.

Surely such an airborne creature should nest in some tall tree-top or, at least, a towering cliff—but no. Our feathered garbageman builds his nest on the ground, preferably in a hollow log or cave. I once found one under a windblown treetop. It contained two babies, so ugly their faces surely must have taxed the love of their homely parents. They were covered with white down. The wrinkled black heads, grotesque beaks, and pinfeathers just appearing, reminded me of two horrid witches huddled in tattered shawls, thinking up evil to wreak on some unfortunate wretch.

A concerned parent stayed close by, occasionally taking an ungainly hop or two in their characteristic buzzard lope. There was no doubt whose home it was. The parents feed the young by regurgitating, and may spill some. It ain't sweet.

But then garbage collection isn't sweet work. It's a job that has to be done, and nature fashioned the turkey vulture admirably for the task. His ugly bare head is easier to clean than one covered with feathers. His eyesight is so good that he can spot a car-killed rabbit from a distance far out of our sight. He has a sense of smell like no other bird, and can even sniff out a winter-killed deer in a cedar swamp.

When I saw that black clad sanitarian cleaning up those smelt I was ashamed of my revulsion at his ugly family. I thank him for picking up after the clod that wasted nature's bounty by catching them and then soiled our earth by throwing them out. 🌿

Birds are nature's public health corp and woodpeckers are the surgeons. Not just content to prey on the hoards of outside insects which constantly threaten our forest, the woodpecker tribe cuts into the ailing patients to get right to the seat of the trouble.

Their chisel-pointed bills are backed up by a special bone structure which permits them to strike blows which would certainly addle the brains of lesser birds. Having dug into the insect's corridor they spear their victim with a special barb-tipped tongue. This remarkable instrument extends from far back in the bird's skull and can be extended well beyond the end of the beak to dislodge their prey.

All woodpeckers have long tongues, but two have unique modifications to fit their specialty. The yellow-bellied sapsucker, which taps living trees for sweet sap and the insects attracted to it, has a bottle brush-tipped tongue to swab up his meals. The flicker specializes in ants. He plunges his bill into the ants' nest, and when they come rushing out he laps them up with his tongue which is as sticky as a strip of flypaper.

Chief surgeon of our woods is the pileated woodpecker, crow sized and with a flaming red crest. He has been caricatured in comics and movies as "Woody Woodpecker." A sure sign of his presence is the large rectangular holes, unlike those made by any other forest dweller.

A pair of these big woodpeckers inhabited a large poplar snag in our woods. Unfortunately it was felled when the cedars around it were logged. They had apparently occupied the snag for years, as it contained four complete nests, one dug out almost three feet below the entrance hole. The whole stub was a mere shell, and since pileateds like to dig a new nest hole each year, maybe they were ready to move anyway. I hope so, for I would hate to lose the benefit of their surgical services.

For the past two years they have been digging for carpenter ants in a large spruce. Some of the holes are over four inches by eight inches, and the ground below is covered with chips. The various-sized holes are scattered all about the lower trunk. They locate concentrations of ants by hearing them and then dig unerringly to their quarry.

No wonder I value their help. Where else would I find a surgeon ready equipped with a scalpel and probe, and with a built-in stethoscope to boot? ✸

One spring day I lay on a Lake Superior beach. A fold in the cobbles raised the April wind above me, a Precambrian boulder pillowed my head, and overhead were the hawks, mostly red-tails. There is something wonderfully sensuous about snuggling in a sun-warmed nook and listening to the windchill. The hawks gave me an excuse for doing it. I was counting their migration—all the red-tails passing overhead for one hour.

Red-tailed hawks are great soarers, in our part of the country only the turkey vulture exceeds them. These had the lift of a northwester striking the dunes. I put the binoculars on one that hung endlessly above me—fanned tail tilted, spread and narrowed, flashing red in the sun. Primaries fingered invisible eddies, adjusting their airholds to stay still in the breeze. Why does he hang there? Earthbound, I can only imagine the delight of truly owning a spot in the sky, my own place to watch the earth below.

My thoughts flashed back to that day when I recently picked up a young gunshot red-tail for delivery to a rehabilitation shelter. What a contrast between this caged cripple and those free spirits riding the spring wind. I wish the man who shot him could see the difference.

This bird's wing was not broken, but X rays showed several pellets. There seemed to be nerve damage. One wing muscle was shrinking, secondary feathers moulted. Wing exercises would be tried on the slight chance of reactivating the nerves.

I think red-tails get shot at more than other hawks. They are our largest buteo and hunt more by soaring. Because they are so conspicuous, they get blamed for all the crimes that hawk haters lay at raptorial doorsteps, but they are almost completely beneficial. At least 85 percent of their food is rodents. They catch rabbits and hares but most of their prey is much smaller.

When a hawk kills, it swings its hips forward and strikes with its feet. At the moment of impact, the talons are traveling much faster than the body. Energy delivered varies as the square of the velocity. The goshawk, our largest accipiter, is 10 to 20 percent lighter than a red-tail, yet it kills much larger prey. Its stoop is about three times as fast as a red-tail and its talons almost four times. The red-tail is built for smaller kills.

I once saw a red-tail catch a cottontail. The rabbit dashed madly but the hawk, wings and tail spread, had perfect control. The strike was a rolling flurry of fur and feathers. It ended with the hawk manteling, wings braced against the ground. A hard kill; the hawk rested before feeding.

I'm afraid our gunshot red-tail will never soar again or make a kill either great or small. Good people will bring him food from road kills. And I will still hope that all hawk shooters will sometime spend just one day watching red-tails in the wind. 🦅

For pure intensity of purpose you can't beat a male woodcock on his singing ground. He has one thing in mind—sex, sex, sex. He doesn't chase the females, they come to him. But man, oh man, what he does to make sure they do.

Each spring I spend a few evenings with the woodcock. Their ardor tides me through the last gasps of winter. Clear sky and a half-moon put extra frosting on a recent visit with them. Timberdoodles come to their singing grounds about when the first star appears. They stay until full night or longer in moonlight. They come again in morning when the stars start to fade.

On our place, scattered openings in a five-year-old poplar cutting provide singing grounds for several males. Each has his spot. Territories are rigidly respected. If a strange male drops in he is immediately driven off. The owner pursues with a clattery "cac-cac-cac" denunciation. Occasionally the combatants collide and fall to the ground, but there are no casualties. By April, all territories are settled. The only visitors are soft brown females to watch the show and mate.

At 7:55 P.M. the first male swept across the western sky and plummeted into the far end of the cutting. Then others came to the left and right. At 8:05 my host helicoptered in almost at my feet—a moments pause, then "gurgle-peent." The "gurgle" is so soft I never before had been close enough to hear it. The "peent" is buzzy and nasal. It seems to come from wa-a-ay down. The whole bird rocks with the effort. He struts and turns, sending his invitation in every direction. Take no chance on some distant female not hearing!

Suddenly he flushes, low across the clearing and over the sprouts, then sweeping round and up, a mere speck against the gloaming. Wings twitter at takeoff, but now, from 200 feet up comes his kissing song, a liquid, wild and musical melody—faint tiny bells painting Venus's backdrop with sound. He zigzags and hangs on fluttering wings. Around he goes, parachutes earthward, wingovers like a falling leaf. Suddenly he is back for more bobbing hiccuping gurgle-peents.

This plump little brown bird with eyes half in the back of his head, and a too long double-hinged beak, has brought special beauty to the loveliest evening of spring. Where in nature could you find a more unlikely artist?

No female comes mating tonight, but the show still goes on. Woodcock nest early. Most hens are already brooding eggs. They alone raise the broods. The nests may be nearby or a half-mile away, but never on the singing ground.

It is a place only for romance, not for rearing families. Strut, bob, and gurgle-peent, fly up and kiss the sky with song. There's always hope for hanky-panky, and that's what he's here for. 🌿

May

If March is a time of battle, May is the month of triumph. Winter's isolated pockets of resistance were mopped up in April. Now spring comes marching up the hillsides, her victory celebrated by flowers scattered beneath her feet: trout lily, trillium, mayflowers in shade; dandelion and yellow rocket scatter nuggets in sunny glades. Ah, there's a switch, gold in an emerald setting.

The trees rush to complete an Arc de Triomphe. Poplar tassels seem to reach out to clasp hands with maple blooms—lemon green and russet. There is a hill I watch each day. In May you can count the female poplar trees. Scattered puffs of smoky green clouds. When they get just so thick they guarantee a dependable fly hatch. Who needs signs to go trout fishing? But, if there is a best time it's in May, when the popple leaves are as big as a kitten's ear.

My wife says Juneberries bloom in May because they can't wait to celebrate. I can't wait to celebrate either. In this second-best time of the year I must be out amongst all God's creatures. No one can be pessimistic in May. Birds sing to announce their territories. They might accomplish the same thing by screeching or screaming. I think the Lord made bird songs beautiful to spread His message of goodness.

May is one time of the year when I never come home empty handed. If the fish don't bite there are always morels, fiddleheads, winter cress, or all sorts of wild greens just bubbling with spring tonic. A creel will hold plenty. Any lingering hint of last season's trout will rinse right off—at least I think it does.

We celebrated May Day with a big mess of mushrooms and a modest bunch of mayflowers. I pick mayflowers from just one spot, a lush carpet far back in the hemlocks. A special trip gets a handful for memory of our first spring together.

The mushrooms were beefsteak morels; big, and brown, and wrinkly. They come earlier than the true morels. I hunt them each year as part of our can't-wait-for-spring celebration. Some people can't eat beefsteaks—allergies I guess. We love them, can't get enough—just one more way we're lucky.

I like May frosts and the wet snowflakes that sometimes fall. They give up so easily. It seems they have to make a token show of cold just in case Boreas, the north wind, might be watching. But, they are caught up in the enthusiasm. At the first gentle touch of sunshine they melt away into droplets, trickle down to rootlets, rouse the robins breakfast worms, and help the plants shout a green hurrah.

The whole world shouts with them. 🌱

The other day, just at sunset, a loon's wild call echoed across our lake. As usual the skin over my spine twitched a little, and for a brief moment I had a flash of some primal ancestor huddled at a fire by a cold lake of prehistory. Surely no sound in nature is more primitive or more apt to stir that spark of nostalgia which still ties us to our distant hunting ancestors. For 50,000 years northern *Homo sapiens* have heard the lonely cry of the loon, and I am sure it must have been indelibly imprinted upon our racial memory.

Down the centuries the loons have changed very little. They are the most primitive of birds, not closely related to any other avian family. Though better adapted for swimming than for flying, they do fly strongly once they get off the water.

The loons' bones are almost solid, completely unlike the air-filled bones of most other birds. They can compress their feathers, squeezing out the air, and gradually sink below the water. With this ability to maintain periscope level at will, loons are the most submarine of all birds. Their feet are set right at the rear of the body like a pair of big propellers. Their legs are almost nonexistent, being encased in the body down to the ankle.

I once encountered a loon crossing a small gravel bar. He stood erect like a penguin, but on seeing me, made two awkward lunges and flopped flat on his breast. Then began the most desperate scramble of feet, wings, and belly slides until he reached the water. However, he made good speed, and I couldn't possibly have overtaken him. In the water he dived at once. I could see him using his wings as diving planes. The contrast with his wild land scramble made his swimming seem the very picture of ease and grace.

Loon fossils have been found in associations with early man. I like to think that the loons' relationship with our ancestors was like the folklore of the Eskimos; something more than just food. However, they probably were eaten. Primitive man ate almost anything. A friend of mine, who once ate a loon while on a wilderness trip, said, "If you are strong enough to eat it you haven't starved enough to need it."

It is good that our tastes have changed, for the loons constantly retreat before us. This feathered relic of the prehistoric wilds doesn't tolerate people. Each year he is crowded further back by the cottagizing of our lakes. As his wild call disappears, that thread of contact with our prehistory grows ever more tenuous. May it never part completely.

Nature has a way of compensating for disaster. The Dutch elm disease is one of the great disasters of our forests. Woodpeckers are one of the compensations. We may never have had as many as we do today. Some southern species seem to be following the elm epidemic north.

A pair of red-headed woodpeckers have taken up residence near our place. Their nest is sixty feet up in an elm snag. They regularly visit our feeders for corn, sunflower seed, and suet. For me it's like old home week. A pair of red-heads always occupied the telephone pole in front of our Mississippi home. To us a woodpecker was a red-head. All other species had special names.

Red-headed woodpeckers are red from the collar up. Scarlet best describes it, but not quite. A friend who carves and paints birds says it is a most difficult color to match. At any rate, the color is breathtaking. The red, white, and black plumage is so spectacular the birds' flight can easily be followed at a distance.

Incidentally, these are the flag colors of the pre-World War I German Empire. As a small child I remember hearing them called Kaiser birds. Some were shot in misguided displays of patriotism. They are a hardy breed and survived this bit of mans' stupidity.

The floodplain woods across our river was about half elm. Two years ago all saw logs over nine inches were removed. Most of the elm was beyond salvage. Now it is an open forest full of ideal woodpecker nest sites. It particularly suits the red-heads, for they are open country birds. Each recent year they have extended their range farther north, but usually along the forest edges. It took a combination of logging and disease to bring them this far back in the woods.

Red-heads like grasshoppers. They catch most of them on the ground, but snap up some and other insects, in the air. They take the hoppers to a perch to hack off the legs and wing cases before dining. They also like fruit and nuts. Down south they store acorns in cracks and cavities for winter use. Here they migrate, yet ours haul corn across the river and poke it into crannies.

Young red-headed woodpeckers have gray brown heads. They will get their red feathers next spring. The black and white flight pattern identifies them. In most woodpecker species the sexes differ in color. Young downy and hairy woodpeckers have a little red on top of their heads. At first moult the females lose all red. The males grow a new patch at the rear. Male flickers have mustaches. Females don't except when young. They moult their mustaches at first feather change.

The colors of the red-headed woodpecker sexes are alike. With such colors, male or female makes no difference. Against those bare gray elms they are just plain beautiful. ❧

Sharp-tailed grouse don't dance like Indians. Indians dance like sharp-tailed grouse—and prairie chickens. Grouse were dancing long before Indians learned how.

When the first men crossed the land bridge from Asia to Alaska and spread south in America, they found three kinds of prairie grouse unknown in the Old World: sage grouse, prairie chickens, and sharp-tails. All three species are polygamous. The cocks gather each spring in traditional dancing grounds to fight, dance and hoot, boom or coo in competition. A few dominant males win all the hens and end up siring that year's generation. The Indians were so impressed, they adopted the choreography. It was a happy adoption, for American Indian dances are among the most picturesque of primitive displays.

A few prairie chickens and sharp-tails still dance in the Midwest. This spring we went to a sharp-taileds' dance. The site was a grassy knoll in one of the great marshes of Seney National Wildlife Refuge. The time—just at first light on a beautiful April morning. By 7 A.M. the show was over.

We heard the dancers before seeing light. Displaying sharp-taileds inflate lavender neck sacs, the birds then expel the air to make a cooing "cac-cac-cac." It has remarkable carrying power. Finally our glasses began to locate white teepees on the dance floor. Sharp-taileds point their tails straight up when dancing. The white coverts show far across the marshland. I think the "cac-cac-cacs" and white triangles must have evolved to tell the hens the show is on.

Soon all the birds are visible. Head down, tail up, wings spread, each cock stamps a minuet on his chosen stage. They quiver with the rapid pitter-pat. Suddenly one leaps two feet in the air, landing turned half around. Two rush together, stop beak to beak, daring. One flips a tail again, again, again. The lesser bird can't stand the threat. He turns away. The dance goes on.

There always has to be a party pooper. One shows on schedule. A rough-legged hawk lights in a nearby tree. The six dancers vanish. Finally, with a fifteen-power scope, we make out scattered lumps on the close-packed grass. Survival by stillness. We want to shout or throw something to drive off the intruder. He leaves in his own good time. The dance resumes as if it had never missed a beat.

Modern communication has put our dancing grouse on television. Anyone who watches outdoor programs has seen them. The real show is much better. The chill of a spring dawn, the backdrop of sere sedges and half-thawed ponds, the sounds, and smells, and feel of a winter wakening marsh just can't be brought indoors. 🌢

If we had a belfry we would surely have bats in it. Since we don't, the little brown bats on our place live in a huge old hollow tree. If they could get in our attic I'm sure they would roost there. Little brown bats are colonial. They like a place big enough for a whole gang. I once counted over a hundred squeezing out of a hunt camp attic. Only about a dozen occupy our hollow tree. In our part of the country if you find a great mass of bats hanging close together in a building or cave they are almost surely little browns. They are our most common bats.

I think most of our bats migrate south in fall, but some may hibernate here if they can find roosts that don't freeze. The first bats show up about the same time tree swallows arrive in spring. That's as early as the first fly hatches. These early flyers may simply have been wakened by the warming weather.

Unseasonable weather may kill early bats. This chill spring I found a little brown squeezed under our garage door. His niche was warm enough, but the cold had kept his food from the air. He was feeble from starvation and soon died. In such an emergency, tree swallows can live on seeds. North American bats are strictly meat eaters. With them it's insects or die.

I thought to help our little starvling, but my wife doesn't favor bats in the house. Besides, what do you feed a bat that's too weak to fly? Incidentally, it's best to handle bats with gloves. Their tiny teeth can't do much harm, but they will bite. Occasionally they carry rabies.

The little brown bats on our place hunt mostly over the driveway. Roadside pools hatch plenty of insects. Bats catch more flies and mosquitoes than any kind of bird. They locate their prey and obstacles by sending out a beam of high intensity supersonic sound and measuring the distance and location from the echoes reflected back to them. Their range is one to six yards.

A bat's reaction is so quick that it flies only four inches before altering course. In controlled experiments little brown bats located tiny flies weighing only one one-thousandth of a gram from a distance of one and a half feet and snapped them up ten per minute. A fly that small can't cause much echo, but a bat can pick up his returning sound if it is only one ten-thousandth of its transmitted strength. They can do it even with interference a thousand times stronger. Scientists, improving radar, are still trying to figure how they do it.

About the only things in nature I really hate are blackflies and "no-see-ems." These little devils make mosquitoes seem pleasant. Little brown bats eat them by the jillion. I love them for it. If they had no other place to stay, I might even build a belfry for their roost. 🦇

It's as hard to be objective about cowbirds as it is about income tax. I just don't like either one.

We built little shelves under the eaves of our toolshed. Last summer a pair of phoebes built a late nest there. This spring they returned and, right on schedule, started building their new nest on the old foundation. These delightful little tenants will often use the same site all their lives. We anticipated this pair's company for years to come.

Suddenly, just as the nest seemed complete, all activities there ceased. The phoebes began frantically trying to build above my bedroom window. The ledge is much too narrow. They have piled the whole length of it with muddy trash. Nothing holds. I placed a shelf across the television brace. In time I hope they will find it and move their nest building around the corner.

I had to know the reason for their desertion. A step stool and a mirror found the answer. A brown-speckled cowbird egg was in the nest. Phoebe eggs are plain white. Imagine, stuck with a stranger before you even get settled! The outraged owners just moved out.

Phoebes don't always desert their nests when parasitized. I examined one nest on a garage light fixture. It contained two cowbird and three phoebe eggs. The pair raised the cowbirds. Their own young were crowded out and died. A second nesting produced four healthy phoebes. Cowbirds lay most of their eggs early. Second nestings are less vulnerable.

It seldom pays to try to help the host birds. I removed a cowbird egg from an ovenbird's nest. The ovenbirds deserted, even though the eggs were close to hatching. Birds will almost never desert a nest with young. A friend found a warbler nest containing a cowbird and two young warblers. The foster youngster was twice as big as his nest mates. Removed from the nest, the cowbird's screams brought the foster parents for identification. They were as concerned as if it was their own flesh and blood.

I favored wringing the young cowbird's neck, but we compromised by depositing it under a bush some distance away. The young Nashville warblers survived to fly, but, you know, I'm not too sure those little parents didn't hunt up that cowbird and raise it too. They were frantic about its loss. His calls were certainly loud enough for them to hear.

Cowbirds pick on small species as hosts. They parasitize Kirtland's warblers so heavily they have become a major factor in the Kirtland's threatened extinction. Cowbird traps are evening the score and giving our rarest of warblers at least a fighting chance.

Biologically the cowbird's habit of picking on the little fellows must be sound, for the cowbirds are thriving. This is one bit of biology I can't like. The cowbird's Latin name, *Molothrus ater*, means dark greedy beggar. It suits them. 🐦

Where we fish all the pike get hungry at once. If we are where the pike are then, it seems every fish wants a shot at the lure. Between meals you can't buy a strike.

Bass are smarter than pike, but day in and day out I think they are easier to catch. They have their feeding sprees too, but bass seem always ready to grab an easy tidbit. Not so with pike. I think they are too dumb to eat between meals. Without the thrust of hunger they don't seem to recognize food. With it, anything that moves is edible.

My first experience with the Esocidae family was skittering for pickerel in Maine. Chain pickerel are small cousins of northern pike. A five pounder is big. Their habits and temperament are similar.

Skittering requires an eighteen-foot cane pole, the same length of stout line, a big hook, and a slab of pickerel belly about six inches long with the two little fins attached. Put the hook through the belly between the fins and taper the far end so it wiggles easy.

My teacher was an artist. He could lay it thirty to forty feet either side of the canoe, dance it around every snag and lily pad, settle it in deep, and snake it over the brush. You could see most of the strikes coming. Give him slack when he hits. These fish want MEAT. Let him stop and chew it. When he starts off again break his neck. It was exciting fishing, and deadly in the hands of an expert.

Our modernized version uses a pork pollywog, weedless hook, and a spinning outfit. In the weedy stump pastures of dam backwaters it's the only method we've found to cover all the water. In good water, during feeding, casts may draw bow waves from twenty feet. Repeat whirls and splashes are common. If a pike grabs the pork and not the hook, you can jerk it away, and he'll grab it again and again until pricked by the hook or scared by the boat. Voracious or just dumb? It doesn't matter. It's fun fishing.

Feeding, pike are the best big fish for youngsters to start on. Any legal pike is big to a seven year old. My grandson and I opened this year's season. We missed a lot of fish. It takes just about all the heft a seven year old can muster to set the hook when a pike clamps down on a pork chunk. We kept five fish, but the big one got away.

A swirl twenty feet from the boat had the deliberate bulge of a keeper. "Keep it coming, keep it coming." Right at boat side three feet of green lightning exploded. For a moment rod bowed, line hummed, foam flew. Then it was over. Eyes wide, arms spread, gaping wide as the print of JAWS on his sweat shirt, "I saw him! I saw him!"

It was a great day. ❦

Every day nature has her life and death struggles. This spring we witnessed one.

The very dry weather guided our morel hunting to the streamsides and damp hollows in the forest. There, my wife and I encountered Michigan's most abundant snake. Garter snakes seemed to be everywhere. At least a dozen of them weaved away over the winter-packed leaves. These beautiful little reptiles derive their name from the decorative striped garters that used to be worn to hold up men's socks. The ones we saw were green and yellow striped, the most common color of the species in our state. They are easily captured and make gentle interesting pets.

Spring is the snakes' mating season, and I am sure that was partly responsible for the concentrations we found. After the long winter hibernation food is equally important. At the streamside we saw proof that in nature, there ain't no free lunch.

One of the garter snakes had caught a toad by its hind legs. The victim had puffed itself up to maximum size and was holding desperately to the streamside grass stems. It seemed to realize that safety was in the water, only inches away.

All snakes have expandable jaws that unhinge at the rear, with the lower jaw connected in front by a stretchable ligament. The teeth are back curved. Each half of the lower jaw can be moved independently. Our garter snake was demonstrating this remarkable adaptation by inching his jaws slowly over his victim. It wasn't easy, for the toad was over twice the snake's diameter, still very much alive and desperately determined.

We watched the deadly tug-of-war for a quarter hour. The toad lost his grip. The snake pressed his advantage by crawling backward up the crumbling sandbank. Dinner seemed almost a cinch, but the toad grasped one last little root and wrenched one leg free. Now the dry sand worked to the snakes disadvantage. Each encircled clod crumbled under the strain.

The battle went on in silence. No violent thrashing about. Just muscles strained in a mortal Indian wrestle. Fraction by fraction the jaws inched up. The amphibian's muscles bulged, straining for freedom at his captor's slightest mistake. Finally it came. Two hops and into the water. Scratched and gimpy legged, but still able to swim a few strokes, he rested in half-submerged exhaustion. My wife gave a rousing cheer for her warty-backed champion. The snake climbed tiredly up the bank.

His struggle must go on. No beans and cornbread supper for him. There are no vegetarian snakes. Every meal is a life and death affair. In our eyes it was a drama—in his just one moment in his normal life. Nature has few champions. She gives each the tools of survival, and they must use them as best they can. 🐾

There are some things best done on your knees. One is smelling mayflowers. Trailing arbutus blooms are seldom more than an inch above the forest floor. To fully enjoy their rich spicy fragrance, get down on your knees. It's a good way to appreciate spring.

Arbutus is slow growing. Its trailing stems are tough. Careless picking may pull up a whole plant. In many places it has been gathered almost to extermination.

The last thing I bought my new bride when we left New England was a handful of mayflowers. In those days each spring found country roads spotted with children holding out fistfuls of mayflowers to passing motorists, a nickel a bunch. The fragrance of that little pink and white handful lasted way into Ohio, long after it was faded and limp. It is our best-loved wildflower.

When we first got this place, we were delighted to find a small patch of arbutus under the cedars just beside the road. We have nursed it, and each year it is a little larger. A spring ritual is to check for buds each day after snow goes and then kneel down to sniff deeply of the first blossoms. It's good for whatever ails us.

Back deep in the hemlocks there is a carpet of mayflowers. We didn't find this hidden wealth for almost a year. Now, with such a luxuriant supply, I cut a half-dozen bloom clusters to renew the memory of our first spring together. They are the only ones we ever pick.

Trailing arbutus likes sandy rocky soil. Recently, in a jack pine stand, we found acres of them. Most were just in bud, but the occasionally precocious plant was a mass of blooms. Who could resist getting down to admire the delicate pink and to sniff? We saw many people doing it.

Michigan is about the middle of the geographical range of this little flower. Yet, it is rare in the southern counties. Maybe it's because the soil is richer there, or maybe there are just too many people. Mayflowers don't take kindly to civilization. They like soil too poor to farm and woods too thick for heavy traffic.

Trailing arbutus is most common north of the forty-fifth parallel. New England is blessed with it in abundance. Its evergreen leaves are often hidden by fallen tree leaves. I expect the reason for its fragrance is so the first spring bees can find it, snuggled so close to the ground.

Arbutus is listed in some states as rare and endangered. Picking, except on your own land, is illegal. If you must pick a bloom, cut the stem carefully. A pull may rip up roots and years of growth.

Juneberries bloom in May, ripen in July, and just add to the greenery in June. Here they are in their splendor by mid-May. Mayberries would be a better name.

Where I hunt morels the Juneberries are almost tree size. The open oak-aspen woods is gloried with huge puffs of white blossoms scattered at random along all the edges—sunlit cumulus clouds dropped upon earth by the warmth of spring. It's reason enough to be out in the woods.

Juneberries probably have more names and more species than any other common shrub. At least six kinds live in the lakes states. Besides Juneberries, they are called shadbush (because in the East they bloom when the shad run), saskatoonberry to mix with the western Indians' pemican, and serviceberry just because they are so good for everything edible.

The problem is that around here they never get ripe. When the kids were home, we had a big Juneberry bush in the backyard. Each year I promised them all sorts of goodies from the berries. They are sweet, juicy, and one of the best wild fruits. We never got any. Just as the berries began to show the first blush of red, robins descended on the tree and consumed every berry. I tried a few at that stage, but no go, too puckery. We never tasted one ripe berry off our tree. I suppose it is still there welcoming the robins each summer.

What the robins don't get, the grosbeaks, waxwings, and squirrels will. Ripe Juneberries are dark purple and delightfully juicy. I can't imagine how our forefathers ever found enough to really use them. The shrub must have been incredibly abundant. I have only had a few handfuls in all my life. At any rate, our pioneer literature is full of June-, service-, and saskatoonberries. We have to be satisfied with a taste in July and a breath of beauty in May.

Juneberry wood is very hard and tough. It makes good hammer and axe handles. It used to be called lancewood. Some of the first fly rods were made from it. If fiberglass ever becomes extinct, here is a substitute. Our woods are full of lancewood trees. When I get old enough to need a cane I'll cut one from a Juneberry bush. It will hold me up, kill rattlesnakes (if ever I encounter one), and hold off the enemy if I'm ever attacked. What a comfort to know such a tool is so handy.

However, berry or wood, today this shrub has just one thing, its resplendence of white blossoms. Other spring flowers keep close to the ground to hide from the wind, and the cold, and the frost. Juneberry stands up and shouts, "Spring is here." I'm glad it doesn't wait till June. 🌿

Who's number one? Among predators in these parts it's the great horned owl. April and May is when they are the most effective. Then both adults are hunting to feed their growing young. Anything under ten pounds is fair game. If food is scarce even larger wildlife may be attacked. Rabbits are preferred prey, but they will take what is available.

Last spring I visited a great horned owl's nest in a poplar clear-cut. The nest was in a huge pine left by the loggers. Sprouts in the cutting showed heavy rabbit damage. The ground was littered with regurgitated pellets of snowshoe hare fur and bones. Three downy owlets' bills wrestled on the nest platform.

A nest near a municipal dump was literally lined with rats, at least a dozen in various stages of butchering. Most nests contain a mixed bag, anything from skunks to other owls. Great horned owls will reuse the same nest, but they usually deplete the local food supply and must move every two or three years.

Great horned owls may be the most powerful of all raptors. Their legs, feet, and talons are enormously well developed—far stronger than any hawk I have ever handled. Great horned owls weigh three to four pounds, but regularly kill animals and birds two to three times their size. When necessary they can carry off a kill greater than their own weight. Since their flight is perfectly silent, most prey is caught by surprise. They can, and do, kill porcupines, house cats, young foxes, and birds to the size of geese and turkeys. If a quick kill is not made, the owl may be injured in the ensuing fight, though the outcome is seldom in doubt once those talons are driven home. The owl just hangs on, driving his talons ever deeper, beating the animal with its wings, and tearing at it with its beak until a vital organ is punctured or the spine severed.

Great horned owls are very aggressive in defense of their nests, but temperament varies widely with individuals. At the nest near the dump we banded two owlets without interference, though both parents were near, hooting and clicking their beaks. As I gathered pellets under the nest containing three young, the female made a bill-clicking pass inches from my head. She left no doubt of her determination.

Years ago, while returning from a late February quail hunt, my partner's little pointer bitch was attacked by two great horned owls as she trotted fifty yards ahead of us. Suddenly there was a whirl of wings and yelping dog. The attack was so silent, quick, and devastating, we never got our guns to our shoulders. The dog's head and back were literally covered with deep cuts. She died two days later.

I remembered that little bird dog as that owl brushed her warning past my head. Our Michigan woods are safe for people, but great horned owls demand respect. They can back up their warnings.

Bracken fern is the most widely distributed plant on earth, and in May it's good to eat. Fiddlehead greens have got to be one of the great spring delicacies of the wilds. There is really no excuse for a morel hunter coming home empty-handed. There are always fiddleheads, and, even if you find plenty of morels, a mess of these spring greens are a fine addition to the menu.

My first introduction to fiddleheads was as a bachelor in Maine. One of my apartment mates was a native Yankee who knew everything to eat that was cheap or free. In May he turned up with a basketful of curley-ended, fuzzy, six-inch stems—fiddleheads—freshly sprouted bracken fern.

He ran them through his hands to knock off most of the brown fuzz and ants, then soaked them in salted water. This chased out the rest of the bugs. Our connoisseur claimed it wasn't necessary to remove all the ants, as they contained formic acid which added a nice tart taste to the greens. I wouldn't know about that. At any rate, ants or not, into the pot they went with a chunk of salt pork, the mainstay of all New England and mid-South cooks. A little water and about half an hour's simmering produced as fine a spring vegetable as ever graced a table.

Fiddleheads should be harvested when they are crisp and snappy. If they don't break clean, skip them. The top six inches is what you want. The first ones will show in sunny spots. By June there will still be a supply in the cool shade, after the first sprouts have long since fanned out into fronds. If you can't eat them all, freeze some the same as you would asparagus.

Bracken is not just for eating. Deer and turkeys find the tender top curls choice sources of spring vitamins. I think bracken is most important as ground cover for wildlife. The broad fronds keep the stems far apart, leaving a miniature green arbor—concealment from flying predators, with plenty of room to maneuver. The roof of this little world may be from one to four feet above ground depending upon rains.

Woodcock particularly love this habitat. They can run about without tangling their bills in a lot of grass. I find them mostly in bracken below ten- to fifteen-foot poplars. One hop puts them through the bracken ceiling, free from ground predators. A few wing twitters puts them out of the aspen canopy. I miss so many birds that way.

The ground stays cool and moist under bracken. Insects live there. Woodcock and grouse come to raise their broods. In autumn its tan brown plateau complements the fall colors. Then it tumbles, to tangle the feet of October hunters and bide its time for next May's cornucopia of plenty. ❧

Woodpeckers aren't the only birds that dig holes in trees. A pair of red-breasted nuthatches are digging a nest cavity in our backyard. They have chosen a poplar snag, well rotted for easy digging. I watched the male at work. Each time he brought out a chip he would leave the hole completely before dropping his burden. Then he would hitch around the hole and reenter. Sometimes he backed out with a chip, but he always circled the hole before reentering. By and by the female took a turn at the work.

When the cavity is complete, these little birds will furnish it with a nest of fine grass, bark shreds, hair, or anything soft. They will stick gobs of pitch around the hole. This may serve as flypaper to keep out insects or discourage other intruders. We really don't know its purpose. The female alone does the brooding. She is careful to avoid the sticky pitch by flying straight into the hole.

Nuthatches are peculiar birds. Nest entrance modifications are just one more peculiarity of a topsy-turvy life-style. Every bird-watcher is familiar with their upside-down travel along tree trunks. It's in the nesting season that each species shows real individuality.

White-breasted nuthatches seldom dig their own nest holes. Natural cavities or old woodpecker holes suit them. They like a large entrance. This puts them in competition with squirrels and starlings for living quarters. If there is an old nest in their chosen cavity, the white-breasteds remove it before building their own. They carry the trash some distance away before dropping it.

When white-breasted nuthatches are settled they bill sweep the entrance. Holding a crushed insect, they sweep their bills in wide arcs both inside and outside of the hole. Both birds do it for minutes at a time. Again, we don't know why.

Down south there is a brown-headed nuthatch, even smaller than our red-breasted. They dig nest holes in dead pines. There is plenty of pitch in their habitat should they want to stick it around the entrance. They don't use it. They bring plant down (cottonwood fluff is usually handy) and caulk any cracks or crannies in their home. No drafts or light leaks for them. But of course, we really don't know if that is the reason for caulking. Some of the cracks aren't deep enough to need stuffing.

Chickadees sometimes dig nest holes in rotten wood. I think they more often use ready-made holes. When they do dig, chicks carry the chips some distance before dropping them. They often dig in low stumps. Hauling chips away helps make it inconspicuous.

Our red-breasteds are building twenty feet up. They just drop the chips. Wind scatters them unnoticed. The important thing seems not where they drop, but the ritual of how they go about it.

Who needs a reason? They do it *their* way. 🜚

The other evening we had a surprise visitor. A badger ambled down our river-side path. He briefly entered some old woodchuck holes and stopped suddenly downwind from the dog kennel. Then, as hastily as a badger can hasten, he departed the way he had come.

Badgers are grassland dwellers. Their distribution in North America conforms approximately to the prairies and deserts. They proliferated in Michigan when logging and fire brought wide grasslands to our state. Now that these openings are disappearing, badgers have become uncommon. In our wet wooded homestead, they are totally unexpected.

Badgers are members of the weasel family, specialized for digging. They are bowlegged, pigeon-toed, and about nine inches tall and two feet long. Their front feet have five long claws powered by burly shoulders. Long grizzly hair enhances the low-slung effect. The head is distinctly marked with black and white. At close range they look like a clown painted face dragging along a dirty throw rug under which it has crawled.

Badgers will eat just about anything that crawls, flies, or runs, but their favored prey is burrowing rodents—gophers, ground squirrels, and prairie dogs. These agile critters can easily outrun a badger, but when they flee to their burrows they are usually doomed. The badger just digs them out.

We once lived in a treeless subdivision that was full of ground squirrels. Several had burrows under our lawn. One morning we found it pocked with great holes and dirt piles. A badger had come hunting. He must have been able to smell the little rodents in their nests, for his excavations seldom followed the squirrel burrows. He just went straight down to home plate. We estimate he moved a half-yard of soil and gravel for each squirrel he caught. We had no more ground squirrels that year, not much lawn either.

Badgers can't run fast, climb trees, or swim very well. They will kill and eat poisonous snakes. They can outfight most anything their size. When all else fails they dig. They have few successful enemies.

A badger and I once surprised each other in an Oregon stubble field. I was empty-handed, not a rock or stick in sight. He spread himself in a depression and hissed like a barrelful of snakes. I've never heard a meaner sound. I wanted no part of that striped-faced blanket of teeth and claws. Suddenly he began to dig. In seconds he was gone. Only scattered clods and a dirt-plugged hole gave evidence of the encounter.

We are glad our surprise visitor didn't stay. Several chipmunks live with us. One has a burrow under the concrete garage apron. I shudder at the consequences of a badger attack on it—might have buckled the house foundation. ❧

The Lord must have been particularly happy when He created wood warblers. I like to think of Him looking down on one of our lovely spring days and suddenly scattering the warblers like confetti over the landscape. They add sparkle to the perfection of His work.

Spring warblers come in waves, heavenly handfuls wafted by the weather fronts. They migrate at night, feed morning and late afternoon, rest in midday. On favorable nights dozens of species may migrate together. After just such a night this spring we found the woods along Lake Huron flashing with their bright plumage.

Black and white, Wilson's, Cape May, magnolia, Tennessee, yellow, black-throated green, bay-breasted, chestnut-sided, Nashville, blackpoll. They get their names from everywhere and everything. Some names fit, some misfit. Prairie warblers are seldom found in prairies. Nashville warblers don't live in Nashville. Magnolias prefer northern conifers to magnolia trees.

Blackburnians are well named by accident. Named to honor Mrs. Hugh Blackburn of England, their orange breast and head colors glow like live embers; tiny torches in the evergreens. Redstarts fit. Watch an orange and black male plucking flies in flight. He has to be redstart.

The northern water thrush does look like a little thrush, and he likes water. They teeter along woodland streamlets like spotted sandpipers. I don't know how they happened to be warblers. Oven-birds are also thrushlike warblers. They are named for their domed nests; like tiny outdoor ovens.

Canadian warblers nest mostly in Canada. Golden-winged warblers have golden wings. Black-throated blues are those colors plus a white breast. Blackpolls are black on top of the head in spring, but not in fall. Black and white warblers are just that, but act like nuthatches. They go headfirst down tree trunks. Common yellow-throats have yellow throats, but they also have a black bandit mask. Yellow-throated warblers have yellow throats too, but no bandit mask.

Myrtle warblers love myrtle berries, but now taxonomists say, "Call them yellow-rumped warblers"—an outrage. Lots of warblers have yellow rumps. Myrtle is a better name.

My first encounter with spring warbler waves was on the Cumberland plateau of Tennessee. I lay on a cliff top and watched them spangle the treetops just below. It was a highlight of my first college spring. For years I didn't try to know or name them. Just enjoying was enough.

Now that I live where warbler waves wash by every spring, I study them. If they will hesitate a moment I can identify even if the name doesn't fit. But, call them what we may, they are beauties—bits of glory scattered to bless the earth. ❧

It looks like we finally have some permanent tenants for our martin apartments. Earlier this spring two pair of tree swallows took up leases and started nest building. Shortly thereafter a pair of house sparrows occupied one apartment and, in spite of the swallows' objections, started carting in volumes of straw, feathers, and grass. It looked like we were going to have an integrated tenement with several vacancies.

Two male purple martins called several times, but were promptly driven off by the tree swallows. In mid-May the martins returned in force, both male and female. About a dozen of them drove off the little swallows and attacked viciously every time they returned. The battles continued for more than a week before the swallows gave up.

The sparrows were made of sterner stuff. They frantically stuffed their nest hole with straw and trash. When attacked, the female defended the nest from inside while the male strutted up and down the porch, daring them to come at him. That little Englishman held the whole martin army at bay. I had to admire his spunk, but the end was inevitable. They couldn't man the ramparts all the time. When they flew the martins were on them like the Red Baron on Snoopy. It took three weeks, but they finally left.

The martins are nest building in seven apartments. The helter-skelter sparrow's nest still protrudes from their vacant room. No one seems willing to clean it up.

Purple martins are delightfully social birds. They gossip incessantly, and there are a few back-fence quarrels. They are most casual nest builders, bringing any and everything—straw, rags, sticks, and mud whenever the mood strikes them. They seem to completely lack the intensity of purpose most birds display. Finally they are almost finished.

Martins insist on a bit of greenery for their nest lining and seem to like to tear off tender treetop leaves. Our only tree is a brand new maple sapling. The martins have almost denuded it, plucking bits of the foliage. Normally martins shun trees. They prefer a nest house well out in the open. However, even while brooding they may visit trees from time to time to renew their nest greenery.

We are happy with our tenants. They will return next spring. This fall we will take down the apartments for cleaning and not put them up until next May. The housing battles were interesting, but we prefer to avoid interracial strife by simply not offering to lease until our regular tenants apply. 🪶

May has more good evenings than other months. The battles between winter and summer are over. Cold has retreated north to lick its wounds and prepare for next fall's sortie. Peace reigns for a while on the weather front. Every month has some fine evenings. May gets more than her share.

There's a place in our woods that looks across a pond to the western sky. It's where to enjoy May evenings; after sunset is best, just when Venus shows. She fills my heart with joy, and each new sight rolls back the years to—"Star light, star bright / First star I see tonight." May I never grow too blasé to make one more wish on the evening star.

May mornings are full of bird songs. Frogs make the music at twilight. A wood thrush may sound his "ee-oh-lee," but the real chorus is amphibious. I don't know how many kinds of frogs and toads live on our place. There are surely a half-dozen different songs. American toads carry the melody. Spring peepers play the flutes. Chorus frogs "crreek" endlessly. The wood and leopard frogs clack and snore. An occasional bullfrog adds "jug-a-rum" for emphasis. It is a veritable panoply of sounds vibrating the twilight air. But it's only an accompaniment.

The real show is the light. I think people who have never lived in the South take their evenings too lightly. Down there when sun sets it gets dark. Here at the forty-fifth parallel, light seems reluctant to quit the day. It throws soft pink fingers against the mares tail clouds and bounces their image against the pool's mirror. It gilds the lemon green leaflets at poplar tips. Each budding aspen illuminates a bit of the forest—but softly, softly. The whole world seems pianissimo.

This is a fair-weather evening. No orange slashes cross the western sky. Just blue and azure, and lavender and purple brushed with some high pink wisps. It is eternal yet fleeting, subtly changing. I'm surprised when the forest no longer has color.

A pair of ducks trace their "To a Water Fowl" path downstream. The hawk that lives in our woods hurries late to roost. An owl "who-cooks, who-cooks" in the distance. Some small night creature rustles leaves at my feet. A few fish flies dance in sky silhouettes.

The little brown bats start their patrols. It's almost time to go, but light's last fingers hold me. Yes, May twilights are beauty personified. They bring peace to my whole being—and I can linger to enjoy for, as yet, there are no mosquitoes. 🦇

June

All of a sudden the wilds are full of mothers. We just can't go anywhere without encountering concerned mothers or parents. Each has their own way of protecting their young.

A robin built a nest on a fence rail by our drive. So secretive were her comings and goings that she had three eggs before we discovered the nest. Our daily walks detoured to the far side of the road. She soon learned to sit tight as we passed.

Another robin, nesting deep in the woods, joined with her mate in screaming alarms and curses whenever we approached. They were never quiet. They chose to fight rather than hide.

Both nests were successful. The fence rail pair showed quiet concern every time we showed their young to visitors. They made no protest until the fledglings objected to being banded the day they started to fly. Then both parents rallied to the rescue screaming every bit as vehemently as the woodland couple.

The tree swallows have my wife completely intimidated. She refuses to go near their end of the pond. Their dive-bombing is fearless. Even the dog circles wide of their nest box. After repeated hair tweaking, he has learned the safe distance.

Recently I helped band hawk nestlings. Red-shouldered and red-tailed hawks usually circled over the trees, crying protests. Goshawks attacked. Always it was the mother. These ferocious birds have a four-foot wingspread. Streaking through the trees screeching their "ca-ca-ca-cas" they looked and sounded like an attack plane on a straffing run. The only sure defense was to hold up one of the young. They would not strike their nestlings.

We have two broods of grouse so far. One bluffed my daughter's car to a stop while her brood scooted into the brush. The other led my dog on a fluttering chase while her family simply disappeared. I would not have seen them had not one panicked into desperate flight across the boat slip. I never thought the tiny mite would make it.

I think woodcock are the best of all wild mothers. They do the most convincing broken wing acts. But many other birds do as well. The other day I saw the unbelievable. I flushed a half-grown family. Three of the youngsters flew well. The mother carried off the fourth clasped firmly between her thighs. The load was so great she barely cleared the braken, but she made it for fifteen yards and time enough to run away in the cover. Instinct, intent, or reflex action? I don't know, but it worked. Woodcock raise a high percent of their hatchlings. Yet, few bird mothers are so unlikely or ungainly looking. Biologists warn against attributing reason and emotions to birds. Instincts guide their actions. Yet, I must believe my eyes.

Erma Bombeck says that God made mothers in a special mold. I think He did so with wild mothers too. ❦

Why are male northern orioles so brilliant orange and black? Closely related to blackbirds, grackles, and cowbirds, they might well have evolved without the flame orange part of their dress.

This year the first oriole arrived at our place the day before Mother's Day. He hung upside down on the suet holder, acrobatic as a nuthatch. We halved an orange and stuck it on a pair of nails. Moments later our visitor's beak was buried hilt deep in a meal to match his bright breast. I think this bird was here last year. He was too sure of everything to be a newcomer. He went unhesitatingly to the suet and was at the oranges almost before we closed the door.

Next day three orioles were at our feeders. The first arrival always placed his left foot on the edge of the orange half, same as last year. Another full-plummaged male stood on the board to feed. A younger bird, his black head mottled with lighter feathers, perched on the orange rim and tried to plunge in all over. This peaceful arrangement didn't last long. When the females arrived, our left-footed gallant laid claim to the entire front yard. The other two were driven off, one to the garden behind the house, the other across the pond.

We hear all three singing to announce their territories. Only Lefty visits the feeders. He has brought a mate to the suet and oranges. She is shy—flies at our slightest movement. He is bold. When he finally flushes, he does so with magnificent arrogance.

We watched him courting. He perched near her, stretched high, then made a series of low bows. Like a blinker he flashed orange breast, black back, orange rump. Always he faced his lady, repeating his jerky ups and downs. She must have liked the display, for soon they were both searching the ground for nest fibers. Surely his bright colors must be a factor in sex attraction.

However, that is not their only value. Our bold oriole dominates the suet when he wants to. He shows aggression by spreading his tail to display the outer orange feathers. One tail spread makes even hairy woodpeckers back away. When Lefty is at the suet nothing interrupts him. From behind he looks mostly black until his tail spreads. Suddenly he looks large and formidable—orange survival value in competition for food.

Of all the spring birds orioles are the most brilliant. Their colors announce that finally there will be no more snow. My wife welcomes their guarantee of warm summer. What a gift for Mother's Day! Three darts of orange amid the green. Another reason for their colors—beauty just for beauty's sake. ✺

This is the year of the caterpillars. In May it seemed that every fruit tree and shrub was draped with their gray tents. An entirely different insect, only slightly less fuzzy, is defoliating our young poplar trees. The woods are full of creepy-crawlies and this year it seems most of them are hairy.

Such an outbreak of insects would normally attract an influx of birds to the feast. In the West during big grasshopper years, there seemed to be a sparrow hawk on every available perch. Even kingfishers deserted the streams to go grasshopper hunting in morning's cool. Spruce bud worm infestations attract supersaturations of warblers, sometimes three or more breeding pairs per acre.

Most birds don't like hairy caterpillars. The bristles are protective like porcupine quills. They prickle the stomach lining. In concentrations like this year, caterpillars may actually drive away birds. I have found several robin's nests deserted due to defoliation of the nest trees by tent caterpillars. In an active robin's nest the eggs are polished. After desertion they quickly loose their sheen. In my prowlings through defoliated poplars I find a noticeable shortage of small birds. It takes a specialist to handle hairy crawlies. Fortunately we have two—the cuckoos.

Black-billed cuckoos are the most common at our latitude. Yellow-bills are more abundant to the south, but this year they are here in numbers. Both species have a thing about hairy caterpillars. They gobble them by the thousands. When their stomachs get bristle matted, they slough off the lining and start slick and new again. How many millenia did it take to evolve such an adaptation? The cuckoos' entire behavior seems to be influenced by their food preference. They are secretive birds, over a foot long, but seldom seen. They sit quietly, seemingly for hours. Caterpillars aren't very fast. They don't require chasing, and many of the hairy kinds concentrate in huge colonies. The cuckoo just sits by a colony and eats. I have watched one tear into a caterpillar tent, gobble a few, then sit and digest or contemplate. I almost expect to hear him burp. Then back to dip into the tent for more fuzzy edibles—repeat and repeat.

Cuckoos are to be heard not seen. Check their abundance by their calls. At dawn their "cow, cow, cows" roll across the woods. The yellow-bills slow to the end into "coup-coup-coup." Black-bills sound softer, "cup, cups," and don't slow. Both call more in humid weather, hence their nickname "rain crows." When the first rain crow's call greeted a May morning I gave a prayer of thanks. Now a dozen or more of both kinds greet the dawns. I think they are gaining on the fuzzies at our place. I listen to their "cow-cows" and count our allies.
ﷺ

One of the nicest things to encounter in the woods is a lady's slipper. Any walk in moist June woods is apt to find them. I like yellow lady's slippers best. Around here they bloom early in June. We have a few spotted along our paths. Right after Memorial Day we start watching for them, yet the first is always a surprise.

Yellow lady's slippers are usually solitary. Sometimes there are two to a stem, and in a few places several plants flower together. They thrive in cool damp shade. The forest always seems more peaceful where I find them. Ovenbirds nest there and veeries sing. The forest floor smells fresh and clean and balsam scented.

About two weeks later the showy lady's slippers bloom. Their big rose pink and white blossoms justify their name. Sometimes two or three bloom from one plant. At our place they live in colonies of dozens. It overwhelms me. Viewed objectively, probably no Michigan flower equals the beauty of a showy lady's slipper. Certainly it puts most hothouse orchids to shame. I marvel at their magnificence beside the dark cedars. But, they intimidate me.

A few small yellow lady's slippers live in our woods. Their thumbnail-sized blooms appear in mid-June. A few live near the showy colony. Always one or two stand in the swampy background. Each year I get wet feet to check their fragrance. Often orchids have no odor. Small yellow lady's slippers are something special.

Wild orchids should never be picked. They produce thousands of tiny seeds, but these have no stored food, so few survive. It takes years for some species to reach blooming stage. Once established, they are perennial from bulblike roots. They are not very tolerant of transplanting and are often subject to diseases or fungus parasites.

Fifty kinds of orchids live in Michigan. All are protected. It would take a botanist to identify most of them and a mighty tolerance of mosquitoes to find them. Most like moist places and bloom when the fly crop is at its peak. In some places maybe the mosquitoes have saved these beautiful flowers from extinction. Everything is tied together. Bugs that bite are just part of nature's plan.

It would be good to know fifty orchids, but I never shall. Yellow and showy lady's slippers, with maybe a few pink and white ones will have to do for me. I like it so.

Any fool can pick a wild flower. It cannot run away. Some flowers invite gathering by their riotous abundance, lady's slippers don't. Meet them in admiration or friendship, and leave them be. You and the forest will be better if you do. ❦

The young grouse that lives near our pond is still working hard at his drumming. Almost every morning I hear a few of his swishing performances. His drumming stage is a sway-backed cedar trunk, barely six inches above the forest floor. Midway between a half-dead balsam and the upswept cedar, his fanning has blown off all the loose shreds. I located it by the polished red bark and piles of droppings.

Grouse drumming is sort of ventriloquistic. It seems to come from where it isn't. When young birds are just learning, they just swish and whiffle. This makes them even harder to locate. Any blundering around will drive the drummer off his stage. It took me weeks to locate this platform, even though it is within sight of our pond dam. Now, with care, I can watch him practice. He is much better than in early spring. On a cool crisp morning he makes quite a respectable rumble.

North of the house an old cock holds sway. His booming rolls fairly peal across the forest. For three years I have searched unsuccessfully for his drumming station. Grouse sometimes change drumming logs. I think this one never has. Every spring I locate him approximately, by listening from all sides. He always quits before I get near. I cheated by bringing the dog. This old rooster led a merry chase, then flushed in the barely audible distance. I have quit cheating.

Each fall I make one or two passes at this old bird. He has yet to hold to a point. I sometimes glimpse his long-tailed shape flashing between the conifers, but never within range. I doubt I would shoot him if I could. Young birds are better eating and not so humbling to hunt. Besides, he drums so well. I depend on him to make the very first announcement of spring.

Another grouse brood hatched this week. A hen and a hatful of chicks scooted out of my way this morning. Part of our place is tag alders. The moist ground is double shaded by all sorts of forbs and ferns. This covey was headed for that happy brood range. It's full of all sorts of bugs and goodies growing grouse need. Each August I take the dog there to practice on young birds. He needs to relearn that grouse are to be pointed, not chased. They need to learn not to perch in trees and "pert" at intruders. The training is mutually beneficial.

Living with grouse is a great pleasure. I enjoy them for twelve months instead of three. As the major predator on the place, I take a few. The feathered and furred predators also get a share. Between us we educate the survivors.

The cock on the north forty has a Ph.D. I hope the youngster by the pond does as well. 🌸

One of the senior citizens of our place lives under a log at the corner of the house. He moved in shortly after I placed the log to retain a flower bed. I watched him one morning as he shuffled and dug backward into the loose sand. He is a very large, and very dignified toad. He, and some of his progeny, keep pests off the flowers. He also cleans up the june bugs which, each night, fall, bottoms up from our lighted windows. He is the only toad we have big enough to handle them.

Common toads may live up to thirty years if they escape predators. They keep growing all their lives. Ours must be very old, for he is a giant of his species, almost five inches long. We think he will be safe with us. He is much too large for any of the little snakes in our woods. The hawks and owls don't usually hunt so close to the house. Our dog picked him up when we first arrived, but promptly spit him out. He must taste terrible, for the dog hasn't touched him since.

Toads hibernate in burrows. In spring they go to ponds to breed and lay their eggs. They arrive about a week behind the spring peepers, our earliest amphibian songsters. I think toads have the prettiest song. It is a high trill lasting up to half a minute. Only the male sings. He does it with his mouth closed by inflating a vocal sac in his throat. This sac stands out above the water, making it easy for the female to find him. She lays her eggs in strings. There may be several thousand in each string. Frog eggs are usually in masses of jelly. Spring peepers' eggs are dropped singly.

Tadpoles hatch in a few days to three weeks, depending on the weather. They are vegetarians, with long intestinal tracts to assimilate vegetable matter. Their tiny mouths are adapted for feeding on algae and other tiny plants. They breathe through gills.

Our new fishpond and the pools by the road are alive with tadpoles. The little black ones are toads. The gray and green ones are frogs. It is hard to tell them apart. They develop fast and colors change.

Before the summer is out the little toad pollywogs will develop legs. The gills and tail will be absorbed, and the mouth widened to accommodate their animal diet. Of all the vertebrates, only amphibians undergo this remarkable metamorphosis. After tasting their first bugs, toads never return to vegetables. No more spinach for them.

Our fat old friend is an extra big eater. One recent rainy evening we watched him finishing off a huge night crawler. He stuffed the last few inches into his mouth with one front foot. Then he heaved his shoulders and seemed to sigh, "I can't believe I ate the wh—ole thing." ✵

"Teacher, teacher, teacher, teach—!" How many times has teacher interrupted the ovenbird's frantic call for attention. Each time I hear this little warbler's call ringing through the spring wood, I see myself eagerly thrusting up a hand to catch the teacher's eye, then realizing I didn't know the answer after all.

Ovenbirds are one of our most abundant warblers. Yet, they are more often heard than seen. I have a terrible time identifying warblers. They are little, and flitty, and beautiful. I find myself admiring them like butterflies instead of studying characteristics that permit quick identification.

I have a friend who knows warblers by their songs. He recognizes calls I can't even hear. Most wood warblers aren't very good singers. Compared with the thrushes, orioles, rose-breasted grosbeaks, and the bobolinks, their songs are feeble chirps.

To me the ovenbird is the most distinctive of the warblers. He has a personality that is strictly nonconformist. He looks like a thrush, may act like a mouse, and has a flight song that would put most of his relatives to shame. Sometimes he sings it in the middle of the night.

The other day I flushed an ovenbird from her nest. She ran, belly down, across the leafy forest floor. Surely this olive gray skittering shape was a mouse disturbed by my footsteps. Fifty feet away she flew up to a twig and paused in a stray bit of sunlight. The broad orange head stripe identified her.

I stood stock still. Six inches from my foot was a little leafy dutch oven. On the fine grass lining were four white-and-brown-speckled eggs. One was slightly larger than the rest. A cowbird had paid this nest a visit. I carefully removed the alien egg, while the mother flitted anxiously back to peer in accusation from each low twig.

Ovenbirds spend more time on the ground than other warblers. They like the bare leafy floor of deep woods. Either bird may sound off their "teacher, teacher" call from a low perch. I think they have definite singing trees from which to announce their territory.

The male has an exuberant flight song. He flies over forest openings, or through the trees pouring forth a burble of melody. In spring it is for courtship, for he always flies back to a waiting female. During nesting he may burst forth anytime as if to assure his mate of joyful love.

The one who cherishes the nest I watch, sings at dawn, and sunset, and on moonlit nights. The melody gushes forth in a tumble of warbles and trills. It ever changes. Yet, each song has at least one "teacher." It's as if he is saying, "This is really what I intended to say." ❧

The fastest duck on foot is the wood duck. We just don't think of ducks as runners. Wood ducks are. Furthermore, they seem to like to run. They do a lot of it.

We put out cracked corn on the river upstream. Each morning and evening the ducks come. Most are drake wood ducks. Their routine is fun and beautiful to watch. They seem to prefer to feed on land. They rush about snatching tidbits and chasing one another. Their ground speed is amazing. Finally they settle down to feed. Then they methodically search out every grain, or tip up in competition with the mallards in the water.

Feeding over, they settle on logs or mudbanks to doze. A few fly up into the trees. I am still amazed to see ducks perched forty feet in the air and walking along the limbs. There are few more beautiful sights than a flock of woodies resting in the sunlight among the lemon green leaves of spring.

The hens are busy nesting. They come down briefly at dawn and dark for a quick bite. As the weather warms they stay longer. They know how long they can leave the tree hole nest without risking chill of the precious eggs. Each hen is greeted warmly by one drake. He attends her intently. The others pay no heed. Mating is settled for this year. In fact, it's all over unless the nest is broken up. The drake doesn't know this, but she does. His attention is to assure fertile renesting if it is necessary. Her preoccupation is to assure care of the eggs. It's nature's plan, not just a whim.

When wood ducks enter a tree hole they grasp the hole lip with their toes and brace with the tail like a woodpecker. When house hunting, they cautiously peer inside. Who wants to be in a tree hollow with a mess of squirrels, or a coon, or an owl? Once their home is occupied, the flip inside is lightning fast. I used to think wood ducks flew full tilt into the hole. Close watching discloses the split second perch before entering.

Wood ducks are not closely related to other North American ducks. Their nearest cousins are the Mandarin ducks of East Asia and Japan. The drakes are as spectacular as wood ducks. Hen Mandarins and wood ducks are almost identical.

Soon the little woodies will be hatching. At their mother's call they will climb to the hollow entrance and leap out. That first step may be a doozy—forty or fifty feet. What a way to start life, and when just one day old!

Still, if you are going to grow up to be a runner, you may as well start right. The first step is the hardest. ❦

Falcons are the royalty of the avian world. Even the eagle, proverbial king of the birds, cannot rival their superb self-confidence. The stoop of a falcon is one of nature's truly breathtaking sights. Unfortunately the only falcon most of us will ever see is the little sparrow hawk. These little kestrels, knights of the sky, are still fairly common in spite of the pesticides that burn so deadly at their vitals. The peregrine, or duck hawk, is just about gone from Michigan.

I recently spent a weekend with three dedicated men who come to our state each year to band birds of prey. Three of the birds banded were sparrow hawks. These hawks nest in cavities. This family had taken up residence in a wood duck box. The three youngsters were about two weeks old. There was one unpipped egg, buff with brown spots.

While the young were handed down in a bag to receive their I.D. bracelets, the parents swooped overhead screaming their "killy, killy, killy." One of the hatchlings posed for his picture. Feet and head up, beak gaped, he was ready for defense even in downy infancy. Our predators bow to no one and the falcons lead them all.

The banding was quick, but oh so careful. The bad egg was measured and stored away for future analysis. Our feathered predators are in peril. These men would find out why.

Sparrow hawks are poorly named. Insects and mice make up most of their diet. They like to watch from some high perch or hover in the wind on quivering wings. They hunt the open fields and are seldom seen in the deep woods. When hunting for their young they take more birds. Any prey is welcome then. I have usually seen them capture birds by direct pursuit. Once I saw one stoop like a miniature peregrine. It was just as spectacular. The little puff of feathers from the stricken goldfinch was like a transistorized copy of the larger falcons' kill. Kestrel is a better name.

Out west I used to fish near a cliff where pigeons nested. Two prairie falcons hunted there. They took the pigeons as they pleased. Many times I neglected a good trout rise to watch the falcons' magnificent flight. Few things in nature can so distract a trout fisherman. That was before pesticides became widespread. I hope the prairie falcons still come to those high bluffs, but I am so afraid.

One of the tragedies of mankind is that we seem to destroy the beautiful and the strong, and preserve the ugly and the mediocre. We poison our falcons and our eagles, while starlings and cowbirds prosper amid our litter. Man cannot live by bread alone. We must hurry, hurry. With each addled egg or silenced call, humanity dies a little. It need not be so. ❦

Mayflies are the most important insects in Michigan. If you don't believe it ask the perch and the martins, the trout and the ducks, the bats, the dragonflies, and the cedar waxwings. Ask all the things that swim, and crawl, and fly, and grow fat on these beautiful little insects. Or ask the trout fisherman with his feathered imitation, and the ice fisherman with his cup of frilly wigglers.

Our lake has several huge hatches of mayflies and many smaller ones. The first hatch this year was a few little gray flies about one-half inch long. The great hatches on our lake are large beige-colored insects over one inch long.

Mayflies spend most of their lives in the water, about a year on the average. Then they are called nymphs, the wigglers that are such good fish bait. They feed on underwater debris and vegetation. In turn they are fed on by fish, dragonfly larvae, and just about anything else that runs across them. This is the most important food form for they are available the year round. In some waters pollution and pesticides have greatly reduced their numbers. The wild species that feed on mayflies have decreased accordingly.

The nymphs swim with an up and down wiggle. When mature they swim to the surface or climb up a reed or twig, split their skin, and crawl out to fly a short distance as subimagoes or duns. In this stage the wings are milky. In a few hours they molt again into clear-winged imagoes or spinners. Mayflies are unique among all insects in molting more than once as an adult.

The spinners have their mating dance at dusk on our lake. Up and down they fly, mating in the air. The female descends to the surface to deposit her eggs, usually in two clusters. They may contain thousands of eggs. The clusters sink to the bottom and eventually hatch into nymphs. Then the adults die.

My wife and I recently sat at the cottage front to watch an evening flight. The air was misty with flies. Minnows dimpled the water at dockside. A family of mallards plucked flies from the reeds, the little ducklings stretching mightily for those just out of reach. Bats flitted among the trees. Birds of every description joined the feast. High up the real aerial hunters, nighthawks, swallows, and swifts gathered the harvest. Flycatchers and cedar waxwings darted out in swift contortions. Ring-billed gulls fed on the wing in comic opera grace, while the herring gulls swam about gobbling everything in reach. Little black terns scooped flies from the air and plucked them daintily from the surface.

Nature was having a shore dinner. It was more fun than kids at a watermelon feast.

Cleaning up the smelly fly windrows next day was a small price to pay for the entertainment. 🐝

William Cullen Bryant would never have written a poem about bobolink if he had lived in the South. This black, white, and buff minstrel of our meadows is a drab yellow and brown-streaked pest on his southward migration.

Thousands of them, mixed with their red-winged blackbird cousins, descended on our grain fields in the fall with disasterous results. We called them ricebirds, and a standard boyhood chore was to defend the crops from these invaders. My earliest bragging bag was sixty-four ricebirds with two charges from a shotgun. They were delicious eating. Now automatic carbide cannons are set in the rice fields to frighten them away. So persistent are the flocks that they soon ignore the noise unless the firing time is changed frequently.

The field where we live has many bobolinks. The handsome males sing from every high weed stem and in flight scatter their tinkling songs like a broken string of sleigh bells falling down stairs. The small, drab yellow females are seldom seen and even less often recognized as mates of our boisterous songsters.

The male bobolink is something of a roué, often mating with more than one wife. Their courtship is most ardent, and the harassed female sometimes hides in the grass to escape. My dog recently flushed one. Two males who must have been watching for her immediately gave chase. Around the field and back into the grass, but one suitor dived in after her. Up again and away but the villain still pursued her. Can we wonder at her retiring nature?

The nests are well hidden in thick grass. The mother, almost invisible when still, never flushes until she has run a safe distance from her nursery. Sometimes the young wander from the nest before they can fly, but the mother finds and cares for them.

The male helps with the insect gathering, but as soon as family responsibilities are over he disappears completely. Actually a complete moult turns him into a slightly larger copy of his drab spouse. The rollicking songs are silent. The yellow and brown families switch their diet from insects to seeds. By August the flocks gather in marshes and on shorelines. They start south early for their winter home in southern Brazil and Argentina.

The bobolink was originally an easterner, but moved west with the white man's migration across the country. He still follows his traditional route to South America, southeast down the Mississippi Valley and the Atlantic Coast. There, as the ricebird, he collects his pay in grain for the farm pests he fed so abundantly to his family in the North. ✹

Each summer I watch for a bird which my grandfather hunted, but I never will—the upland sandpiper, a shorebird that shuns the shore. This week when I saw one striding across a neighbor's lawn my first recollection of them came back to me.

When I was growing up these big sandpipers were so rare that it was an event just to sight one. I remember the tales of hunting them from a chaise. A driver handled the two-wheeled buggy while the shooter sat with one foot on the step ready to hop out quickly. The birds were easily spotted in the open fields, and the horse would be set to briskly circling nearer and nearer the selected target. At the crucial moment the gig would pull up and the shooter hop down to fire at the flushing bird.

One hundred years ago this was a popular summer sport. Now it is both illegal and unsporting by our standards. Upland sandpipers were hunted in July and August. Their long trip to Argentina requires an early start and only in the Deep South did they offer fall shooting.

When I first came to Michigan I was thrilled to find them nesting here. Each year there seem to be a few more. They are gradually recovering from overshooting, but not so fast as some other shorebirds. Their competition with human activities for nesting space is probably the reason.

These plovers are unexpected-looking birds. With heads too small for their bodies, they resemble a fat woman with a crew cut. They often perch on fence posts. On alighting they hold their wings straight up a moment as if to stretch before settling down. Their long pointed wings make them appear larger than woodcock, but they aren't. In flight they seem to use only their wing tips. Maybe they have surplus wing area to help on their long migration. Their whistle is drawn out and melodious, much more musical than their killdeer cousins' worrisome cry. This weird song and their peculiar appearance makes them an interesting addition to the outdoor landscape.

Their habit of nesting in hayfields causes many broods to be destroyed by mowing. While brooding they sit very close so that sometimes even the adult bird is caught by the mower. This is tragic, for they are the farmer's good friends. They feed very heavily on grasshoppers, cutworms, and other farm pests.

Few birds so love the wide open spaces. Golf courses, airports, and mowed fields are their habitat. Easily seen but hard to approach, they are extremely wary. They have excellent eyesight and are fast afoot or awing. No wonder they taxed nineteenth-century gunners' ingenuity. ✤

Poets write about the "murmuring pines and the hemlock," "the spreading chestnut tree," and "the shade of the old apple tree." Our pioneer forefathers were "tough as hickory" and "great oaks from little acorns grow"—but nobody writes about poplar.

Beloved by beavers and porcupines, choice fodder for elk, bread and butter for the deer, rabbits gnaw on it, mice nibble at it, grouse live on it, and heaven protects it. Eliminate the poplar trees and half the game in the upper lake states would starve to death. No other forest tree is so chewed on, bit off, drilled into, or pecked at. Its seeds are so fragile that almost none of them sprout, and the seedlings so feeble they seldom survive. No wonder one of our poplar species trembles in the slightest breeze.

The aspens, for that is the proper name for our poplar trees, make up 50 percent of all the trees in lower Michigan. Quaking and bigtooth aspen are the most important. A third species, balsam poplar, is of less value as animal food, but has a medical history which led to its nickname "Balm of Gilead."

How could such trees take over half our forest? The answer is fire. After the cut out–get out logging of our virgin forests, fires swept through the slash repeatedly between 1900 and 1920. To compensate the aspens for feeding the forest fauna, nature gave them the ability to sprout from roots. Whenever a tree is killed suddenly, suckers sprout from the horizontal roots. One tree may produce suckers over an area fifty or sixty feet wide. If enough parent trees were present, sprouts may come up forty to fifty thousand per acre. It was these dense stands of poplar sprouts which fed the developing deer herd and big grouse population of forty years ago.

Now with the modern protection from forest fire, poplar has lost its most friendly enemy, for aspen trees cannot reproduce in the shade of others. Even grass or bracken fern will choke off poplar seedlings. If a poplar is killed in a mixed forest, any few sprouts that do spring up will die a lingering death in the shade of their elders.

But poplar has found a new friend in the modern logger. After ignoring it for centuries, man is finally finding its true value. Half of all the pulpwood cut in the lake states is poplar, and the logger has learned his lesson from the fire years. To grow poplar you must destroy the forest. Then, like the Phoenix, new poplars will rise from the ruins. No other tree can return so fast and that is according to nature's plan.

A young forest is a busy forest, full of birds, and animals, and insects. They must have plenty to eat and the poplar is their grocery.

One of the choicest wild foods in Michigan is probably the least exploited—crayfish—freshwater lobster. They abound, free for the taking, in almost all our lakes and streams.

Supermarket shrimp have just about priced themselves out of our menu. We have a seemingly limitless substitute right at our front door. Every time I filet fish, I stick some scraps and backbones in the minnow trap and toss it in the river. Next morning it usually contains two or three dozen crayfish.

The crayfish in our stream are carnivorous. They have big strong pinchers. In proportions they are almost exact miniatures of the big saltwater lobsters we caught in Maine. A nearby lake contains vegetarian crawdads. Their pinchers are smaller. Bread is the best bait. My front field contains vegetarian crawfish that live in the underground water table. They push up mud chimneys from the tunnels they excavate. Most any warm rainy night will find them crawling about the field. Their eyes shine red.

There must be dozens of kinds of crayfish in America. Down south we had big black ones, and red ones, and several smaller varieties in various shades of green. I caught them for years as crawfish and crawdads before I ever knew that the proper name was crayfish. Still sounds kind of prissy to me.

Our river craws average three or four inches long, plus another inch for pinchers. Some go over six inches. We usually boil them with salt, red pepper, and spices. Five minutes is plenty. We put ours in cold water and turn up the heat. As the water warms, the crayfish relax, go to sleep, and stay nice and tender.

We like them cold for weekend lunch. Allow plenty of time. Twist off the tail and peel it, then pull off the little dorsal flap, starting at the body end, and discard the mud vein. Pop the choice morsel in your mouth or, if you can wait that long, shuck enough for a cocktail or salad. It beats shrimp and it's free! We also like the claw meat on these river crayfish. A nut cracker is handy for this work, and it leaves plenty of time for leisurely conversation. My New England in-laws say it's just like eating crabs. You can starve to death right at the table. T'ain't so.

Fried crayfish are choice. Pour boiling water over to kill them— instant and humane. Shuck the tails, remove the mud veins, roll in cornmeal, and fry quickly. Euell Gibbons recommends dipping them in tempura batter to make a few go a long way. We like batter made of beer and Bisquick. It puffs up and tastes delicious. In fact, it tastes so good we are going to have some tomorrow.

Better go set the trap out right now. ✹

The two life-forms that most seriously challenge man's domination of earth are rodents and insects. It is dangerous to make such broad generalizations, for we have allies in both enemy camps, but generally these groups eat the same things we do. Often they are quite successful in this competition. Some rodents and insects transmit dread diseases. A few insects even eat us. Right now those "people eaters" are at their peak.

The worst people eaters belong to the order Diptera, flies and mosquitoes. There are 15,000 known species in North America—about 80,000 in the world. Only a handful actually bite us, but in May and June, what a handful! On my dawn meanderings the swarms of mosquitoes are sometimes dense enough to obscure vision. Only mosquito-proof clothes and plenty of fly dope make them bearable.

Around here we usually have two big crops of mosquitoes. The first comes in April, shortly after the snow leaves. The larvae live in snowmelt water. In the arctic some mosquitoes lay their eggs in dry depressions. The eggs hatch when flooded by snowmelt and may stay viable for several years. Our little snow mosquitoes may reproduce the same, for none appear in dry springs, such as this year. When they do appear they last about two weeks.

The second mosquito crop hatches a few days after big May rains. They are larger and last longer, well into June. This year there is a bumper crop. Only female mosquitoes suck blood. Males fast or suck plant juices. I would almost swear this year's crop is 90 percent female. By the end of June mosquito population drops to a tolerable level. Usually a blaze orange hat is all I need to keep them away. Most outdoor pests seem to dislike that color.

Fortunately our homestead does not have blackflies. My first experience with those devils was forty years ago on a June fishing trip in Maine. Those flies crawled into buttonholes and down collars. They seemed to like our old-fashioned tar and citronella fly dope. On that trip I also learned about punkies. They came through the camp screens with their wings spread and covered us with stinging needle pricks. June is supposed to be the best north country fishing month. I'll take fewer fish and fewer flies earlier or later.

We are fortunate that these people eaters are small and only suck blood. My hunting uncle used to tell of a large mosquito, fortunately now extinct. It flew only at night. "I was late getting out of the woods one evening. Just as I got in sight of the levee I heard one of those Mississippi skeeters coming. I dodged behind a big cypress. That skeeter drove his bill through the tree, uprooted it, and cleared half an acre of ground before I could kill it with my axe." Our little modern mosquitoes aren't really that bad after all.

𝕸

Chimney swifts have a unique life hazard in cold late springs. Some nest in residential chimneys. If the homeowner starts a fire to ward off an unseasonable chill, the smoke may suffocate roosting swifts. This is one price these birds pay for the nest and roost sites man has brought them.

Before the white man came to America, chimney swifts occupied large hollow trees. Available nest sites limited their numbers. Now they use chimneys almost exclusively. In migration, flocks roost in large industrial or commercial chimneys. They scatter to nest, but several pair may occupy a large chimney. One of our local groups favors enclosed church belfries. Some nest in silos.

Years ago the South was dotted with huge old chimneys left when cotton gins were converted from steam to electricity. I remember each fall watching the swifts come to roost. There was a tornado of birds circling tighter and tighter. Finally the bottom of the funnel centered the chimney and changed wing pitch. A torrent of birds fluttered out of sight. In a few minutes it was over. The chimney must have been shingled with feathered bodies. In Georgia bird banders captured and counted 7,377 swifts in one chimney.

Swifts almost never alight except on vertical surfaces. Grounded, their legs are too short and wings too long for takeoff. Young birds cling to the chimney wall until they are accomplished fliers, for if they ever flutter to the ground, they might never fly again.

Chimney swifts gather nest twigs by snapping them off the tops of trees in flight. The twigs are transferred to their beaks in flight and stuck against the chimney wall with saliva. During nest season both males and females develop large salivary glands. The nest is a rigid half-saucer lattice with no lining. The glue is not waterproof. A heavy rain may wash the nest down. Chimney swifts lay four or five eggs. The little nests quickly get overcrowded, so the nestlings climb out. Their entire life will be spent flying or clinging.

The quills of chimney swifts' tail feathers extend a bit beyond the barbs making stiff spikes to brace against the wall. The tails are too short to help in flight maneuvers. Swifts steer by varying wing speed and pitch. Sometimes one wing moves faster than the other, making it appear they are flapping alternately.

Swifts aren't related to swallows. Their wings are longer and more crescent shaped. They have wide gaping mouths to catch insects, but no wind scoop whiskers like swallows. They fly faster than swallows and generally higher. Swifts are the most aerial of all birds; may even mate on the wing as pairs frequently make contact in the air.

Swifts like our small towns. Our chimneys are their homes. They pay rent by insect eating and, when traffic noise eases, you can hear their twitters and chatters. It is a gentle sound. ❧

If wild strawberries were as big as cultivated ones they would sell for $2.00 a box. They are that much better. At their normal size they are priceless. You have to pick your own.

The best way to pick wild strawberries is to high-grade. I wander about our field listening to the bobolinks till I find the best patch. Then I sit right down amongst 'em.

Wild strawberries grow in little clusters on separate leafless stalks. My New England mother-in-law taught me how to pick them. She picked the whole cluster, gathering the stems in her left hand like a bouquet of violets. When she dropped a bunch in the basket it was enough for one serving of shortcake.

In good picking you can get a whole bouquet without moving. I like to skooch around in the patch on my bottom to save getting up and down. The stains on my pants would make a hit at a teen fashion show—carmine and green and some brown smears from deer droppings.

Everything eats strawberries. We have some early patches in openings near the river. Coons get almost all of them. Every June coon droppings on the place are loaded with strawberry seeds. We get our share in the field because there are just too many for everything to eat.

We call our place "Strawberry Banke" after the shore of the Piscataqua River where the Pilgrims first settled in New Hampshire. It's now a part of Portsmouth, my wife's hometown. The spelling is correct. Those early Yankees didn't understand modern language.

I do the picking. We hull them together. Eve makes the shortcake. After that it's everyone for himself. If there is any left over I usually find it before bedtime. Use real whipping cream. Don't insult wild strawberries with any of those pressure-canned synthetics.

Weather permitting, we plan on wild strawberry shortcake the first day of summer. This year hit it right on the head. The sun was warm. The breeze was cool. The bobolinks tinkled song, and the upland plovers cried alarm. Wet weather had made a bumper crop. Some berries were fingertip large.

I screwed up my self-control to prevent nibbling and sat down in the first patch. Picking cultivated berries, the farmer tells you where—that's business. For wild ones, the berries tell you where—that's fun.

My mother-in-law picked with Yankee efficiency. She said putting one strawberry at a time in the basket was time wasteful. She was right. But, anyone who picks wild strawberries has plenty of time. ⚹

Some of the small print in our history is written in lilac. This time of year you can read it in domes of pale purple blooms. Each of them marks what once was a home. The men who homesteaded this part of America brought apple trees. Their womenfolk brought lilacs.

In much of northeastern Michigan, particularly along Lake Huron, the soil is thin and rocky, barely covering the great deposits of limestone. After the logging much of it was farmed. Today all that remains of these farms is gnarled apple trees and those ever present mounds of lilacs. Search beside each and you will find a rough stone foundation, maybe a well hole, lost or broken tools. A record of failure? I think not. There were hopes, and plans, and dreams. You don't plant lilacs unless you are going to stay. They will not bloom tomorrow, or next year, or maybe the next, and then only for a few brief spring days. You cannot peddle the fragrance, or even store it except in memories.

Each spring I visit these old farmlands. Apple blossoms fill the air. Hedgerows of wild plum and chokecherry hide tumbled stone walls in white lace. Every so often the scent of lilacs drifts downwind. Lilacs love lime. In this land they thrive. They reproduce by suckers, so that each bush is marked by an impenetrable dome-shaped thicket yards across and clothed foot-deep in pale purple.

Man has carried many plants in his migrations. Some, like dandelions, escaped, moved on the wind, became truly wild. I've never seen a wild lilac. Our familiar variety grows wild in Bulgaria, first found there in 1820. Long before, it was a domesticated shrub in the Near East; brought from Constantinople to western Europe in 1554 and to North America in the seventeenth century. The French and English brought them. Now there are about 500 kinds ranging from white, cream or blue, to lilac and deep purple. Some have no odor. Don't look for the fancies on abandoned farms. Our pioneers brought lilac lilacs with one plant in a thousand blooming white.

Except in the South, everywhere we lived we've had lilacs. We bought a big old house in Oregon because of the big lilac bush blooming by the back door. Here suckers from a wilderness farm struggle against the annual deer pruning. Someday they will bloom.

Lilacs restore my faith in man. Our forefathers came to wrest a living from a strange land. They were burdened with tools, and babies, and food-producing seeds and sprouts. Often they walked. And in that conglomerate of necessities they found room for lilacs. It places us one step above the beasts. 🌿

July

My wife's dachshund spent her last summer feuding with our chipmunk. She was a very old dog, and he was a very old chipmunk. Through four summers of taunting and pursuit they learned mutual respect and established a set of rules. The dog had long since given up trying to move the woodpile or excavate the toolshed foundation. The chipmunk had learned the exact point of no return between shed and woodpile. Each sunny day she settled in her selected spot, and he manufactured errands between his sanctuaries along the route that provided the most exciting combination of danger and safety.

This summer neither contestant appeared on the field of battle.

Such relationships are not unusual in the animal world. Most species enjoy games either with their own kind or friendly enemies. Chipmunks are particularly prone to establish themselves with people, or their domestic pets, whenever the opportunity offers.

These little animals are solitary dwellers. We know ours was a male, for no young ever appeared. Early each spring he disappeared into the woods to find a mate, but was always back in residence when we arrived for the summer.

Five years is a long life for a chipmunk. He must have built an elaborate burrow in that time. Chipmunks are real do-it-yourself architectural engineers. They keep improving their homes all their lives. A larger bedroom, new storerooms or even a second toilet may be added.

The toilet is always the lowest room, a sound and sanitary design. The bedroom is elevated to avoid flooding. The bed is made of shredded leaves and grass and may be king-size, almost a foot across.

The burrow's entrance is usually well hidden and free from fresh earth. Another hole may be opened some distance away to remove excavated soil. After a pile is dumped, the hole is plugged to confuse predators.

The chipmunk doesn't really hibernate, but he seldom appears above ground in winter. He stores quantities of seeds and nuts in his various storerooms. The favorite storage is under the bed. What could be handier? By spring he may have eaten his bed supports almost from the ceiling to the floor.

Chipmunks have cheek pouches for transporting food. Packed full they resemble an outlandish case of mumps with the animal's head over twice its normal size. They can pack two or three acorns in each pouch, loading them alternately to maintain balance.

Handsome, fun loving, and with built-in market baskets, no wonder these little sprites are favorite tourist attractions for small children. They're one of my favorites too. ❦

Phoebes say, "phoe-bee." Pewees say, "pee-a-wee." It's a good thing they sing out their names, for these two little flycatchers look very much alike. Right now we have lots of both kinds. Pewees whistle their name. It has sort of a plaintive quality, sometimes sounds like "dear me." Phoebes don't whistle. They just call their two syllables, clearly annunciated. The two species are easily identified when they speak up. In midsummer they don't.

Field guides tell us that phoebes have all black bills, black heads, no wing bars, and wag their tails. Pewees have wing bars, yellow lower mandibles, head and back the same color. Both birds are dull olive gray, light breast, erect stance, and fly from a perch to catch their prey. O.K. so far—but young phoebes do have wing bars, their heads aren't always black. Sometimes they don't wag their tails, sometimes pewees do—confusing!

My wife and I sat on the balcony watching the flycatchers do their thing. In mid-June five phoebes fledged from the nest under our toolshed eaves. They found good hunting in front of the house. Suddenly we realized we had too many flycatchers. One of the phoebes had been scooped up by a sharp-shinned hawk the day he left the nest. The old phoebes were renesting, yet we surely had six or seven little birds snatching flies. The extra ones were pewees.

The pewees nested high in an oak over our rustic bridge. Their nest was a little cup tied by spiderwebs tight in the crotch of a horizontal dead branch. Camouflaged by lichens, it looked like a tree knot. Pewees are the only birds I know that often build on dead limbs. They arrive late in spring, usually lay three eggs, and raise only one brood per year. They are not shy around the nest, since they seem to know there is no way I can reach it. Let a blue jay or red squirrel come close and they are real furies—fierce as kingbirds.

Phoebes and pewees catch all kinds of insects, but show a decided preference for flies. Our place has plenty. We have the usual houseflies, plus deerflies from the river and horseflies from the mucky pond outlet. Without some control, our balcony cocktail hours would be impossible. Phoebes and pewees are the controllers and provide entertainment as they work.

Both species perch, then fly out to kill. Pewees work a little higher than phoebes. Their hunting overlaps at balcony height. Both are amazingly adept and very tame. They pluck flies from the screen without touching the wire, scoop them from the air within arm's length. You can hear the phoebes' beaks snap when they make a catch.

Martins and swallows get publicity for mosquito catching. For us deep-wood dwellers, flycatchers are the stars. Phoebes and pewees make our balcony livable. We love 'em both. 🌿

There aren't many red wild flowers in our part of the world, but we do have one that's super. The slender spike of the cardinal flower is so intensely scarlet it literally smites the eyes. There is no redder red.

Each day I walk through our river's floodplain. In summer the path is in a waist-high sea of wet-loving plants: mints, touch-me-nots, speedwells, goldenrods, nettles, and marsh grasses. Iris are scattered about, and in the shadiest spots cinnamon ferns raise bouquets of fans. It is a pleasant place to visit. We stick to the paths so as not to disturb the plants. If we do wander, the nettles quickly warn of trespass.

There is a succession of blooms, most of them lavender, white, or yellow. Suddenly, in July, one is red. I expect the cardinal flowers, yet the first one is always a surprise. Like so many summer flowers cardinals are tall. In our woods they aren't the tallest, but their color makes them tower over the rest. The bloom spikes seem to shoot up overnight. The flowers open in succession from bottom to top, yet I never see them unbloomed. They seem to bide their time in the crowd, then shoot up a foot and burst open a dozen scarlet tubes.

Cardinal flowers belong to the lobelia subfamily of the bluebell family. All their relatives around here are blue or violet. I wonder what happy quirk of evolution caused this one species to be so red. They are perennials, so we always find them in the same place but scattered, never in masses like the mints and goldenrods. They seem to like late goldenrod for company. This lets them finish their blooming chores before their neighbors spread their golden counterpane.

Cardinal flowers are pollinated by hummingbirds. It would seem that their bright red blooms should fear no competition, yet they choose blooming time of special advantage. They peak in early August. Then on any day, dozens of their flames may be scattered across our flats. The wild bergamot is faded, wild mint reduced to a few violet whorles near the tips. Touch-me-nots are just opening. Goldenrod still sleeps in lush greenery. The competition for attention is absent. Then the cardinal blooms come on like a flourish of trumpets.

You can transplant cardinal flowers, but they don't like it. Despite the best of care they will die out in a few years. Better to leave them in their home and go to visit. Yet, each year I pick one. My wife loves red, and every year I bring her the first cardinal bloom.

The Indians made a love potion from the cardinal flower. When I bring that scarlet spike to my bride, I believe it works. ❧

Young evening grosbeaks are the most fun. Each July our feeders are deluged with fledglings of all kinds. Evening grosbeaks are the most dependent on their parents. We get many a chuckle as we watch the apron strings being severed.

This year the first two arrived July 8, two more arrived two days later. They are apparently all from the same brood, for we have not seen more than one pair of adults. Young evening grosbeaks are colored like their mothers, but their beaks are grayer and straighter. They do not acquire the massive Roman-arched adult beak until the fall moult. The adult grosbeak can crush a cherry pit and easily bite through the skin on the back of your hand.

Both adults shuck sunflower seeds and feed them to the youngsters. The straight beak gives the young bird's face a sort of pinched look. Crest feathers stand like a pompadour pushed back with wet fingers. Breast down, head back, and wings aquiver, the begging is irresistible. Even I want to help. Seeds are consumed at an amazing rate.

After a few days the most precocious fledglings begin to imitate their parents. They poke about among the seed shucks, handling and discarding empties, occasionally finding a loose kernel. Full seeds are rolled about haphazardly between the mandibles. I think the first crackings are purely accidental. The bird seems surprised at finding the goody inside and, of course, we are delighted.

The adults continue to supplement the youngsters' feeding efforts. Always there seems to be one idiot child that just can't learn. Oh, but he is pitiful, fluttering and begging ad nauseam—longer and longer between feedings until hunger finally does the job. Then he quickly catches up to his siblings in seed-cracking skill. By August all the new brood are self-sufficient.

Evening grosbeaks formerly nested north and west of the Great Lakes. They have been extending their range east and south. When we first moved to this conifer swamp, we made a deliberate effort to hold evening grosbeaks for nesting, plenty of sunflower seeds year round. For three years everyone left in May. Then one spring we watched a female gathering grass rootlets from our garden. They use these for nest lining, and now it's an every year occurrence for one to three pairs.

Evening grosbeaks build on horizontal branches high in conifers. We have never found a nest. This year I found a dead nestling on the ground, searched every overhead branch with binoculars. Nothing—but the adults were about carrying insects. It's always a surprise to see that thick Roman beak holding a big green caterpillar.

If the years and sunflower seeds hold out, we will eventually get our confirmed nesting record. Meanwhile, we anticipate each July for the fun of watching a new evening grosbeak generation grow up. They are so much like people. 🌿

Disaster struck our red-headed woodpeckers. A night windstorm destroyed their nest. Later I sat with them for a while.

The limb broke midway of the nest cavity. One young was in the top half just below the entrance. I removed his body from the floating snag and set it ashore to dry. It didn't help, but birds shouldn't be so wet. He was almost ready to fly, killed just before his first driver training.

A parent brings food to the top of the shattered snag—a big black beetle, whacked soft on a butcher block, wing cases akimbo—a choice morsel. It's poked into the hollow top of the shattered snag. No takers. If young are there they didn't survive. The beetle drops unnoticed to the ground. The parent flies to another tree to sit and look, and then flies back and away again.

The other parent works nearby. There is no way to tell, yet I feel it's the female. She is digging a new cavity—a western exposure like the old place, but more practical, in a short husky snag below the wind. She doesn't work very hard. Stops and sits a lot, just looking.

The red-heads are delightful neighbors. As the young grew, they were eternally busy at the suet and corn of our feeders. But they must have a balanced diet—beetles and grubs from the dead elm bark, grasshoppers from the pond berm, mayflies snapped over the river. Ah, there's a sight, a red-head fly catching. Beauty and skill against a cloud-dappled sky.

Woodpeckers don't just live in a hole in a tree. Their home is spacious. Our red-heads have a pantry—a broken top elm where they store chunks of suet, and corn, and other eatables that won't spoil. They keep other birds away. There is a butcher block on another stump for preparing tough food, and a high tip for viewing and to call from. There are bone-hard limbs for ringing out tattoos and special roost holes for the parents—no room in the nest with young so big.

The male brings a suet bit from the pantry, then takes it back. He starts a new hole ten feet below the old one. I hope they won't nest there. The whole trunk is split. Another storm may bring it down. Soon he's through the bark, chips fly. It's a nice neighborhood. Cedar waxwings nest across the slough, very stylish birds. The oriole family spatters the foliage with color. Sapsucker fledglings tear about— nice kids, but noisy. A doe has her nursery below, such well-behaved twins.

He hitches to the old nest for one more look, then back for a few more chips. Off to the view point to wait and look. She comes to wait with him.

I do not know if woodpeckers grieve, but we can. We grieve for them. 🐦

We have a three-ring circus in our backyard; eight purple martin families occupy the center ring. Tree swallows have the west side, barn swallows the east. Last year we had only the martins, but this year the tree swallows worked so hard at dispossessing their larger cousins, that we took pity and installed a single nest box on the west power pole. It was occupied at once.

The barn swallows came last. Their first act was a suspense drama as they balanced their mud ball nest on a five-eighths-inch molding. It just couldn't stick to the smooth aluminum. Yet, up and up it tiered in ever-widening semicircles. Now it is six inches high, and they are brooding in a snug feather-lined cup under the eaves. Surely man's early architects could have learned structural engineering from these winged masons.

The martins provide the main musical score. All the swallows have soft liquid twitters, and the small ones join the chorus early and late. The martins are never silent. Apartment living must develop gossips. They seem to discuss all manner of things. Even now, with feeding the young, the conversation is only slightly muted. It's surprising how many insects a martin can carry—and they can talk with a mouthful. One pair has a problem. I suspect it's parasites in the nest. They continue to bring bits of fresh green leaves. The whole colony denuded our maple sapling with the first nest building. It has releafed, but this couple brings their greenery from the woods. Theirs is the west apartment. Maybe the fresh leaves help cut the afternoon heat.

Right now the best act is the tree swallows. Their five young are flying. What antics they display. They swoop about in joyful grace. Sometimes two vie in midair rough and tumble.

The parents demonstrate capture tactics on the mayflies. The youngsters sometimes venture a try. Real meals are still served up by the old folks. The nest box remains the favorite feeding spot. One youth seems always to sit, head poked out, waiting for a tasty mouthful. They must take turns, for sometimes Mom and Pop refuse to deliver.

All swallows fly the first time from the nest. We watched three of these make their maiden flights. They never crash. Their nest box is six inches square. With five fledglings practicing inside, imagine the confusion. For days before they flew there was a constant twitter and flutter. I believe they establish a brood pecking order. The most aggressive practices more and flies first. There always seems to be one timid soul who has to be enticed out last. Pity him not. How could any birds learn to fly in a six-inch box without some sort of order.

So each day nature shows us her ways—ruthless logic and delightful surprises. We are lucky to have such graceful teachers. ❦

Woodchucks don't chuck wood, but they are certainly the second best dirt chuckers in these parts. This summer one chose our yard to demonstrate her prowess. It was a disaster.

We were away for three days, boarded out the dog. Our return found several wheelbarrow loads of sand piled against the chimney and front door. Five years of ivy growth was pulled down from the chimney. At the base of the pile a sizable hole led under the garage apron. My first thought was that the badger which visited us earlier had returned to dig out our resident chipmunk. Tracks proved me wrong.

A woodchuck has four toes on its front feet. A badger has five and is more pigeon-toed. He also has longer claws. The badger has to be the best digger, because he gets his food by outdigging other diggers. Woodchucks dig for shelter, but eat plants. They can take their time at digging. Our invader had simply liked the chipmunk's choice of building sites and appropriated it.

We examined the rest of the property. Woodchucks like to start their holes in corners with the first excavation at a rather shallow angle. A twelve-inch underground obstruction will divert them. This one had made several tentative holes around the house footings, disturbed the flower beds, scattered minnow traps stored in a chimney corner—no serious damage.

There was a hole started from inside the vegetable garden. Oh, no! The heart was gone from every head of lettuce, succulent tidbits from this parched summer landscape. This garden has a mesh fence, one foot buried, three feet high, plus strands of electric wire. We use the electricity only at night to keep out coons and deer. Woodchucks, which feed in the daytime, had never learned to climb over or dig under. A young one had found the electricity off and "goodbye lettuce." We chased her from her hideout in the asparagus patch and turned the electricity on full-time.

No woodchuck would live permanently under our front door—too public—bound to move. From the upstairs window I saw a veritable explosion of sand from the rock garden. Dirt was thrown eight or ten feet. I watched—fascinated. The chuck would disappear among the rocks, moments later a heaving plug of sand appeared at the entrance and exploded. It was a young female. She was pulling the sand under her belly, then backing out to kick it away. Looked like fun, but this gal had to go. Scattered bulbs and flower stalks made a scene of wreckage.

Woodchucks are easy to trap, and this one was no exception. Execution was quick, but now I'm sorry. She couldn't get back in the vegetables with the electricity on. It really wasn't much of a rock garden anyway, and she *did* move from under the doorstep of her own accord. We miss her. 🌿

No pterodactyl, 180 million years ago, looked more primitive than the great blue heron that came winging down our river. All angle-winged and trailing-legged, stately and reptilian, it undulated through the crest of the morning mist. For an instant I imagined wings spanning the river's tree-lined tunnel, fierce beak about to snatch me up, the hapless victim.

Too much science fiction—a startled "groark," scrambled pattern of wings, neck, legs, and beak—the heron recognized me with a desperate change of direction.

Great blues don't trust people and make no bones about it. Other birds know this. When I hunted ducks down south, a great blue heron sometimes landed near our spread. The ducks accepted his judgment and tumbled into the decoys. Why bother to circle and check when Daddy Longlegs stands so surely there?

One great blue heron has made our place a favored hunting ground. It has been an education in stalking. In a few places, he stands motionless. He must recognize schooling spots for small fish. He returns repeatedly to the same place and invariably spears several victims.

Sometimes he strides purposely along the river shallows, neck cocked for instant thrust. Anything he flushes is fair game. I saw him catch a dragonfly and a snake. The spotted sandpipers give him a wide berth. He is a jump shooter with all seasons open.

Usually he spots his prey well ahead. Then he is motionless locomotion. He moves without moving. His steps leave no ripple, stir no mud. His forward lean is slow as a mountain's shadow. His lightning thrust leaves no time to know what happened. Frogs and crayfish are most often captured by this technique. Most of his jabs are fruitful.

Herons are more efficient hunters than hawks. I think 90 percent of most hawks' stoops are missed. Maybe falcons bat over 500. Our heron friend does much better. I watched him catch three frogs and two crayfish in succession.

He must be feeding young. Twice a day he hunts. Always he comes and goes from the same direction. I have spent hours seeking the rookery. It is miles away in a great roadless swamp. Great blue herons head there from all directions. Distance and the leaves hide it from curious humans. Years ago they nested near the river. The big elms were logged and too many people came down the river.

The herons sought more private land. It is good that there is still some for them to find. Next spring, before the leaves arise, I may find their rookery. I have no real business there. The stench and clamor of their socializing will rival our great cities. It will readjust my perspectives. Then I will leave them their primeval privacy. ❧

July 15 is one of my dog's favorite dates. That's when he gets his bell back. He doesn't wear it all the time, just when we go for a walk. When I slip that bell collar on, he knows it's time for him to do what he was born for—HUNT BIRDS!

Michigan law prohibits running hunting dogs between April 15 and July 15—helps protect nesting birds—a good law. My Brittany loses his bell about the time rabbit season closes. Without it he must stay in sight, on the roads or trails within fifty yards. It takes about a month for him to get resigned to the rules.

In grouse-woodcock country all bird dogs should wear bells. The best hunting is in heavy cover. You follow the sound. When it stops, get over there fast. In early season bracken I often flush the bird before I locate the pointing dog. Zeroing in on that last bell tinkle usually gets me close enough for a shot.

With his bell on, the dog can follow his nose. He does the hunting. I just follow and shoot. Upwind is the way to go. Before July 15 he can't do what he knows is best. Often he will swing into the breeze and stop—head high, sniffing, sniffing. "Can't you see that they're out there?" I don't know how far a dog can smell a grouse. In season I've followed mine hundreds of yards upwind. No way is he going to leave the woods with a nose full of grouse. He's plumb stubborn about it. In summer I think he pities me. At least his looks say so when I call him off a scent.

The bell knocks off six years. He's a pup again. Around and around the yard. Listen to it clang. "Now, let's go. With raspberries ripe, they are in the berry patches. Been there every morning. I'll prove it." The bell stops among the briers. Out come a half-dozen young grouse. Some light in trees, crane necks, "pert" at us. "Ain't this fun."

Until September 15 we'll check out the covers, count the hatch, pick a place for opening day. Then we can bring the gun. My dog is good on woodcock, but he just accepts them. He's too enthusiastic for grouse, flushes a lot. When I do hit one, he never loses it. Sticks his nose in the feathers and takes a dee—eep breath. Lovely odor.

December 1 is another good date. He gets his bell again and, with snow on the ground, he's allowed to chase rabbits. If there are no grouse, rabbits are better than nothing.

Yes, my dog lives for three dates, July 15, September 15, and December 1. They are important to me too. People who don't find them so miss a lot. ❧

Anyone who doesn't know how to pick wild raspberries should learn how. It's more fun than picking cultivated berries, it's free, and they taste better.

When picking farm berries you are supposed to stay in line. Snitching a few from the next row is a no-no—may get you a dirty look. In the wilds, pick anywhere. Farm pickers should pick clean; get all the ripe berries in one pass. Picking wild, it's O.K. to high-grade. There are plenty of other pickers coming behind, and some will have already been ahead of you.

Grouse are the best wild berry pickers. They may spend all day in the patch. All sorts of passerine birds come to the feast—grosbeaks, robins, orioles, waxwings, sparrows and, of course, the catbirds who lay claim to every berry patch.

Chipmunks are messy pickers. Juice drips down their chins. Deer mice are dainty—nibble one berry at a time. Coons pick at night, as do foxes. I find seeds in their droppings. All sorts of insects are on hand. Yellow jackets and bees feast on berries that have been nibbled or mashed to free the juice. They make a nice droning background of chamber music. I respect these musicians and have never been stung.

A good wild berry picker is quick with the fingers and slow with the feet. Some of the best berries are in slash piles. Hurry and you may fall and spill your pickings. Pick handfuls at a time. Your fingers gather the berries. Pail them when the hand's full. Some-times you can pick double handed. Usually wild raspberries are so tangled it is faster to hold the cane with one hand and pick with the other.

Raspberry briers aren't bad, but it's best not to wear shorts. A good belt to hang the pail on is a must. I use a three-pound coffee can tied close to my belly. It doesn't hang up when I push through the tangle.

Some people worry about snakes. Down south where they were expectable, we had a rule. "Stir around a little to run out the snakes." Talking won't scare snakes, but foot stomping will. It will also stir up any yellow jacket's nest. In Michigan they are far more dangerous than the snakes. I've never seen a snake in a Michigan berry patch, but watch out for the hornets.

By the time you've learned how, you will have enough for a shortcake. On the first picking that's a good time to quit. My wife's the best shortcake maker in the United States including New England. She makes them like drop biscuits with extra shortening, melted butter is best, no sugar. Put sugar and vanilla in the whipping cream, real, no fizz-bottle synthetics. Use plenty of mashed berries sugared to taste. Thank the Lord for his bounty and dig in. Thank yourself for picking enough for seconds. ❧

Canada geese have a babysitter service. I frequently see it on our wildlife sanctuary where dozens of pairs raise their families in close proximity. The other day I watched one pair of adults riding herd on thirty goslings. The old birds were constantly alert while the half-grown youngsters grazed on the close cut park grass. Meanwhile, the other parents took their leisure in the private yards across the street. They preened, rested, or wandered about in desultory feeding. You could almost feel them enjoying the freedom from responsibility. Finally, back to family cares. The old birds held up traffic as they paraded back to sort out their broods. Soon the park was again scattered with family groups.

These geese usually lay five or six eggs. I saw one family of nine. Four is probably average. The young grow rapidly, doubling their size in one week. They quickly progress from cute balls of fluff to long-legged clowns. Size differences make the different families easily recognizable in a babysitting group.

I don't think Canada geese use sitters for the very young. Then the family sticks close together. They swim—gander front, then the young. The goose brings up the rear. The old birds are fearless in defense of their family, in fact, family ties are probably stronger in Canada geese than any other birds. They are one of the very few species in which the family stays together throughout migration. Young birds don't leave their parents until they return to the nesting ground in spring. Then the young birds gather in teenage flocks for their first summer away from parental care. They do not mate until two years old. The flocks of grown geese we see flying about now are these nonbreeders.

Mated birds seldom go far from their young even when they have babysitters. The slightest hint of danger sounds an alarm from the sitters which brings a rush of concerned parents to the rescue. In some cases even the unpaired teenagers come to help.

In our sanctuary there is constant feuding between the swans and geese over nest territories. This spring we accidentally flushed a goose from her nest. She was immediately attacked by a huge cob whose mate was nesting nearby. The alarm brought the gander tearing and, moments later, two dozen young geese, honking loudly. The cob broke off the attack. Too proud to beat a hasty retreat, he still knew the odds called for discretion. The goose slipped quietly back to her eggs. The young birds left after a little parading. The gander watched the swan disappear. Then he passed his neck over and around his mate to reassure her, and returned to guard duty at the waters edge.

Yes, geese have babysitters—and a rescue squad too. But, for raising a family, good parents are what counts. Geese are the best.

There are many blue midsummer flowers, but the bluest of all is chickory. Only the fringed gentian equals its color. Gentians hide in woods and wet meadows. Chickory hoists its ragged blue sailor flowers from unmanicured roadsides and ditch banks. Men brought chickory from Europe, so you will only find it where men have been.

Chickory is a morning flower. Except on cool cloudy days it closes tight by noon. A weed-grown road where I ride each morning is blessed with a host of tall chickory plants. I stop each day for a soul-stirring drink of their beauty.

It would be nice to think our European ancestors brought chickory to America for its beauty, but no, they brought it to eat. Chickory is closely related to the dandelion and is every bit as good as an early spring green. Like dandelions, they quickly turn bitter so you have to get the first leaves that show. To get tasty greens from older plants, cover either dandelions or chickory with a flowerpot. In a week or two the leaves will be blanched sweet and tender. Don't forget to plug the pot hole.

My first experience with chickory was in coffee. My father was from Louisiana. My sister lived there for years. She learned to prefer coffee with chickory. Many Louisiana groceries sell coffee blended with chickory root. Down there be sure to read the coffee label.

The chickory root used commercially is imported. It's the same root that supports our blue roadside flowers. Dig some up and scrub them well. Put in the oven and dry at low heat till they are brown and brittle. They should snap like a dry twig and be dark coffee colored inside. A good blender will grind them to coffee-size grains. Brew like coffee, but use less or mix some with your favorite brand. It's not exactly like coffee, but it's better than the instants that have been boiled to a powder and then reconstituted with hot chlorinated water. Cheaper too and fun to make.

The pretty chickory flowers hold a volatile essence with great soothing properties. Put a quart of flowers and a quart of water in a kitchen still and collect the first cup of distillate. Modern kitchens don't have stills, but with a little ingenuity you can make one from a stainless or crockery pot. Don't use other metals as they spoil the brew. Add one-half teaspoon of boric acid to the chickory distillate and cork tightly. Soak pads in it and lay them on tired bloodshot eyes for half an hour. Better than those fancy cosmetic eye brighteners.

So that's chickory: a warming brew, a tasty dish, and a soothing touch for tired eyes—all this in just one plant with flowers so blue they alone are reason enough for being. ❧

You learn faster when you are hungry. Kingfishers prove that when teaching their young to fish. I have been watching a pair training their family.

The male captured a two-inch crayfish, whapped it repeatedly on a log to soften it up, and then swallowed it with much jerking and head shaking to tuck all the legs and claws down the hatch. All the while, junior sat by watching, almost literally with his tongue hanging out.

Another dive brought a three-inch chub. Whoppity-whop on the log and the stunned minnow was flung back into the water. As it drifted swiftly downstream, junior leaned over with interest, but held tight to the perch log. Splash—Poppa snatched the struggling fish and gulped it down before the starving sibling.

The lessons moved up and down the river. All our frontage is in this pair's territory, and they have several favorite perches. Sometimes there is a long wait between dives. I can almost see the youngster's appetite increase. Occasionally a tidbit is given to the begging young bird. The parents aren't about to let their family starve, but each day the free snacks get fewer. The route to the brain is via an empty stomach. Eventually the young kingfisher takes that first dive. Thereafter skill develops quickly.

Sometimes kingfishers hover in midair. This must be college level stuff. I have not seen the young being taught to fish from hovers. Maybe they will learn it later. In one section of river where there are no good perches the old birds hover before a dive. They do not fish this section while teaching.

When a kingfisher hovers, his body is almost upright as if he were flying vertically just fast enough to resist gravity. The head is bent forward for better watching. To dive, the kingfisher flips tail up and goes in beak agape, head first.

Some hawks also hover when hunting. They do so with their bodies horizontal. Hawks seize their prey with their feet. I have watched sparrow hawks slowly lower their hover as if slipping up on their prey from midair. In a fast stoop they go head first, but bring the talons forward just at the moment of strike.

Here we have two carnivorous species that have evolved variations of the same adaptation. The differences are slight, but they are what works best for each bird's method of capture.

I don't know how many young these kingfishers have. Each parent seems to teach only one pupil at a time. The female, readily identified by her brown bellyband, holds forth in one section of the stream. The male holds his class out of sight around a bend.

Group classes aren't held, but the teaching method is the same. Keep showing—when they get hungry enough they'll learn. 🌿

A "picket pin" is a gopher—cute, pesty, but beneficial. He is a thirteen-lined ground squirrel, but lots of the lines are rows of spots. At any rate, if you see a little gray-brown striped animal that runs like a toy choo-choo train and stands erect like an oversized clothespin, it's a thirteen-lined ground squirrel.

They like roadsides, golf courses, mowed fields, and lawns. Hawks eat them, little boys love them, and farmers distrust them. They eat grasshoppers, weed seeds, grain, bugs, birds, and eggs. Yesterday I caught one in a minnow trap. He dropped dead from fright.

The thirteen-lined ground squirrel is the most widely distributed ground squirrel in North America and the only one common in Michigan. Chipmunks don't count, though accurately they are squirrels that live on the ground. I like to give picket pins distinction—the only ground squirrels east of the Mississippi.

There are many ground squirrels in the West and North; some big fellows up to two pounds, some with bushy tails like the tree squirrels. Only our little striped gopher keeps pushing east. Every new opening seems to invite him. He moves right in.

We live back in the woods, a quarter mile from good ground squirrel habitat. Several years ago we cleared some cedar swamp and built a pond. The dam was seeded with clover. You can imagine my surprise to find a picket pin in a minnow trap I had discarded after catching fish bait. The little fellow was still breathing, but all efforts to revive him failed. There was still plenty of bread from the minnow bait, so I can only conclude panic killed him. I remember similar happenings to mice live-trapped years ago.

The amazing thing was, this little short-legged animal had traveled so far through strange country to find my clover. What primal urge sent him through that dark cedar swamp so shadowed from his beloved sun? You have seen these little fellows scoot across a highway. For them, a quarter mile of woods must be an incredible journey.

Picket pins love the sun. They sleep half the year, then sleep every night in summer. Sunny days are their time. Seeing is their thing. We once lived in an oft-mowed new subdivision. Thirteen-lined ground squirrels lived with us. The grass was always short enough for them to stand and see over. They loved it. Marsh hawks came for miles to hunt them. Badgers dug them up. Weasels explored their burrows. Yet, still they prospered.

I examined one I caught—a female, and found their secret. She was equipped to nurse ten babies at once and often does twice a summer. No wonder the species survives—but what a way to make a living! I wonder what the father does? ❦

Nobody sleeps late at our house nowadays. A male yellow-bellied sapsucker has found our aluminum ladder. He uses it to rap out his territorial warning each sunrise. No bird in this part of the county has such a fine sounding board. The raps fairly peal across the woods—and through the bedrooms. Two competitors pounding tree limbs across the river are muted by comparison.

Sapsuckers do not have a continuous rhythmic hammer. Their beat is staccato—a series of taps and pauses. No other woodpecker does similar drumming. Right now they are hammering more than any other species. Hairys and downys lead the chorus in early spring.

Last year a pair of sapsuckers nested across river. Four young showed up in July. They tasted the suet, but spent most of their time practice drumming on a misplaced wren house. I finally moved it to prevent demolition. This spring we were overrun with sapsuckers. Six at the suet was common. Several have established nest territories in the area.

One pair nested in a poplar by the garden. The male started a hole before any female arrived from the South. He drummed up a mate. The pair put on a fine bobbing courtship dance, complete with typical woodpecker screeches. Then she started a new hole on the east side of the tree. That one was finished and occupied. They fledged only one young.

Now suddenly all the male sapsuckers are hammering again. Territorial fights are common. Maybe renesting is in progress. We have seen few young birds this summer. Possibly the weather caused failures. At any rate, it provides a noisy, interesting show.

Sapsuckers are unique among woodpeckers. There are two species, both native to America. They drill square holes through the bark of deciduous trees, eat the cambium layer and lap up the sap that oozes out. Ants and other insects come to the sap and are swabbed up. The sapsucker's tongue has a bottle brush end to facilitate this diet. They also like berries and other small fruit. About half their diet is vegetable; more than any other woodpecker.

A sapsucker will lay claim to a tree and drill patches of holes about half an inch apart. They return year after year, and eventually the tree may die due to disease or rot entering the holes. For valuable trees a liberal application of asphalt base paint will some-times discourage the birds. We find the sapsuckers more interesting than the trees.

We could move the ladder, but the drummer intrigues me. He is a handsome fellow with red throat and crown, yellow belly, and black and white trim. His drumming is a businesslike warning to competitors, but he really seems to enjoy it. When he rears back to listen to the feeble answers from across river how can I take his drum? We just go to bed a little earlier. ❧

Any time you can, it's good to be in the woods. Some times are better. Some places are best. Occasionally they are all together. The other day I was there. So were a lot of friends.

One of my favorite places is where a hardwood run crosses our drive. Logging removed the cedar on one side years ago. The swamp hardwoods are full of dead and dying elms. Tag alders, poplar, and young fir hangs a green cliff all across the old cutting. Goldenrod and ripening raspberries line the road. The pools by the culvert have shrunk to green-covered puddles hiding all sorts of wiggly life-forms. Across the road old conifers shade vistas sliced to glimpses by towering trunks. The wind is still, but the forest is full of movement. A Solunar period is at peak.

A family of orioles stirs the green cliff face. They come and go through invisible trapdoors, shake the twigs, and occasionally pose head down as they look under leaves for crawlies. After nesting, orioles seem to disappear. They don't sing. Suet and oranges don't interest them. Insects are better eating and more abundant.

This family may be from the nest above our compost. They fledged a week ago. The dull yellow young are already expert caterpillar catchers. Poppa hasn't shed his paternal instincts. Occasionally he pokes a choice morsel down a still-willing youngster.

Rose-breasted grosbeaks search with the orioles. The young seem more dependent, begging always. One brilliant male stuffs a two-inch-fat larva into a pleading fledgling. It isn't possible, but a few vigorous pushes gets the squishy green wad down the hatch—a whole beefsteak in one swallow. The young grosbeak sits a moment, neck stretching, looking surprised.

A quiet tapping shows a sapsucker adding wells to his sap field. This is an old field. Neat rows of holes tattoo square feet of the maple trunk. Four young yellow-bellies wait nearby. One explores dead elm bark. The others watch the well drilling—learning or waiting for a handout? I won't know. Other actors get my attention.

A big cock grouse paces the road, stretches on tiptoe to pluck raspberries I missed. A half-grown snowshoe hare clown foots past, too young to fear me or too careless to notice. No wonder so many things eat them—easy pickings.

A half-dead elm holds a flock of chickadees. I think sick plants attract bugs. Chicks must know this, for they find a feast among the curling yellowed leaves. A young mourning warbler joins them, slim and bright beside his plain companions.

Everything but me is busy, busy. There must be millions of insects about my box seat. I see almost none, but the birds do. How would the trees and I survive without them? 🌿

When not used to honor some prominent person, Latin names for our wildlife can be wonderfully descriptive. The kingbird's name, *Tyrannus tyrannus*, "tyrant of tyrants," is particularly appropriate. Certainly within his chosen territory this fightingest of our birds is a true tyrant.

Small birds are usually tolerated. Hawks, crows, and most other large birds are attacked almost on sight. The kingbird is not satisfied to defend only his nest area. He flies out to attack the enemy on the aerial high seas. Diving for the back, he screams his fury as he pecks and nips. I once saw one of these little furies actually light on the back of a hapless turkey vulture and tear out a small feather.

The demonic ferocity of a kingbird's attack is a sight to see, but I am more impressed with his obvious fighting skill. I suspect his fierce shrieks serve the same purpose as the frightening yell of the karate expert. Our little fighter surely deserves a black belt, and he seems to know it as he returns to his perch after routing the foe.

I have been watching two families of kingbirds this year. One is nesting in a roadside maple by our field. The nest is large and unkempt outside, small and neat with three young inside. Typically, it is in a crotch of the trunk, not concealed at all. These birds depend on their fighting skill to protect their home. They sit more erect than most birds, with head thrown back, daring any intruder. This pair hold sway over most of our field. The crows, which occasionally forage there, confine their activities to the most remote corner. Even there they are sometimes attacked.

Our other monarchs are in a spruce at our cottage. The huge mayfly hatches on our lake attract many birds, and we usually have a pair of kingbirds. A dead limb nearly above the nest and the removal of some nearby cedars by my neighbor is what made the site attractive. These birds demand a handy perch where they can see all their territory. They use this throne to guard their home, and also as a takeoff point for feeding. All flying insects are their prey. They dart out quickly, snap them up, and return.

On this wooded site our feathered rulers man a much smaller defense perimeter. They usually ignore the numerous gulls, but occasionally strike one just to keep them in their place. Other large birds are rare here, but even innocent visitors are not ignored. Our spaniel pup has twice had his back hair tweaked, and no longer turns his back on that spruce tree. Even when he doesn't have to, the kingbird emphasizes his royal prerogatives. 🐾

Each morning when I walk up for the paper, a male horned lark meets me and my dog near the highway. He tries to lead my pup away so I know he has a nest nearby. This will be their second nesting, for the field already has many young larks. They resemble their mother, like a faded copy of their handsome dad. I am sure the first eggs were laid almost before the snow left.

Horned larks are the only New World relatives of the European skylark—"the blithe spirit" immortalized in poem by Percy Bysshe Shelly. Our little lark doesn't have the grand opera voice of his famous cousin, but he has every bit as much spirit. He flies aloft in undulating spirals scattering his simple little song in bright tinkles from the sky. His was the first bird song we heard this spring, and a welcome sound it was.

We first noticed them in February, searching the snow-plowed shoulders for seeds in the stray tufts of grass. As soon as the first ground bared, the male began his courting song—the season's optomist of the bird world. Even the late snowstorms didn't dampen his spirit.

Our field has many tall weed stems and a few low bushes. Sparrows and bobolinks use these regularly, but I have never seen the horned larks alight anywhere except on the ground. They walk or run, never hop. In flight they clasp their wings tightly after each stroke. Their hind toe has a long straight claw. This gives them a distinctive footprint, one of the few small bird tracks I can positively identify in the snow.

Their nest is built in the open, a slight depression lined with grass. When covered by the drab-backed female it is almost invisible. I happened upon one two years ago. The mother deserved an academy award for her crippled wing act. The five eggs must have been near hatching, for she was most persistent in her efforts.

She does all the brooding, but he encourages her with song and stays nearby to help lead intruders away. Both birds gather insects for the young, which hatch in ten or twelve days, and are ready to fly in another two weeks.

The grown birds feed almost exclusively on weed and grass seeds, some of them the most unnourishing-looking bits of matter imaginable. Last winter I marveled how they could stand our field's fierce windchill on such a meager, chaffy diet.

Tomorrow my tufted friend will meet me again—running down the pavement, then flying away and back to try once more to escort me from his home.

So much spirit in this little mite of a bird starts each day a little brighter. 🌼

To pep up the forest you can't beat a midsummer rainstorm. The other night we had a gully washer. I spent the next morning sloshing around the wet woods. The storm had flushed a myriad of insects from the foliage. The birds were trying to cut 'em off at the pass before the crawlies got back into hiding.

The liveliest of all the bunch was a family of winter wrens. These little bundles of vivacity are one of the most delightful of all birds to watch. They are hardly larger than a hummingbird. With their tails straight in the air they look even smaller.

Suddenly I was surrounded by wrens. I stood on a footbridge over the little stream from our pond while four brown beady-eyed mites made like a dozen. They were everywhere at once. One examined my shoe seams for bugs. Another searched the bridge rail with gimlet eyes. Detail was lost to movement as every cranny was searched.

Winter wrens are usually as hard to see as mice. Wren watching is usually wren listening, for their enchanting song is larger than life. They are aggressively territorial and sing often to announce it. For a short while after fledging, the family hunts together. It was such a group that now kept me bubbling with chuckles. They passed all too soon.

A scarlet tanager appeared in the path. How can such a brilliant bird be so inconspicuous? They are with us all summer, but seldom seen. Treetops are their home. There they prowl so deliberately that movements seldom attract attention. The rain-washed insects brought them to the ground. Female scarlet tanagers aren't scarlet. They are greenish and yellow. One joined her mate. Their almost lethargic feeding was a perfect contrast with the pert activity of the wrens. The tanagers seldom made a false move. They looked, then picked. The wrens picked, looked, probed, and flipped all at the same time. Both consumed insects at a great rate.

A water thrush flitted through the brush piles and sprouts. Here is a warbler that looks like a thrush and often acts like a sandpiper. The ones at our place live by the trickly pond outlet. Now it is a torrent, driving them to new feeding ground. They joined other warblers in the new cutdown. Little greenish yellow birds were everywhere. Most of them were young birds.

There are about a dozen wood warblers whose young are so similar, I just resign them to unidentified entertainment. Eye rings, wing bars, tail spots: such precise specie codes weren't detailed from feeding flocks. I'll leave summer warbler identification to the bird banders and museum students.

Summer rains are made for bird watching. So who minds wet to knees and rejuvenated mosquitoes? Not I. Birds are too much fun!

August

I'm a putterer. Midsummer is a good time for puttering. There is such a teeming of life outdoors it is hard to concentrate on one thing.

August is the most quiet summer month. Most birds quit singing, but cardinals don't. They greet almost every sunrise with song. Purple finches sing all summer too. Orioles almost vanish after the young fledge. How can such brilliant birds be so inconspicuous? They haven't left, for they show up in the berry patches. Bobolinks don't disappear. In August the males disguise in female dress and quit singing. The fields suffer from their change.

Brown snakes have yellow neck rings when they are young. They are easy to mistake for ringneck snakes which keep neck rings all their life. It doesn't make much difference though, for both these little snakes are good to have around. They eat slugs and lots of other crawlies that I battle in the garden.

Herons swallow fish head first. Their Adam's apple goes up and down just like mine, only more so. Hawks swallow snakes either end first. I watched a broad-winged swallow one tail first. The snake kept moving about and running out its tongue until it disappeared. Now that's real fresh meat.

The little seedpods of yellow wood sorrel have a nice sour taste. A handful adds zest to summer salad. The leaves are good too, but better in spring. Summer rains bring up all kinds of mushrooms. I'm not sure enough to pick them, but some look good enough to eat. I'll wait a while for the stumpies.

A gray tree frog lives in one of our log birdhouses. When it's not too hot he sits in the entrance like a gray old man watching the world go by. Spring peepers like the berry patches, lots of insects there. I marvel how they can climb about the brambles and not get scratched.

If you want hardwood brush for a hunting blind, now's the time to cut it. The leaves will stay on. Cut it when duck season opens and they will fall off in a day or two. Woodcock are in the willow swales—the only damp places. What a miserable place to work the dog, but he needs it, full of fat from easy living. A half hour is enough; too hot; find a brook to cool in. I think the woodcock want rain too. They don't like the swales, too grassy and leather leafed. They like less tanglefooted cover.

The fawns have almost lost their spots. The hen grouse still looks after her young, though they are almost as big as she is. She bluffed my car to a stop in the drive until her two youngsters got away. I wonder what got the rest of her brood? Kildeer have two black collars, but their juveniles have only one. I wonder why?

Puttering in the outdoors there's plenty of time to wonder. ❧

Blue jays are the street gangs of our bird feeder community. They will gang up on other birds, or even one of their own species.

Normally, jays at the feeder are just pushy and bad mannered. We accept that as part of the price of their amusing antics and beautiful colors. Currently, we are overrun with young blue jays. Sometimes they aren't amusing.

Recently several of them attacked a young evening grosbeak. They got him down, and would surely have pecked him to death but for my wife's intrusion. Such behavior is inexcusable.

Several of the young jays this year have bald heads. Baldness varies from a light cover of pale down to a few pinfeathers or simply high foreheads. Two of the latest arrivals also have poorly developed outer tail feathers. I think the affliction affects two families, six or seven birds. It may be due to a diet deficiency or maybe they are just too young to be fully feathered.

The bald jays are accepted by the others, but they are at the bottom of the peck order. This seems to be almost by acclamation. Normally peck order is established by individual bird confrontations. Most is simply aggressive display with few fights. There is lots of that right now among the young birds. When a bald jay tries to push in among his fellows, several of them will drive him back. I haven't seen this in any other species.

All bird watchers are familiar with the mobbing tactics crows use on owls and hawks. Jays are their close relatives and join in the fracas at every opportunity. Both species seem to thoroughly enjoy the fun. We have several hawks on our place. Mob scenes are almost a daily occurrence. I think they are most often started by the jays. They far outnumber crows here, but their big cousins come quickly to their screams of profanity. I don't fault this mobbing even when it involves the little sparrow hawks. To most birds predators are the public enemy. Why not try to drive them off?

A half-dozen jays came to our feeders all summer. We found one nest a couple hundred feet from the house. The adults were as well behaved as jays can be. We enjoyed them in the bird lean nesting days. The first teenagers showed up in July. Some were so young their parents fed them. Now we have dozens.

The families are close-knit. They stick together even after the young have lost most of their immature characteristics. That may be why jays are successful parents. It's always a good idea to know what your youngsters are doing. Blue jays keep an eye on theirs all the time.

Now I know why jays are such rowdies. Hell, their parents show them how! ✺

The first fish I ever caught was a catfish. We fished in a bar pit by the protection levee that ran through our Mississippi Delta farm. I was a little leery about worms, particularly real wiggly ones, so I usually stuck two or three loops crosswise on the hook and tossed it in the water. One quick dip of the cork and the bait was gone. A friend showed me the right way. He was a lot older, at least a year, and knew most everything about fishing. He pinched about one inch off the end of a worm and threaded it lengthwise on the hook. He showed me the hook tip just under the skin waiting to catch a fish. The front end of the worm is best. Don't let the hook show. Spit on the hook.

This time the cork went under and stayed. Pole, line, and fish swept a high arc, landed in the grass up the bank. It was a beauty, a mud cat (black bullhead) all of five inches long. My friend showed me how to string it on a willow switch. I could hardly wait to scoot the half mile back to the house for show and tell.

Lord knows how many miles of worms have been threaded on hooks since that long-gone day—plus minnows, crayfish, crickets, grasshoppers, or anything else that wiggles and squirms and might appeal to fish. Bullheads lost their glamour. There were "brim" and crappies and bass. My first bass plug had five treble hooks, rainbow stripes, spinners on both ends; then to a fly rod, bass bugs, streamers, wet flies, and finally dry flies on a New England trout stream. For a while I got real snobbish about dry flies.

Memories came flooding back this summer as I threaded on a big worm. I had come a full circle, again after catfish, but this time channel cats, the aristocrat of the tribe. The mouth of our river, where it enters the big lake, is just loaded with channel cats. In summer they may be our most reliable fish. It's a good place to take a kid fishing. One of my young neighbors was with me. We trolled slowly with crawler harnesses and when we found the right spot we caught a sackful.

To love fishing, a kid has to catch fish. Little water with small fish is best for getting started. Enjoying is more important than learning how. When he really loves fishing is time enough to learn to catch fish that fight back. That's the time for channel cats—no long runs or fancy leaps, just yank, yank, and yank, and bore for the bottom. For intensity personified watch a kid's face with a large cat on his line.

Oh, trout and salmon, bass and pike are fine, worth all the fancy boats and tools to catch them. But for plain fun give me a kid and some channel cats. They make more fishermen than all the glamour fish, and, oh, such memories. 🎣

Nature's camouflage artists choose many things to imitate, but one of the most unusual choices was made by the American bittern. He disguises as a bunch of reeds or grass. In his marshy habitat this is an eminently logical choice and he is truly an expert. When approached he will almost always hide rather than flee.

One spring I slipped up on a flooded patch of willows to watch the spring peepers in their annual concert. As I crouched at the water's edge, waiting for them to resume their chorus, I suddenly realized that I was staring eye to eye at an American bittern not five feet away. Bill pointed skyward, his streaked breast and neck blended perfectly with his surroundings even though he was at least a foot from the nearest willow switch. His yellow eyes fixed me with an unblinking suspicious gaze. Point your nose straight up and then figure where your eyes would have to be to permit you to see forward. That's where a bittern's eyes are, almost at the corners of his mouth. As I moved away down the shore, the bird turned, slow as time, to keep his streaked foreparts facing me. Surely he would have been undiscovered had I not happened to stop right beside him. On a windy day I have seen one sway slightly in time with the blowing reeds.

Bitterns are common nesters in our wildfowl refuge. Their "onk-ka-chonk" love song echoes throughout the spring morning and evening. It sounds like an old-fashioned pitcher pump and gives the bird one of its nicknames, thunder pumper. It is worth the effort to slip up on one of the singers. He sucks in air to swell his throat and crop, then belches it out with the most awful convulsions. Surely some of our televised stomach remedies would help him. He needs them not, for he is engaged in serious courting. His belching hiccoughs are accompanied by a display of white plumes erected from his shoulders. These are normally concealed under the drab brown plumage and are spectacular by comparison.

Bitterns nest on the ground in thick reeds or cattails. Many predators seek them, but few succeed. The mother is a fierce defender. Some years ago my Labrador retriever stumbled on a bittern's nest. Only a too early strike saved him from losing an eye. The female was fluffed out twice her normal size, neck cocked like a coiled rattler, dagger beak constantly aimed for the face. A more aggressive dog could have been badly hurt.

In nature it is often thus—hide if you can, fight if you must. The bittern is expert at both. ✹

Left alone, wildlife usually does a pretty good job of taking care of itself. Sometimes we can help. This year I saw a little help go a long way.

For the past several years common terns have had a tough time on Lake Huron. High water covered most of the island beaches. Gulls took over what was left. The terns were relegated to mainland nest sites. Two years ago a colony nested on the riverbank of a local factory. Dogs destroyed every nest. Last year a large colony on a suburban sandbar was also destroyed. Half a dozen nested on the dyke of a local factory wastewater pond, some within inches of the road. They fledged three young.

This year the terns returned to the pond dyke, at least a dozen pairs. Part of the dyke is a finger, free of traffic. This was protected with snow fence loaned by the county road commission. The terns settled in that little sanctuary. They nest on the ground, turning round and round, kicking backward to scoop out a hollow. Three eggs are usual.

Both parents take turns brooding, three or four weeks depending on weather and their diligence. The young leave the nest after a day or two, but if they wander too far, other adults will peck them home, sometimes with fatal results. How fast they grow depends on the food supply. Around here it's alewives, jillions of them. Often a parent will stuff in an oversized fish. The youngster just sits with the tail hanging out. An occasional gulp finally gets the meal down. By August 1 most of the young are flying. This little colony fledged at least thirty.

The young birds have a white forehead and shorter outer tail feathers. They stick with their parents who feed them for several weeks until they learn to catch their own fish. Some never learn. First year mortality is very high. Even among adults annual mortality averages 23 percent, so good hatches are essential for specie survival.

Common terns from here migrate east to the Atlantic, south to Florida, then west across the Gulf of Mexico to winter on the Gulf Coast or the west coast of South America. Young terns usually spend their first year in the wintering grounds. They don't breed until three or four years old.

Terns are site tenacious. They will return to their hatching place, or to the nearest suitable nest site, year after year. Barring disruption, we can expect the surviving young from this year's hatch to eventually return to nest beside their parents.

Each day I stop a moment to watch the terns, sea swallows, bringing minnows. Every shore rock wears a white-fronted fledgling. A roll of snow fence, a few minutes work, and the respect of workers who passed their way put them there. It wasn't much, but it's big for them. ❧

Anyone who has to eat every fifteen minutes has a right to be a freeloader. Sometimes a hummingbird is just that. This spring, before too many flowers were out, I watched a hummingbird sponging off a yellow-bellied sapsucker. It wasn't begging. It was outright thievery, and it wasn't appreciated.

Sapsuckers tap tree bark for fresh sap and the insects it attracts. One pair established a battery of holes in a birch over our garden. With a brood to feed, the sapsuckers made frequent trips to their honeycomb of sap holes. Hummingbirds fed there too. The sapsuckers didn't like it.

Repeatedly the hummers were driven off. The first we noticed was a ruby-throated male. He invariably backed off and perched six feet away on a bare fir twig. As soon as the sapsucker left, he was right at the buffet snatching sweet sap and insects. A moment later the tableau was repeated.

Sometimes the female appeared. When driven away, she simply hovered at a respectful distance. Imagine such self-confidence—like treading water after being driven off by sharks. There was simply no way she could be frightened. She knew she could return when she would.

Our hummers got really hung up on freeloading. One of them followed the sapsuckers everywhere, even to our front yard suet. Hummers don't eat beef fat, but one would hover patiently near while the sapsucker stoked up. That's how they found our hummingbird feeder. We hung it on a front rail and finally it was noticed. Now the ruby-throated family visits regularly.

We seldom see the male. He has no family chores. The female made regular trips for sugar water. Now two young also come often. Two bubbles up the feeder tube must be a filling. Then they hover a bit or perch. Seldom do they return to the feeder at once.

They can't live on sugar alone. Spiders and tiny insects supply protein. It is essential for growth. Right now they probe the jewelweed, in full bloom and full of tiny crawlies, seeking the nectar. I tore open a few blooms, and almost every one had some tiny insect inside.

Hummers have a tongue like a soda straw. They can suck out the nectar and, I suppose, any bugs that come with it, at least far enough to meet the beak tips. Down the hatch to fuel those energy-consuming wings. There is simply nothing among warm-blooded animals to rival them. Their energy output per unit of weight is ten times that of a man running nine miles per hour. If you or I flew like that, we would have to consume 155,000 calories per day. That would take 270 pounds of potatoes and 77 pounds of beefsteak.

At today's prices I'd be a freeloader too.

Goldfinches justify thistles. It took a long time for me to find that out. I think I was almost born a thistle hater.

To a small boy barefooting the summers away, there were many sticker weeds. Lots of them were thistles and the bull thistle was the worst of all. A patch of them towering four or five feet was a barrier to be reckoned with. I developed such an abiding hatred that they are still the only weed that I won't tolerate in my chronically weedy garden.

Goldfinches live by thistles. Any kind will do, but I think bull thistles are their favorite. They time their nesting by the maturing flowers. Thistledown lines the nests. Thistle seeds are the staple food all throughout the family raising.

June is peak nesting time for most birds. August is peak for goldfinches. Some wait until September. I once found an occupied nest on an October grouse hunt. It all depends on the thistles. There are more than a dozen kinds. Some are in bloom from June to frost. Most thistles like sunny places. So do goldfinches.

A goldfinch nest is a masterpiece; a neat down-lined cup. The female does all the building. When thistles are ripe she can build a nest in four days. While she is brooding, her mate swallows thistle seeds and feeds her by regurgitation. When the young first hatch she regurgitates to feed them—thirdhand cereal. Later both parents gather thistle seeds.

Until this year we never had summer goldfinches. Two years ago we cut a couple acres of conifer swamp near the house. Now most is in six-foot poplar sprouts. Bull thistles took over the openings. It's goldfinch heaven. We first realized the change when paired goldfinches visited our summer feeders. In winter we have dozens, but they usually spend the summer rollicking the fallow farm fields. This year they were almost our only June visitors. In July they crowded in with the grosbeak and purple finch fledglings. Suddenly in August they were gone. I found them in the cutdown. One morning the path was jeweled with thistledown, each fiber dewed with infinitesimal pearls. I sat down to watch.

A male goldfinch tackled a ripened head. "Don't wait for it to open and scatter the goodies. Dig right in." Deftly he opened the prickly pod, snipped the seeds. A gentle breeze took the down, a miniblizzard in August, but softer than snow. Goldy swoop-swooped to the nest in an alder stump sprout. His mate's wings quivered like a fledgling as she fed. In a moment he was back.

As the yellow bird made snow mid the purple prickly flowers and the new sun gilded the dew, I finally knew why thistles were. ❧

Maybe we are gaining a little. Ever since Rachel Carson's *Silent Spring* opened our eyes, any careful observer could read the tragedy of our poisoned planet in the declining bird life. Finally, in our bumbling way, we began turning off the poison. Banning DDT was one of the steps.

The other day a most unlikely messenger brought a note of hope. A double-crested cormorant beat across the industrial waterfront and skidded to a landing. Later I watched him feeding close to shore.

Cormorants are high density birds. They ride low in the water. They can change their specific gravity. Sometimes they swim with only their heads above the surface, periscoped submarines. The clear water gave me a good view of this one's maneuvers. At the surface he paddled alternately like a duck. Underwater both feet pushed together. He moved with a jerky putt-putt motion, but fast. Half-opened wings gave extra thrust for quick twists and turns. Every few seconds he surfaced, an alewife in his hook-tipped bill. If the fish wasn't headed right he would toss it in the air and gulp it down headfirst—neat trick.

Cormorants used to be common nesters around the Great Lakes. They disappeared in the 1960s. Cormorants feed almost entirely on fish. DDT accumulated from our poisoned waters caused thin eggshells. No young survived. Ospreys and eagles nesting on Great Lakes shores suffered a similar fate.

A few double-crested cormorants continued to pass here in migration to less-polluted sites. In fifteen years there was only one small nesting attempt in 1972. Cormorants are long lived, twenty years or more. Finally in 1977 the first nesting south of Lake Superior fledged young. Now several islands in Lakes Huron and Michigan have healthy colonies. If we keep the poisons turned off and don't turn up any new ones, they may again enliven our waterfronts.

Cormorants are more common on the seacoasts. Forty years ago we watched thousands in Maine. There they were called shags. We watched them catch sardines. Hundreds of the black goose-sized birds would surround a school and herd it together. Such a splashing and gulping you never saw. Gulls and terns joined the fray. Cooperative competition, a wild exciting display.

Cormorants' flight feathers aren't waterproof. No rest on the water for them. They find a rock, or buoy, or pile and spread their wings to dry. With their snaky necks and orange gular pouches, they make a prehistoric landscape effect.

I sometimes visit idle eagle nests on the lakeshore. They give me an awful down feeling. This midsummer cormorant gave me a lift. My grandchildren may someday see the shags' fishing frenzy and later watch them drying their sails. It will be a better world when they do. 🦋

The other night it rained toads. The dripping sunrise found our road covered with little three-eighths-inch-long ones. A few were larger, with a rare giant of three or four inches. A day earlier no toads could have been found. If the old wives' tale of raining toads had never been told, I could have invented it then—and proved it.

Toads are amphibians. Except for breeding, they live on land, but must have moisture to survive. In dry weather they find it by burrowing in the ground or under logs and forest litter. Dewy nights bring them out. They are seldom seen in daytime.

What I was witnessing was the emergence of this year's toad hatch from the hiding of their first extended dry period. The rains had stopped just about the time little toads lost their tails and left the roadside ponds. Before they could scatter far, dry weather slowed their dispersal. The summer storm brought moisture and food spread everywhere on the ground. Toads are mainly insect eaters. They will tackle anything they can swallow. For a three-eighths incher that isn't very large, but somehow they find a living.

Now they were rejoicing in the damp comfort of the road spread with all sorts of goodies washed from the trees. There was no place for the bugs to hide. Hunting was easy. The toads hopped reluctantly aside as my dog and I took our morning walk. Occasionally I paused to watch a big one feed. The youngsters were much too small to see detail.

A toad's tongue is attached in front and loose behind. It can flip out an amazing distance to lap up an insect. Toads only distinguish movement. If a bug stays still it's safe. I watched the stalking of a beetle struggling in the mud. The toad didn't hop. He walked, step by deliberate step. Suddenly the tongue flashed out—no more beetle.

Toads don't cause warts even though they have plenty themselves. If handled roughly, their warts exude a poison irritating to mucous membranes. My dog long ago learned toads were not for him. One taste was enough. After handling toads, wash your hands before touching eyes or mouth. My grandson is a great toad catcher. He handles them gently and never suffers discomfort, though I seldom see him wash his hands without prompting from mother.

Most toads don't survive their first summer. In spite of their built-in "Off" system many things eat them. I've caught bass on tiny toads. Some birds eat them. Around here snakes are probably the main predator. Garter snakes are abundant and eat plenty. Hognosed snakes prefer toads to all other food.

The other day I saw a broad-winged hawk catch a big snake in our road. I didn't know whether to mourn for the snake or rejoice at the toads who were saved. ✻

Beauty is a white egret in blue water against a green shore. A common egret has chosen one of our streams for a late summer vacation. Nostalgia flooded over me as I watched him stalking minnows and crayfish in the sunlit shallows.

Our visitor was snow white, over three feet tall, with yellow beak and black legs. He was as breathtaking in the riffles as a single cumulus cloud in a summer sky. I watched till lengthening shadows reminded of evening chores. Childhood memories of Mississippi summers came flooding back.

Egrets were just starting their trek from near extinction when I was first learning the outdoors. Late summer always found the mud flat lake banks lined with herons of all sizes and colors. Most of the white ones were young little blue herons. Occasionally a snowy or common egret was cause for excitement.

Egrets are herons that have beautiful long nuptial plumes. Around the turn of the century these plumes were in great demand to decorate women's hats. Plume hunters almost exterminated egrets when their plumes, called aigrettes in millenary trade, reached a price of over $32.00 an ounce. I remember a picture of my grandmother, a magnificent woman, with twenty-inch plumes sweeping back from her hat. Even if Audubon wardens and legal protection hadn't saved the egrets, social changes might have. Such finery wouldn't fit into autos or be tolerated at a movie or ball games, even if you could get modern women to wear such a hat.

At any rate, as a boy I occasionally saw a common egret or their smaller snowy cousins. Snowy egrets can be recognized by their black beaks and yellow feet. One of my first wildlife lessons was that these birds were something special. We never saw them in nuptial plumage. Nesting colonies had long since been exterminated near our home. After nesting, egrets shed their plumes and scatter in random migrations. The ones we saw must have come from the handfuls of survivors deep in southern swamps.

Now I can lean on a bridge rail and watch the product of one of conservation's success stories. Egrets again reach to Canada in their late summer wanderings. Some now even nest along the lower Great Lakes. Rookeries are common throughout the Deep South.

Lengthening shadows brush white feathers with blue. Yellow beak spears one more chub. Two steps and stately wings carry our guest toward some private roosting place. I gaze upstream for one last glimpse. Then home again, glad I'm a human being. Only man would care enough to save another species. I've just seen beauty that's part of our reward. 🦢

A nighthawk isn't a hawk. A bullbat isn't a bat. Both are goatsuckers and the same bird. Their closest relatives are owls. They don't suck goats. They only eat when flying.

Add to that a set of whiskers and a built-in comb on their middle toes and you have as improbable a bird as you are apt to see. In addition, they sleep most all days. When they do stop in trees they perch lengthwise of the limbs. Their open mouths are bigger than their heads. If you look closely you can see the backs of their eyeballs through the roof of their mouths—weird.

We were entertained by a family of these remarkable birds while blueberry picking last week. The berries were few and far between, so it was a real relief to hear the "vroom-m-m" of a nighthawk's power dive. When courting, the male nighthawk makes spectacular dives and pullouts. His "vrooms" come from wind passage through his wing feathers at the pullout. Now the young birds are flying. I think the parents are teaching them to "vroom." It's certainly too late for courting.

The jack pine barrens where we were berrying is a good place for nighthawks. They like to nest on open sandy-gravelly ground. No nests, just a spot that looks sort of like the buff-speckled eggs they lay. Many nest on gravel-roofed buildings in cities, but too much insect spraying will drive them away. I don't see as many in town as I used to.

The other day I saw a young, just-flying nighthawk dodging traffic right downtown. At car door level it weaved a block or more before resting on a gravelly vacant lot. Apparently similar terrain to its hatching place led it to safety. On my return an hour later, I was amazed to find the parent bird brooding her young. How did she find the young wanderer?

Nighthawks fly like crazy. They seem to not know where they are going. When I was a boy, we used to deploy along the levee on fall evenings to shoot bullbats. Anyone who could score on nighthawks could hold his own in any shotgunning. We ate what few we killed, and they were delicious. Fortunately shooting them is now illegal. Their numbers have been sadly depleted. We need them desperately against our insect enemies.

I watched the four nighthawks, bullbats, goatsuckers, against a cumulus background in the evening sky. Their erratic aerobatics made all their improbabilities seem probable. Then when they swept down from flyspeck height to pull out in a "vroom-m-m-ing" dive, I knew they weren't crazy after all—just one more family of neighbors having fun on a summer evening. ✺

Each animal species is unique, but if it were possible for uniqueness to be superlative, the star-nosed mole would be the most unique of all. Certainly around these parts there is nothing quite so improbable as these little mammals.

This morning I found one dead in the road, tooth marked by some small nocturnal predator. This little fellow was about four and one-half inches long with a three-inch hairy tail. Its front end began with a bare pink nose, fringed at the tip with twenty-two short rosy tentacles. Eyes were pinhead size. There were no visible ears. I'm sure moles have necks, but they don't show outside. Short powerful front legs were the only sign of the torso's beginning. The front feet were set well to the side, broad, and with strong, close-set claws; certainly one of the most efficient digging tools ever devised by nature.

The fur was dead black and wonderfully soft. Most animals' hair has a definite grain, lying backward from head toward tail. Mole hair rubs both ways. It lies equally smooth stroked either toward head or tail. This is an adaptation for living in tight-fitting tunnels. When a mole backs up, its hair doesn't stand up and dig in. It simply folds the other way so its owner can slide smoothly without getting earth under its fur. Moles live in moist soil, yet don't get dirty.

We also have eastern moles. They are slightly larger than the star-nosed. Their noses are bare and pointed. The tail is naked. These are the critters that make ridges and hills over lawns and golf courses. Star-nosed moles are most common in the North near lakes and streams.

One of our first summers in Michigan was spent in a lakefront cottage with a colony of star-nosed moles. My wife had a dachshund—an impossible combination. One by one the dachshund dug out our little neighbors and deposited them (eleven in all) proudly on the back steps. Star-nosed moles don't usually make ridges. Their tunnels are deeper down. They occasionally push up a foot-wide hill of earth to clear them. We could have tolerated the moles, as they did little damage and kept the grass roots free of grubs. When Tammy finished her excavating, we had to replant the lawn.

Star-nosed moles like damp places. They swim well, dive expertly and often catch aquatic insects. They live mostly on earthworms, but consume any small animal life they encounter. They may eat twice their weight in a day. That takes lots of digging. Believe me, they really work for a living.

Their senses seem pitifully inadequate. Almost blind, no external ears at all, a poor sense of smell—but boy, can they feel. With twenty-two fingers on the tips of their noses, you can't beat their sense of touch. ✺

A turtle is a reptile with a shell. They have been reptiles with shells for over 200 million years. The order Chelonia, to which turtles belong, is one of the most conservative of all vertebrate orders. Modern turtles are basically not much different from their 200-million-year-old ancestors.

I think one of the largest turtles in Michigan lives on our river. She has spent the last two summers in a logjam just upstream from our house. I estimate her shell is almost twenty inches long. She must weigh close to fifty pounds; certainly the largest snapping turtle I have ever seen. As snappers go, she must be very old. She likes to bask on top of her logjam. Most snapping turtles seldom bask. She is out almost every good day. All old animals I have known enjoy a bit of sun.

Her years have been good to her. She is bulging with fat. The yellow brown skin at the base of her legs pushes out beyond the edge of her carapace. She could not draw in her head and neck if she wanted to, but she doesn't need to. Nothing on this river is tough enough to tackle this old lady.

I think this turtle is female despite Ogden Nash's famous quotation that the turtle's "plated decks successfully conceal its sex." Male snappers never grow this big. Male turtles have other distinguishing characteristics. Their tails are longer, and their plastron (bottom shell) is often concave as opposed to the flat or convex plastron of the female. As Nash said, it is indeed, "clever of the turtle in such a fix to remain so fertile."

Turtles are very fertile. A big snapper, like our neighbor, might lay up to eighty eggs. They are round and leathery, resembling Ping-Pong balls. She lays them in a hole she digs about six inches deep. If a coon or skunk doesn't find them, they hatch in about three months. If it's too cool, the young may overwinter in the eggs.

I once had a baby snapper pet. It was the hungriest, meanest baby I ever saw. After two finger nips I set it free. Snappers' tempers don't improve with age. They are ugly in appearance and disposition. On land, when one elevates its rear, watch out! It can lunge and strike like lightning. If you step on one underwater it will sulk. You can pick it from the water by the shell, but grab the sides not the ends.

As I watch this old snapper spraddled out on her logjam, I think of Carr's description of turtles' conservatism. "They remained turtles while the dinosaurs bellowed toward their doom—as the mammals rose to heights of evolutionary frenzy. They kept on watching while 'Eohippus' begat Man O' War, and a mob of irresponsible and shifty-eyed little shrews swarmed down out of the trees to chip at stones and fidget around fires and build atom bombs."

She still watches. 🌿

How would you like to find a snakeskin in bed with you? That's what baby great crested flycatchers often find in their nest when they hatch. Their parents like to decorate their nests with something shiny. Discarded snakeskins are one of the few naturally shiny materials suitable for nest building.

In my boyhood I had a birds' egg collection and searched out every nest available. Every crested flycatcher's nest had a snakeskin. I will never forget the start I got when I first discovered this. Then I believed it was to frighten off intruders.

In the North snakeskins are not so easily found, so the great crested has gone modern. Cellophane, wax paper, and plastic are often found woven into the nest. These birds nest in hollows and require a large hole. They are no bigger than their close relatives, the kingbird, but they collect a remarkable amount of nesting material.

Several years ago a pair nested at our hunt camp. Hollow trees are normal sites, but these chose a discarded vent pipe almost a foot in diameter. It lay on a lumber pile about six feet up. They almost filled it with leaves, bark, and bits of mineral wool insulation. The second year they returned to the same nest and added strips of aluminum foil from the Air Force's antiradar litter.

The great crested is the most colorful and largest of our flycatchers. He has a yellow breast and reddish brown tail. Other local members of the family are either gray, olive, or black and white. Even the kingbird, best-known member of the family, has only a few red feathers to decorate his crown, and these are concealed till he elevates his crest. The family has some vividly colored members, but they live in the southwest and the tropics.

In the South we often found crested flycatchers nesting near wasp nests. I thought this was only a coincidence, but later found it is a deliberate protective practice of the flycatcher family. Like the kingbird, all members of the flycatcher family aggressively defend their nests. When allied with the hottest stingers of the insect world, they are just about invincible. I haven't found stinging allies near the two nests I've watched in Michigan, but I never fail to look closely. I'll never forget one of my boyhood friends getting zapped on the back of the neck just as he reached a great crested's nest cavity.

I don't know if these flycatchers have switched to modern materials in the South. When I studied them, we had not spread our civilized litter so liberally in the wilds. I hope they still use snakeskins. It's a great thing for a boy to come home and tell his folks about.
🐝

Snake doctor, mosquito hawk, devil's darning needle, dragonfly, all the same thing—good luck if they light on your fishing corks, and they'll sew your mouth shut if you talk too much. In my youth, these were absolute facts.

Dragonflies zipping about kept noisy fishing companions quiet. If one lit on your pole or cork, you didn't dare move. The only thing that could safely disturb it was a brim, or a catfish or, praise be, a big ole German carp pulling your cork under. Believe it or not, this is usually what happened. I still think snake doctors are good luck.

In those days all fishing bobbers were brown. We didn't need fancy red and white floats to hold our attention. Most bottles came with cork stoppers, so a ready supply of bobbers in assorted sizes was available. My favorite was a slender vinegar-flavored one. With the right amount of weight it rode at a forty-five-degree angle. The slightest touch at the bait would tilt a warning. With my lucky cane pole and a dragonfly resting on that cork, there was just no way I could come home empty-handed; particularly if I had remembered to spit on my worm after baiting up.

Last night these memories came flooding back as I watched the dragonflies harvesting mosquitoes over a roadside pool. I watched till the light faded enough for the bats to take over the pest control.

Dragonflies catch winged insects in a net made by flexing their slender bristly legs. Mosquitoes, a mere mouthful, are scooped up and eaten on the fly. Larger insects, such as bees and beetles, are carried to a perch to be torn apart.

Dragonflies rest with their four wings horizontal. In flight, the pairs move independently. When the rear wings are down, the front pair is up. They are the deftest of flying insects. They have extra-large compound eyes which gives them particularly good motion vision. Any insect that crosses a dragonfly's hunting patrol is doomed. They can change direction in a flash or hover motionless. Even a bat can't match them in flight skill.

Dragonflies lay their eggs in water. The nymphs are just as fierce predators as their parents. They eat hundreds of mosquito wigglers and other aquatic insects. The larger ones catch small minnows and tadpoles. They have an extensible lower mandible like a grapple hook. It can snap out almost one-third their length to grab luckless prey.

Dragonflies are one of the best of arguments against broadcast pesticides. Contact poisons easily kill them. For every one that dies, thousands of mosquitoes and flies are saved. There has got to be a better way. It doesn't make sense to kill our allies.

Besides, they make the fish bite better. ❦

August is the getting ready month, the first time of year when suddenly I can see, way off in the distance, the glorious days of October. One morning it's cool enough for a jacket. The dew-laden bracken sends goose pimples up my spine. The air seems full of new odors.

The dog's too fat. He was yesterday too, but now I notice it. He will suffer those early season days, and maybe I had better take off a little. Somehow it's always too hot September 15. Then I find wood-cock and grouse in blackberry tangles. Brier-proof clothes are too hot for comfort, but I wear them then and sweat. If the dog will enter such miserable bird cover, then I must too, just to keep his respect. Sometimes the shooting is terrific.

Sporting magazines are fun to read, but I'm suspicious of their pictures. The hunters I know don't look like them. I never saw a dedicated bird hunter that didn't look sort of like a scarecrow, tattered and torn. Their dogs are too neat. Even before opener my Brittany looks sort of moth-eaten from trimming off burr-knotted hair.

All spring and summer he and I have stuck pretty close to the paths. Can't disturb wild nests and nurseries. When I go serious nature studying he stays home. It's legal to train dogs after July 15, but July just doesn't feel like hunting. We wait till August.

Now it's time. I whistle, signal left. He noses into a tangle of popple sprouts and raspberries—thirty feet and his tail takes an ultrasonic tempo. I push to keep up. Dew pours down my neck, smears my glasses. Stop to wipe them. Point!—"whoa"—one step, a whole family of pats explode. One stops six feet up and "perts" at the dog. Who could hold a point now? Crash! "Whoa! Whoa!" Glory be! He stopped. I stroke his back. "Whoa—Good dog. Go—ood dog." We ease up. Young birds sputter off at every step. He stretches his nose two feet ahead, walks on eggs.

"Good dog. You're the best. Let's go. Heel." We head back to the path and down to the flats. Drought drives woodcock to the riverbottoms to feed. There we find them in the nettles and switch ash. Nettle stings carries through my wet pant legs. Dog ignores them and points like a champ. Ah, woodcock are the birds to prac-tice on.

We stop on a sun-dried knoll. My fingers find burdock and beggar-ticks behind his ears. I carry little scissors to snip them out. The dog gets those he can reach—spits out white tufts. I feel him all over. Miss anything? He loves it, and so do I. It's part of getting ready. Won't be long now. 🌾

September

The trouble with dogs is you fall in love with them. Then, about the time you admit they are something less than perfect, it's too late to get a new one.

Since I was fourteen all my dogs have been hunters or, at least, they were supposed to be. I've had rabbit dogs that ran deer and deer dogs that ran rabbits; bird dogs that pointed turtles, tweetie birds, and anything else that gave off scent, including a few quail; and one lovely setter that couldn't smell bologna hung around her neck. All had one thing in common. I was their god. Mean, thoughtless, or just plain dumb, I could do no wrong. Good or bad, they earned their keep by making me the most important thing in their world.

About this time each year I get dog-preoccupied. September air causes it. It smells like grouse and woodcock and sounds like geese in the distance and duck wings swishing close at dawn.

All summer our daily walks have stuck to roads and paths. For a time in spring he couldn't understand. His nose found all sorts of things worth checking. My "stops" and "come backs" just had to be wrong. Finally he accepted my errors—trotted half a gunshot ahead, or waited patiently while I wasted time on unimportant things like gardening or building fences.

Now suddenly I've regained my senses. We poke through the bracken and briery tangles. He points out the woodcock that he knew were there all along and apologizes for earning a licking chasing grouse. Now if I'll just get the shotgun, my recovery will be complete. He will have once more brought me back to the real world.

Every hunter is entitled to at least one fine dog in a lifetime. I've been blessed with several. The first was a dropper, named Dan. He pointed quail or rabbits, or treed squirrels with supreme indiscrimination. For a boy with his first shotgun he was perfect.

A big Chesapeake would retrieve all day in Maine's icy salt chuck, but the ducks he brought were his and mine. Other hunters risked an arm to collect their bag. He would wait for me to come home from work, then drive the kids behind the sofa till he had made his welcome.

Memories glow of the Lab that seldom put a foot down wrong in field trials and the Brittany, Pepper, that taught himself to circle and stop a running pheasant. But they are gone.

Now I'm lord almighty to a Brittany that pushes grouse too hard and sometimes mashes birds he brings. But joyful greetings and adoring eyes make even those sins not really very bad.

And now it's September again. 🌾

Beauty is in the eye of the beholder, but—only its parents could think a young turkey vulture beautiful. This thought ran through my head as I held a young vulture to be photographed for an Audubon publication. He was magnificently ugly.

A local outdoorsman discovered this vulture's nest in a ramshackle chicken house at an abandoned homestead. He reported it to me. We decided to band the nestling. Not many turkey vultures are banded. The young are unpleasant to handle. Far more important, the nests are very difficult to find.

Turkey vultures nest on the ground, usually in hollow logs or under blow-downs. Caves and rock crevices are welcome homes. We heard of one nest in a doghouse at a vacant hunt camp. Our bird nested in the hayloft of the old chicken house. When we arrived the young bird was three-fourths grown and had left the loft. We found it in the grain bin on the first floor of the shanty.

Its wings and tail feathers were almost full-grown. Its body was covered with gray down. On our approach it turned its back, squeezed into a corner and hissed like two barrels of snakes. An unpleasant sound, it would have discouraged any predator. It certainly slowed me up.

A vulture's major defense artillery is regurgitation. It can be an effective weapon. Aware of the hazard we carried a gunnysack to smother the discharge. A little maneuvering and the bird was in hand. The soiled sack was discarded to set the pose for the photo.

We think of vultures as being nasty, filthy birds—'t ain't so. They are as clean as they can be under the circumstances. This nest area was not smelly. The milky droppings had been deposited neatly aside and apparently dried rapidly. Even the young bird's vomit smelled clean. It seemed to have been recently fed from a freshly killed animal. Nowadays vultures make a good living cleaning up road-killed animals. They seldom leave them long enough to spoil.

I think turkey vultures are gradually moving further north, like so many southern birds. Last spring I saw a flock of eighteen circling in the thermals as they skipped from one cumulus cloud to the next. I wonder how much further north they went? It was as graceful as any display in nature.

This beauty on the wing was quite a contrast with the bird I held. He weighed no more than two pounds, but was remarkably strong. His wingspread was already over four feet. It would eventually exceed six feet.

Our photographer angled for a close-up of the black wrinkled head. His only remark was "Homely, ain't he." ✘

I like weeping willows. So do deer, and beavers, and even muskrats. I like willows to look at. They like them to eat. It looks like I'm losing out.

For four years I have been poking weeping willow sticks into every stream- and poolside opening. Most of them sprout. I had visions of slender pendulous branches reflected in summer water; of yellow twigs and lemon leaflets announcing spring. One of nature's best displays of wild beauty is a weeping willow struggling with the wind. I wanted these shows for our place.

Around the forest edge and roadside pools, the deer nipped every sprout before one summer's growth. They ignored native willows all around, to browse the exotic newcomers. None survived.

Willows like sunlight. First plantings were away from other trees. Next time around I hid my sticks among the brush. They grew more slowly, but a few won the first game of hide-and-seek. If they stay undetected two more years, I can remove competing trees to help them out.

The place we mostly want willows is on the stream before the house. Our bachelor beaver disposed of the first planting. He disappeared two years ago. Our sproutlings thrived. A few more nibbled by muskrats, but by last week, dozens were poking their limber tops above the streamside growth. Our hopes rose—too soon.

A young beaver took up squatters' rights on an abandoned burrow just downstream. Usually two year olds leave home in spring. This one got a late start and settled in a ready-made den. First evidence of his arrival was fresh-angled stumps in the streamside brush. Soon he had drag trails down the bank from cuttings in the woods. A pile of branches built-up in the river, anchored in the mud for later use. Here was a beaver in the best tradition, storing fodder against the winter's cold. We welcomed our industrious new neighbor. There were plenty of alders where he chose to live. A little thinning would do them good.

Of course, he had to check the neighborhood. He visited the boat slip upstream. A dozen thriving willows surrounded it. It must have been like a candy store. Every twig was cut. Beavers eat small twigs like stick candy. Larger ones are peeled for the tasty bark. Our new neighbor had a feast.

Last night he found the weeping willows in front of the house. Now all but one are gone. No use to hide another planting. They can't grow too big for him to cut.

We'll have no weeping willow in our front yard. These trees come from China, and our neighbors like Chinese food. ꭗ

Summer rain doesn't bother anyone but people. Wildlife pretty well goes about business as usual. They have showerproof built-in feathers and fur. Wet is just another normal state of affairs.

Thunderstorms are dangerous. Hail can kill, and even big raindrops may bring down small birds. Wind-thrown debris and lightning dictate shelter. But just plain rain, the good old soakers that come down by the hour, that give wives and children cabin fever and make taxicabs vanish in our cities, are just no bother to most birds and beasties. The other day we watched wildlife through a rain-dripped window.

There was no end of activity at the feeders. Grosbeaks, purple finches, chickadees, and nuthatches swarmed to the sunflower seeds. Hairy and downy woodpeckers, blue jays, and even a brown creeper came to the suet. Aside from an occasional shake to shed droplets, there was no change in feeder activity.

The hummingbirds' wings made a halo of mist as they shattered the raindrops. It may take more energy to fly in wet weather, but it didn't show, just wing music made visible by water. The hummers preened a little longer between syrup visits.

A cottontail hopped to prune the volunteer sunflowers. Woodchucks like sunflower leaves too. I can't imagine why. I tasted one—prickle hairy—but rabbits reach on hind legs to get them. This rabbit shakes his head frequently. He does it too when there's no rain. I think he has an itch, not water in his ears. All rabbits don't shake so. His hair doesn't even look wet.

I don rain gear to walk the dog. Smoking hot tracks show an otter's way. The scent trail leads over the dam. Runoff has muddied the river sending the fishermen to clearer water. A kingfisher perches overhead to try his chances too. Maybe rain makes hunting harder for the predators. Winterkill left no fish in our pond. The frogs and tadpoles will make slim pickings.

Back at the house a broad-winged hawk has made a pass at the feeder. This is unusual. They are poor bird hunters. Frogs and mice are more in their line. Must be hungry. You don't see many hawks flying in rain. Still they must eat. Maybe for some wildlife rain is a problem.

But the droplets in my face and patters on my hat felt good. I remember walking, too many years ago, just for fun, in the rain with a special girl. And now we are more "civilized" and set in our ways, and rainy days seem dreary. So we watch birds and rabbits in the rain and envy them a little. ❦

Today I watched one of nature's deadly games; blue jays playing Russian roulette with a sharp-shinned hawk. The sharp-shinned had intruded on a flock of jays at breakfast. Peace, and the chance for a meal disappeared with his discovery.

Several jays would approach the hawk, limb by limb. There was no raucous profanity. This was a silent deadly game. How close could you get?

Suddenly the hawk would choose a target. Instant takeoff, deft maneuvers through the trees with his battle cry, "I'll get cha, get cha, get cha." Invariably the jay flew a wink sooner, twisting and turning, both birds shedding a few feathers against the branches. Usually the chase was short and twisty. Occasionally a jay made the mistake of choosing an open path. Then the hawk gained quickly. Only a last-minute dart among the branches prevented disaster. These careless birds screamed in terror. They retreated to the conifers to screw up courage for another dare. Death had been but inches away. Recovery takes a while.

A sharp-shinned is not much larger than a blue jay, but it is perfectly capable of killing one. In fact, they commonly kill birds larger than themselves. However, their main diet is on small species; sparrows, warblers, chickadees, woodpeckers. Birds make up over 90 percent of the sharp-shinned's diet.

There are three accipiters in North America; sharp-shinned, Cooper's, and goshawk. Their sizes let them cover the entire range of feathered prey. They are undoubtedly the fiercest of all the hawks. Falcons show a similar range in size from the little sparrow hawk to the rare gyrfalcon. They are birds of the open country; ultrasonic fighter planes with swept-back pointed wings.

Accipiters are hunters of the forest. Rounded wings and long tails give them the maneuverability of a crop-dusting plane, but enough speed to get the job done. They hide among the trees and make short dashes to seize unsuspecting victims.

The sharp-shinned I watched was a juvenile. An old bird might have quickly ended the game with a kill. This youngster was completely frustrated. Finally the jays left. The hawk perched over my head, smoothed his ruffled feathers, and then sat still.

A warbler appeared searching leaf tips. I expected momentarily to see him snatched to death. Suddenly the jays returned with reinforcements. There were fully thirty of them. Now the game had purpose. "Get this villain out of here so we can have breakfast." They crowded him. His chases shortened. Sometimes he sulked, sighing "fee—fee" crys of exasperation.

His tormentors led him away from the oaks, dash by dash. Finally he reached a decision. I could almost see him growing to maturity. "Why should I tolerate this rabble."

He flew midstream up the river, retrieving his dignity. The jays did not pursue. Out of the trees he was death inevitable. Even a mob won't risk odds like that. 🌿

In every September suddenly, one day, it's wool shirt time again. Got to get that dog straightened out. Bird season opens next week. Where's the bell for his collar? Better take along a bag. There may be some early fall mushrooms—and binoculars too, the warblers are migrating, and we ought to check those beaver ponds for ducks.

So begins the very best time of year. The shadows are cool. The sun is warm. The first red leaf floats on a roadside pool. The whole world seems busy getting ready. No frost yet, but it won't be long now.

On our way to the grouse grounds a flock of geese crossed low, wings cupped toward a green field. Stop and watch them settle in—man, they didn't even circle. Must be fifty in that bunch. The dog whines impatiently.

From the car to the popples, the trail threads through an oak woods. The dog minds the signals well in the open cover. No birds here, but good practice at quartering. My mind wanders to the treetops. Binoculars show a bumper acorn crop. Withered oak twigs on the understory advertise the work of squirrels. I smack my lips over next week's squirrel and gravy. There's a gray barking near the hilltop.

Head-high blackberry canes mark the edge of a six-year-old cutting. A hatful will be just about enough. I ignore the dog as I gather the thumb-size fruit. From the corner of my eye I see him flash to a stylish point, then forget everything he knows, and dive into the berry patch.

Suddenly all the grouse in the world are in the air. Young ones light in the trees and "pert" at me and the dog. He goes stark-raving crazy. The smell of PARTRIDGE is just too much to bear. Surely he can catch one. Before I can find my whistle without dropping the berries, he is almost out of hearing, chasing the last of the birds. He returns repentant with a foot-long tongue.

All business now, the next covey is handled nicely and, in make-believe, I tumble two on the rise. Visions of blackberry cobbler appear in every glade. I get back to picking. Suddenly, wings sputter again through the popples. How long has he held that lonesome point? I apologize as best I can. He finds one more pat to prove a point. I finish filling my hat with berries. Then we sit by the pond, warm sun on our backs, and watch the wood ducks scatter duckweed as they come in to feed.

You can't do three things at once, but, Oh Lord, in September it's so good to try. 🌿

Ospreys fish feetfirst. Almost all other species that feed mainly on fish catch them by fishing headfirst. Only ospreys and, with somewhat less skill, the eagles catch their slippery prey with their feet. Few fishermen are so skilled or so well equipped.

An osprey's feet are super-duper fish grabbers. The toes are tipped with sharp down-curved nails. The underfoot pads are covered with short sharp spikes. They can move their outer toes to the rear, so as to grasp with two toes on each side of their prey. Even an eel can't slip away when they grab hold.

I have seen ospreys miss. I've seen them release a fish too big to carry, but I have never seen one accidentally lose a fish they once grabbed. Ospreys fish by flying over water 50 to 200 feet up. They sometimes hover. A fish on or near the surface brings a closed wing dive that sometimes takes a bird completely under water. They come up flying. A few feet up they shiver all over to rid their feathers of water in a glistening shower of spray. It's spectacular. Grips are adjusted to turn the fish headfirst and, off to the nest or favorite feeding perch.

At one mill where I worked, a brook through the mill yard was a favorite osprey fishing ground. Suckers concentrated just under the high voltage wires from our power plant. Hundreds of times we watched the big black and white birds plunge between the wires to seize a meal. I'm sure work efficiency dropped almost to zero when one of the ospreys came fishing. Finally the inevitable happened. The big female held her wings too wide. She died amid a shower of sparks, darkened lights, and halting machinery. The male did not find another mate. Next year their nest was empty. The mill never seemed to run so happily afterward.

Most osprey nests on our Great Lakes and northern seacoasts have long since disappeared—destroyed by pesticides that prevent reproduction. Even with controls it will be years before our big waters are pure enough so fish won't pass these deadly chemicals to their predators.

Inland ospreys do better. A floodwater near us hosts twenty pair. This lake gets no pesticide runoff. Nesting pairs have increased from eleven in 1966. Twenty-six young were banded this year. Most nests are on artificial platforms. The old nests were in flood-killed trees which often collapsed and drowned the nestlings. Conservation for Survival, Inc., saved these birds by providing nest sites in one of our all too few poison free habitats.

Man wreaks much destruction by his thoughtlessness, but he is the only species on earth to show real concern for another.

It is another mark of his superiority over the beasts. ❦

Catbirds like grapes, cherries, and raspberries, but they lay personal claim to the blackberry patch. They resent anyone invading these briery fruit thickets. It's almost impossible to go blackberry picking without hearing the meowing protests of catbirds.

Now, I'm not really sure that catbirds resent blackberry pickers any more than they resent raspberry or blueberry pickers. I do know I encounter more catbirds when picking blackberries than when following any other outdoor activity. This may be because blackberries ripen last, after all the catbirds' parental chores are over. Young birds have to be fed protein for growth, and insects are our song birds' primary source. But, catbirds prefer fruit, and blackberries come along just about the time the last broods are fledged.

Over half of all catbird food is fruit. Even when feeding nestlings, the parent birds often make their own meals on berries. They take anything in season from strawberries to poison ivy, but of course, their real bonanza is in the late summer when nature literally floods the landscape with succulent goodies.

I join them in the brier patch. Blackberries are choice. The other day I visited a poplar cutting to gather my season's supply. Here the berries were patched at random among twice head-high saplings. My favored stands had been covered by earlier pickers. I had to find new canes.

Blackberries don't grow right among dense poplar sprouts. They are in the little openings that always intersperse such new forests. However, looking for a glade in a ten-year sprout thicket is as bad as seeking a bus stop in a London fog. I searched aimlessly almost an hour before I began to listen.

The fifty-acre cutting I wandered was full of catbirds, but they weren't everywhere. They were where the berries were. I finally realized that their protests would lead me to the best picking. I simply followed their "meows" to the choicest stands. I think these birds prefer their berries dead ripe, for they had abandoned the picked-over patches. They repeatedly led me to small virgin groups of canes loaded with thumb-size fruit.

In an hour I had our season's supply, while the catbirds sat at arms length and protested my invasion. They would skulk ahead through the foliage each time I moved, then come up to watch and meow when I stopped to pick. No one knows what, or if, a catbird thinks, but I could almost feel resentment. It bothers me not at all. He protests too much.

Blackberries are tough to pick because they fight back. No other wild fruit is so well equipped for protection. Anyone who can stand the briers will find it O.K. to ignore the catbirds' claims. ❦

When I was a very small boy down south, we had a grove of pecan trees out back of the house. One of them bore particularly choice nuts, but never more than a few quarts. It was fully as large as it's neighbors which gave bushels of lesser quality.

After one fall's particularly skimpy harvest, our yardman, Parson, said "Dat ole tree jes' lazy. What she need is a good whupping." Parson was a keen observer of nature, and we had learned to respect his judgment regarding all matters of soil and plants. He was given the go-ahead, and proceeded to give that tree about a dozen good hard whacks with his axe. He didn't quite girdle it, but he hurt it plenty.

Next fall the tree was loaded with nuts. All us kids rejoiced, because it was the only tree we had that grew pecans we could crack easily.

I remembered that experience vividly yesterday when I saw that the porcupines preferred to feed on a tree they had damaged almost to death the previous year.

Two years ago I was hunting squirrels south of here, and stopped near a lightning-damaged oak. I shot four squirrels without moving out of my tracks. All the trees had plenty of acorns, but the squirrels seemed to prefer that one. It was almost as if, being hurt, that tree was producing extra special seeds to insure survival of its line. Nature works in wonderous ways. The many acorns the squirrels buried and never found might be just what was needed to insure another generation of oaks. Maybe she made those nuts extra choice to attract the squirrels and increase the chances of some being buried and forgotten.

A report on ruffed grouse from the University of Minnesota Department of Entomology, Fisheries, and Wildlife, indicates that the flower buds of male poplar trees are the favorite winter and early spring food of grouse. Also it states that possibly injured or off-site aspen provide a richer food resource than more healthy trees. Again we run into wildlife preference for sick trees.

Male poplar flowers are rich in oils and protein. Studies of some gallinaceous game birds have shown that the level of vitamin A in the early spring diet is a critical factor in their reproductive success. Do poplar flowers also contain vitamin A? Do sick trees produce more vitamin A than healthy ones?

I'm not about to go out and try damaging poplar trees to increase the grouse population, but it would be an interesting study.

Sometimes there is nothing quite like a good bath. Most birds bathe occasionally. It may be an important part of their health and feather care. Baths may vary from a brief splashing to a thorough hub-scrub soaking. Of the birds we watch, waterfowl are the most regular bathers. They usually dip a little water over their backs and shuffle it under their wings after every feeding or mating—sort of washing up afterward.

The other day I watched a family of Canada geese *really* taking a bath. It started with one of the adults diving below the surface, then turning somersaults in the water. A great shuffling of wings and more somersaults. Soon the whole family joined the action. Some floated back down kicking the air, rolling over and over, wings splashing. If ever I saw birds having fun, these were having it. The show went on and on. Finally the whole family paddled ashore and spread their wings to dry in the sun. Sheer luxury.

I've only seen geese engage in such aquatic gyrations late in summer. It may be a part of preparation for migration or conditioning operation for new feathers. During June and July, while the young are completing their growth, the adults have a postnuptial moult. They lose all their primary feathers at once and can't fly. By the time the young birds can fly, the adults have regained their flight plumage, and all the family are fully feathered for the fall migration.

Waterfowl's feathers are structurally waterproof. Their shape and position shed water when the birds want to keep dry. Oil secretions from the preen gland on their popes nose may also help water resistance. Bird feathers are controllable by skin muscles. They can be fluffed up to increase insulation in cold weather. I think position changes also help wet the feathers in bathing. The bathing geese looked fluffy. Tumbling and splashing worked the water through the feathers.

Mallards sometimes bathe vigorously too. A friend kept tame ducks in a dry pen. When they were occasionally taken to swim, their feathers were barely waterproof. They swam heavily, got soaked. A day or two on the pond with strenuous bathing soon put their plumage in shape. They rode high and dry.

I think the goose family was feather conditioning. But they were having fun too. As a kid I bathed because I was made to. It took years for me to learn the joys of bathing. Those young geese were learning just like I did. I felt a tremendous urge to join them.

To hunt squirrels you mustn't work too hard. If you do the squirrels will disappear. Squirrel hunting is just about the best excuse I know for out and out loafing in the woods.

Bird hunting is fun, but it takes lots of effort. Grouse like briers, tanglefoot brush, grapevines, and little trees. I never saw a really dedicated grouse hunter that didn't end the season vaguely resembling a weathered scarecrow. On almost every hunt I have at least one desperate battle with malicious vegetation, while the biggest grouse of the day flies safely from my vine-tangled gun.

Duck hunting is even worse. Decoys have to be set, blinds built. Slog in hip boots through knee-deep mud, then sit in a drippy-nosed chill while the rain decides whether to change to snow. Oh, it's lovely when the mallards drop their flaps, and the blue-bills rip the air to shreds. But, you can row yourself blind chasing cripples, and the decoys weigh a ton going home.

Give me the squirrel woods on opening morning. That's the best place to start the fall. Sunrise found me across the river prospecting for fox squirrels. Walk a little, look a lot. Careful where you put your feet. Lean against a tree to break your silhouette. Listen—listen for the pitter-pitter-pat of acorn crumbs. Put the glasses on that brown spot—just a wad of leaves. How the gold September sun tints the treetops. Only burr oak trees here. No acorns at all this year. Should have gone to the red oak woods.

A crow calls in anger. Others come from all around. What are they mobbing? A red-shouldered hawk winds through the dead elms, shrieking irritation. The crows keep respectful distance, telling all the world. I hope he gives them the slip soon. He is the hawk that hunts red squirrels at our bird feeder. They need thinning out. He can't hunt with those black rascals around.

One lone fox squirrel barks near the river. Ease over to that big basswood. Careful—scarce squirrels are skittish. Wait him out. Wood ducks fly up the river. How slowly they go when not afraid. The drakes are just starting to color up.

Suddenly the treetops are full of warblers—feathered butterflies in stripes, and yellows, and olive. A black and white one hangs head down on the trunk above me, almost like a nuthatch. Why try to identify them? It's just fun to see their beauty.

Guess I'll wander home. Leave that old squirrel for seed. Besides, he's too smart for me. No hurry. I wonder if there are bass below the rapids. Ought to try them sometime.

There are no unsuccessful squirrel hunts. But, on some of them you shoot no squirrels. 𝕫

One of our does has a problem. In fact she has three problems. She has triplet fawns, and they are late, still red and spotted in late September. The chances of their surviving this winter are mighty slim.

In our woods triplet fawns are common. Farm crops provide excellent food. For the past three winters there hasn't been enough snow to cause yarding. Deer visited the fields all winter. There has been some logging every year. The bumper fawn crop proves how well the deer wintered.

This year I noticed the first triplets in early June. The big doe that lives at our field edge has done it again. She had triplets last year too. Does superficially look alike. Living with them year round we learn to recognize individuals. This big gal has lived in the same patch of brush for at least three years.

I think deer like to nurse their fawns where there's not too much tanglefoot. This one often nursed hers right in our road. Almost every morning I saw tracks of the operation. Nursing fawns push their muzzles at their mother and stamp their feet—real eager eaters. It leaves a patch of tiny prints beside the doe's big tracks.

Twice I saw the triplets nursing. It is possible for a doe to nurse four at a time, but I never saw more than two suck at once. The extra youngster would crowd in. There was always some place changing. All three fawns seemed to be about the same size. By mid-September their spots were gone.

The other triplets first showed September 18. I was surprised to see a tiny spotted fawn almost in our backyard. A search with the glasses found the doe and two more fawns standing among the cedars. Next day I watched two of them nursing. The third was lying down. I estimated them to be less than two months old.

Does usually come in heat about November 1. By mid-November most are impregnated. The rutting season is about over. If a doe is not successfully bred the first time she will come in season again in about twenty-eight days and even a third time a month later if necessary. Bucks are in breeding condition from September to February to be sure there's always one ready for any available doe.

This late mother is quite small, but she must surely be over a year and a half old. First-year does usually have only one fawn; an interesting mystery for the biologists. Why was she so late? No shortage of bucks around here.

It's basic in animal biology that more young are produced than is necessary to carry on the species no matter whether it's elephants, deer, or people. By one way or another some must die. This little family is a product of the system; insurance for specie survival. We don't need the insurance this year. If the snow is deep all three will be discards. ❧

The hummingbirds left the third week of September. They lingered awhile after the first frost, dining at our feeder, but most of their favorite blooms are gone. They must be off to a land where there are flowers all winter. Our hummers will probably cross to South America. Some may stop on the Gulf Coast.

Before they left, our hummingbirds fought a running, or rather flying, feud over our feeder. Their adversaries were yellow jacket wasps, one of the few sugar eaters adept enough at flying to challenge them.

We first discovered the wasps while mowing around a birch stump. The thrashing mower blades brought a squadron of yellow-stripped fighters from their underground hangar. The stump wore an unmowed border from then on. We have no quarrel with yellow jackets, but we respect their privacy and they respect ours—sensible arrangement.

The wasps discovered our feeder shortly after the young hummers started using it in numbers. Before they arrived the birds were unchallenged except by the male ruby-throat who had laid personal claim to the syrup bottle. He couldn't stay all the time, so the other hummingbirds got plenty of our homemade nectar. The small insects it attracted were snapped up as sugar-coated tidbits.

The yellow jackets had the strength of numbers. They set up a shuttle between feeder and hive. There seemed to always be one of the little stingers on hand. If a bird did get in for a sip he was usually interrupted by attack.

We have watched the hummingbirds fearlessly dive at yellow-bellied sapsuckers that came to sip. Around the nest they would attack anything including me. They never battled the hornets. It was strictly evasion, like an out of ammunition Spitfire dodging a Messerschmitt. It was an exciting aerial show repeated dozens of times daily.

No hummer ever got stung, but they had hair-raising escapes. Having felt the power of the wasps' armament, we feared for our little friends. A zap by one of those stingers might be fatal to such a tiny bird. We even considered a gas attack on the insects' citadel, but abandoned the idea as the birds worked out their own solution.

The hornets were late risers. They had to wait for the sun to warm up their engines. They also went home with the first cool shadows of evening. The hummers ganged the feeder early and late. Their normal sip was two bubbles up the feeder tube. Now they took four each time. They still dared midday forays, but usually got just one bubble before attack.

Frost grounded the yellow jackets for three days. The birds stoked up undisturbed to head south. Hummers live in an eternal flower garden. And, with snows coming on, a flower garden life doesn't look too bad, even if it does have a few hornets. 🌿

There are sixty-nine kinds of goldenrod. About two dozen of them grow in Michigan. I ran into this when my wife and I decided to list all the wild flowers that grow on our place. We bought a book, *Field Guide to Wildflowers* by Roger Tory Peterson and Margaret McKenny. It lists twenty-nine kinds of goldenrod. The first two we checked weren't on the list. We finally identified them by studying a library book on Michigan flowers.

Goldenrods are so showy they discourage close examination. Our identification search made us really look at them for the first time. It was educational. The individual flowers are tiny yellow-rayed blossoms not too much different from daisies. Sure enough, they belong to the composite, or daisy family.

Composites are the largest family of flowering plants and probably the most recent to appear on earth. The flower heads are clusters of many small flowers growing tightly together. Sunflowers are composites. Goldenrod blooms have the same arrangement in miniature.

Goldenrod is the undeserved butt of many jokes about hay fever. It is insect pollenated and produces only modest amounts of pollen. Some species are quite fragrant. On one clump I watched bumblebees, and honeybees, and yellow jackets all busy at the same time. The real hay fever baddie is ragweed, another composite. It is wind pollenated; produces great masses of pollen. Since it doesn't have to attract insects, it has inconspicuous green flowers. Blooming at the same time as goldenrod, it escapes notice, and the showy goldenrod gets blamed for the sneezes.

To identify goldenrod look at the flower heads. They may be plumelike, graceful; elm branched; clublike, showy; wandlike, slender; or flat topped. The leaves may be feather veined or parallel veined. This helps narrow the search. Then look at details like arrangement of leaves, fuzz on stems, etc. Looks easy. It's not.

I took our book to a stump in a cutdown where clusters of goldenrod had appeared by magic behind the loggers. The first clump was a foot tall, graceful, and plumelike, but unlike anything in the book. Nearby a three-foot clump was similar but with broader leaves, also a mystery. Both had been browsed by deer when young and tender, which added to the confusion by messing up stem arrangements. A third group proved to be late goldenrod, large showy plumes, smooth stem, toothed parallel-veined leaves. Near the river, in rich soil, this species was over six feet tall.

Samples of the unknowns accompanied me to the library, but not until I had soaked up a lot of quiet time outdoors. Goldenrod blooms from June to October. They have always been beautiful. Now they are fun. I'm glad there are sixty-nine kinds. 🌿

When I was a child I think all the primary schoolbooks must have been written in the North. They said robins came in the spring, when even the dumbest kid in Mississippi knew they came in the fall. One of my earliest school memories is of a young teacher who reprimanded me for insisting robins didn't come in the spring. My Dad had to show her a flock of thousands in our pasture to set her straight. It was years before I got over my suspicion of anyone from up north.

Right now the flocks that caused that mix-up are building up as they head south. Most territories that bustled with their red-breasted activity all summer are now vacant. Little bunches of robins are regularly on the lakeshore points where I go to watch migration.

Most fall birds are youngsters. A pair of robins may nest three times with three or four eggs in each clutch. In spite of high mortality, birds of the year far outnumber their elders. Newly fledged robins have speckled breasts. So do bluebirds. Both species start with spots to remind them of their ancestry. They are thrushes: a spotted-breasted family whose members usually retain their spots throughout adulthood.

Young robins start to shed their spots by moulting as soon as their first feathers are fully grown. By migration, most are dull copies of their parents. It takes a close look to tell a fall robin's age.

The other day, right in the midst of a wave of migrants, I saw a short-tailed speckled-breasted robin begging worms on a lawn. Robins like small-town people habitat. This is good for us humans, for they eat our insect enemies and decorate our lawns. Unfortunately it exposes them to predation by our pets and all sorts of hazards like insecticides, cars, and general people activity. This late youngster I saw was probably a final effort to reproduce in spite of the hazards of city nesting.

Robins are great fruit eaters. A cherry tree we had in Illinois was invariably picked bare. Where wild fruit abounds they aren't so harmful to orchards. Down south they eat chinaberries. These hang on the trees in winter and often ferment. Some birds get so drunk they can't fly. They get hangovers too. We used to catch the drunks to save them from cats. Their frowzy looks were perfect copies of some folks I've seen on New Year's morning.

But drunk or sober, cherry stealers or bug catchers, robins are our most popular bird. They live wherever we do from Alaska to the Gulf. We'll miss them for a while, but it will make their "cheerily-cheerilys" all the more sweet next spring. 🌿

What can you expect from a late summer bird feeder way back in the woods? Lots of blue jays, lots of rose-breasted grosbeaks and, suddenly, a proliferation of white-breasted nuthatches. Most of these birds are young. Some of the jays still have half-developed head feathers. Many of the grosbeaks are reluctant to cut the apron strings, constantly begging for a handout. The nuthatches are self-reliant and aggressive. Besides eating, their preoccupation is to establish their pecking order.

Nuthatches have frighteningly aggressive displays. They raise black feathers and lower their heads to give a belligerent grotesque shape. Wings and tail are spread, head moved side to side. Repeatedly two birds will alight near the feeder and assume these fierce attitudes. One always backs off. Over and over this is repeated as the two or three families come in for seeds. It looks like every bird wants to be a bully. But, really nobody bullies nobody. It's all part of a plan.

Each species must establish a social order, a way of living in peace together. Man and some other animals have mostly one offspring at a time. This automatically establishes a certain amount of order. The first born is usually bigger, stronger, and is first to leave the home. Just suppose we had litters, broods, or clutches instead of single babies. Which one would eat first or last? Who is first out of the nest cavity or first gets to use the family car?

Nature is much too methodical to leave such things to chance. The nuthatches are following a ritual evolved over eons as one more better step on the road to survival. Someone has to be first, someone has to be last. Most times there is plenty for all: plenty of trees to search for food, of mates to be had, of territories to live in. What do you do when there aren't? A species can perish if its members squabble over each crust. Better that one should eat and survive than all fight until survival is impossible. That's what the pecking order is for. Each wild family, and each species establishes one. That is the show we see at our feeders. The birds are deciding who will be first, and second, and third, and last.

The blue jays seem well spread by age groups. The early litters dominate the late. Rose-breasted grosbeaks will soon migrate and will probably live in less-competitive situations. The nuthatches will live here year-round. This year many seem just the same age.

This generation is setting up their manners, their ethics, and their laws. Now it looks brutal, ruthless, but amusing. But soon, the right-hand driver will have the right of way. It will be ladies, elders, or royalty first. There will be peace among the nuthatches at the feeder.

"Manners maketh man," and it helps other species survive too.

"I can stand anything in a duck blind except a shortage of ducks." Anyone who hunts ducks long enough will have to seriously consider if he really means that. Things happen to duck hunters that shouldn't happen to a dog.

In fifty years of hunting ducks, I've been accused of being crazy by parents, wife, various school and business associates, just about everyone except fellow duck hunters. Any sensible person would go back for the forgotten lunch or to turn off car lights—but if we do we miss the morning flight. Come back when things slow up. The wind blew a gale, and we couldn't get back for hours and hours.

The car lights finally went out. The ducks came from everywhere. We shot some and then just watched them pile into the decoys. We learned a lot about ducks that day—how they act in a windstorm and what they do with decoys when they swim among them. We never thought of that five-mile walk till we got back to the car.

One year we had a floating brush blind on a tideflat. At high water there were whistlers and broad-bills, scoters and sheldrakes. At low tide there were black ducks. One day low tide was at sundown. We waited too long for the blacks and then couldn't leave; half a mile of rocky mud to floating water.

It was the December half of a Maine split season. If there is a colder place than that December mud flat I haven't found it. We waited. Even the dog shivered. Then the blacks came. We listenend to their wings and their puddling and muttering among the eelgrass. We watched them silhouetted against the stars as they wing stepped from the sky. Finally, the water came back, but still we waited. Then the blacks left and we went home. We didn't talk much.

When there is no cover, you lie down. Once we hunted a bare mud flat—air mattresses to lie on and burlap for cover. Mine sprang a leak. I laid in the mud all day and never knew I was wet until quitting time. Ducks can do that to you.

Nowadays I notice cold is colder, water is wetter, and the wind blows harder against me. I spend more time with a bird dog and less in hip boots. They don't make them as light as they used to. But, one day last fall, I found myself flat on my back in a cut cornfield; a duck call at my lips and burlap for cover.

The mallards swung that field a dozen times. When they lowered their flaps almost on top of me they still had that old magic, for that bare ground wasn't cold and hard at all. ✻

I stood under a maple tree in the middle of a *big* cornfield. It was gnarled, with dead limbs stark among the foliage. A sentinal crow had flushed from its peak at my approach, warning the hundreds fattening on milk tender corn. Near its base a stone pile guarded a fox den. Now deserted, flattened weeds testified to the tumbling play of the pups whelped there last spring.

Way off a tree line marked the wooded river bottom. Another view held a pasture, a big barn, a small house, and dozens of black and white cattle lining homeward for milking. Here was an American farm, not the biggest or smallest. Its cash crop happened to be milk. It might have been potatoes or beans, wheat, pork, or any of the thousand and one things that feed the human race, and, in America, most of the wildlife.

I wondered about those trees in farm fields. Most fields don't have them. Those that do have big ones. I don't ever recall seeing a small tree alone in a cultivated field. Why are they there? What's their purpose? I visited some. A doe sprang out of waist-high weeds at the foot of an ash. She couldn't have picked a safer place, clear view in every direction and forty acres of beans spread around for dining.

An apple tree, standing ankle-deep in clover, held a kingbird's nest. One of its residents darted out to snatch a grasshopper, then settled back to watch my approach. On their home ground kingbirds are disdainful. This tree was his. I had no business there. His whole stance told me so. Each tree is a little neighborhood. Each has a story.

In hunting across and up and down America, most of my time has been spent on farms. I expect 80 percent of the game I've shot has been farm grown. The rest of it came from wetlands, much of it part of operating farms. The volume of wildlife on any tract is directly related to fertility. In America most all fertile land is in farms, their fertility maintained by annual fertilization, crop rotation, and a variety of management techniques. They feed us and the wild things. Some crops even provide a place to live. Watch the coons skedaddle when a farmer picks the last few rows in a cornfield.

I asked some farmers about those trees in their fields. "What are they for?" "It's a place for the coons to go when the hunters come." "A shady place to rest." "The kids climb in it." "The apples are good." "Deer come there in evenings." "I can stand by it and shoot ducks." "It's pretty against the sky."

So now I know. These people love the land—and, horrible thought—suppose they didn't? Suppose the trees were cut so the tractors needn't go around, the river bottoms cleared to run off the deer and other crop freeloaders? Who then would give the earth tender loving care? God bless and keep the farmers. ❦

October

Morning arrives when the night is still deep in darkness. Long before dawn lightens the eastern sky, suddenly indefinably it is morning. Night still must play out its finale, but day stands ready in the wings, silent, invisible, but now for sure it is there. For me it is a magic hour.

I am not usually up and about so early, but on October's glorious days I cannot wait for dawn. The sky is a blanket, midnight blue. It has a texture, soft and friendly. I can almost feel its pile, gently against my face. It cradles a half-moon and a scattering of stars and planets. Some moonlight is good for amateur sky watchers. It blanks out the lesser stars, leaves only the important constellations for us to recognize. A clear moonless night is too full. The universe overwhelms me. October half-moon makes the sky simple and friendly.

A south breeze brushes my cheek—mild and damp. I can almost smell the faraway gulf from whence it came. We need rain. This moist wind will help break the drought if it holds. The south winds of fall are different from spring winds. They have a lingering quality, bid reluctant farewell, but not sadly. Parting is sweet, and October's south wind lingers to prolong the ecstacy. The earth is the south wind's lover. Each year's departure makes their love more strong.

A barred owl "who cooks" way off in the distance. His voice is bigger than he is. It rolls across the woods, a noble sound. Nearby a small animal screams, just once. The woods are never so silent as after a death scream. Everything listens: predators to pinpoint the kill and possible opportunity; prey to pinpoint the killers and make safety sure. Finally, at my feet the leaves rustle. Some small citizen goes on with the business of living. Nature has no time for regrets.

Something splashes. The pond is a bed with a silvery counterpane. Soon enough the morning breeze will throw back the covers, but now night must have it all neat for a little while. See how she smooths the wrinkles, chases the wavelets ashore.

Is there more light? Look to the east. The stars have lost some luster. The sky has lost some depth. It is closer and paler. Shadows laid down by the westerling moon evaporate in the eastern light. Two wood ducks etch silhouettes toward the river. Far away a farm dog barks.

An October day steps forth for another splendid performance. The whole world applauds. 🌾

If you haven't stocked your larder, better get with it. That's the word around our place in October. Some of our wild things have gotten the message. Others ignore it.

Wildlings have several ways to handle winter. Migrants just leave it, or at least, move where the food supply is ample. Most of our summer birds go south. We get winter species from north and west.

Hibernators fatten up and sleep through it. Woodchucks are our local experts. In October they go inside and lock the door. Body processes slow almost to a stop. If they are dug out in midwinter, it takes hours in a warm room to rouse them. Despite the legend, they are unaware of Groundhog Day, they don't wake up till it's warmer.

Foragers gather food as they need it. Winter diet may be different, but they have learned to live on what the seasons offer. Ruffed grouse do it well; bugs and fresh greens for the young, poplar leaves and berries, clover, ground greenery, nuts, and mushrooms till snow falls, then tree buds in winter including the flower buds from my apple trees. Darn 'em!

It's the hoarders that are busiest in fall. Some try to store food to last all winter. Many forage when they can, visit their larders when necessary. Chipmunks are the most diligent hoarders. They spend the winter inside, but don't hibernate. A favorite storage spot is under the bed. They sleep a lot and like to have food handy. Chipmunks do have to get out of bed occasionally for the toilet chamber is away from the bedroom at a lower level. They had inside sanitary facilities before man invented the outhouse.

Tree squirrels both hoard and forage. Fox and gray squirrels bury nuts individually in the ground, find most of them even through deep snow. The lost nuts sprout to regenerate the tree species that provide the food. Red squirrels store in caches. Around here they put acorns in hollows, mushrooms in tree crotches, and birdseed in ground holes. Their favorite winter food is evergreen cones. This year the cedar cone crop is great. The squirrels have pruned cone-laden fronds till our road through the swamp is paved with greenery. The reds lug the cone bunches to a midden, usually in a cool damp spot where the cones will not open and spill the seeds. Dining spots are marked by piles of scales, some very large and used for years.

All the tree squirrels visit our feeders on nice winter days. Our resident birds come snow or shine. Jays and nuthatches are compulsive hoarders, sticking sunflower seeds in every nook and cranny. Jays also use hollows and old nests. I've never seen these species reclaiming hoarded food around here. Our feeder is too handy. But they take no chances. Better to be safe than hungry. Who am I to change their saving ways? 🦋

Life in the wilds is hazardous. Most birds, newly fledged, do not survive to breed. Among raptors about 75 percent don't make it. We are watching a hawk whose survival rests on a razor's edge. He has a lame leg.

A week ago the young sharp-shinned stooped at sparrows under our feeder, missed, swept up to perch. We never saw him kill. When he returned each day we finally discovered his bad leg. Occasionally he flexed it; moved the talons. They worked O.K. but he never put weight on that foot.

Beneath our feeder the ground is cleared. Bracken fern grows knee-high all around. Migrating sparrows, come to the clearing to feed; hide in the bracken. In the past sharp-shinned hawks have lit in the open, run into the bracken to chase sparrows into fatal flight. I suspected something was wrong when our current visitor hovered over the edge of the bracken, one leg extended. Occasionally a panicky sparrow flushed, but then darted back to safety. A ground chase would have foiled this tactic.

Mostly our sharp-shinned chases blue jays. They are the street gang and self-appointed vigilantes of our dooryard. Two or three jays keep an eye on the hawk while the others feed. In dense cover the security guards will edge close, provoke attack. It's a dangerous game. A jay brushed by talons screams in fright, and is quickly relieved to recover.

A male sharp-shinned is blue jay size, but much stronger. He can kill birds that outweigh him by a third. If our hawk had two good legs, we would have seen him kill by now, if not a blue jay then a sparrow or woodpecker which come to feed as the jays bait the enemy. Chickadees and nuthatches place no faith in jay security. They stay strictly away when the hawk is near.

This spring we watched a sharp-shinned kill a hairy woodpecker. She struck it down into a snowmelt pool, stood waist-deep treading and stabbing with both feet. She dragged it ashore, plucked it, and dined until the carcass was light enough to carry away.

Our current visitor would kill the same way, but half his killing tools are out of fix. A blue jay would be a hard fight. The bad leg might be injured again. Yet, if he does not kill soon he may never. Do we see his flight not quite so sharp, so strong?

Nature swings a wide scythe to force survival of the fittest. Some of the strong are reaped with the weak. We see no evidence our little hawk is a weakling. He is a skilled determined hunter. We pray for him to make one good kill. It might give him time for that leg to heal. And if it does, he just might live to make the next generation of sharp-shinneds a little bit better. 🦅

"There's a skunk in our garage." A background babble of excited children emphasized the seriousness of the crisis. This phone call was important.

Fall is roving time for skunks. The young, who have followed their mother through midsummer, spread out to find living space. Adult females, freed from family chores, start fattening for winter. They also look up other females, for often several will den together in winter. Males are solitary, have no paternal responsibilities, and are already fat from a summer of easy living. Still, they roam in fall. This time of year skunks are our most persecuted pedestrians. Our highways are littered with them. Gentle and fearless, they just never learn about cars.

Skunks will eat almost anything. Their consumption of insects and mice makes them one of the most beneficial of mammals. They also eat bird eggs and will take poultry if it's handy. Garbage is an irresistible attraction. Plastic trash bags are an invitation to explore. Only a tightly topped can, too heavy for tipping, will thwart their searching.

Most skunks don't smell bad. Males fighting during the breeding season, sometimes spray each other. We have plenty of skunks on our place. We find their tracks and the little pits they dig for grubs, but we never smell them except those hit on the highway almost a mile away.

But how do you get a skunk out of a garage? Skunks are nocturnal, they like dark places. If discovered unexpectedly, it will retreat to shelter. Most garages have something they can hide under or behind. If it is night, simply open the garage door. Turn the garage light on, outside lights out. The skunk will leave—in his own good time. If you clean up the garbage, he will leave sooner. In daytime get behind him, away from the door. Tap his hiding place gently with something light like a fish pole. Don't hurry. Keep the door open and free of kids. He will leave.

You don't scare a skunk away. You invite him to leave. If you push him too hard, he will stomp his front feet and raise his tail. This is a warning. Back off, let him calm down. Skunks are well-mannered little animals. If we match their good manners, they will leave in peace. Next time lock up the garbage.

Beware though if a skunk acts aggressively, doesn't hide, comes toward you. Keep away. He may be rabid. This is rare, but it does happen. Call the police or shoot him when he's away from buildings. Warn the neighbors. Don't panic. ✷

I recently had to spend several days in the crowded southeast corner of our state. I was lucky, stayed in the suburbs about thirty miles west of the city. It is pretty country, hills with bits of forest and tiny marshes scattered in the land folds. A few working farms hugged the byroads, shoulders hunched against the subdividers. To urbanites it must seem like real country.

But everywhere there are people, no view without rooftops, no breeze without the sound of motors. On clear days jet contrails sketch flight plans in disappearing ink, small planes wander aimlessly below. East wind tells of freeway traffic, west and south bring local road noise just in time to drive quiet back to hiding. There is no silence. I wake late and listen at the window. The sounds of civilization still crowd upon me. It presses down my spirit, makes me sad.

The University of Michigan's Matthaei Botanical Garden is a gold mine for the serious botanist. I stopped there looking for a lift of spirits; found it in the garden trails along Fleming Creek.

I lingered under a big cottonwood tree. Leaves rustled in the wind. High above, planes pass, disembodied, their noise masked by the leaf whispers. Cottonwoods are great rustlers. The slightest breeze makes them talk. On summer days they told tales of Indians and Mississippi riverboats, of catfish long as your leg, and all the dreams ever dreamt beside a southern pond. It was good to hear them again.

Burr oaks, 200 years old, made a rampart against road sounds. Big trees are best. They keep noises from jumping over. Underbrush catches those that sneak below. Trees understood acoustics before we did. We build houses and freeways too close for trees to grow and then erect concrete fences to stop the noise. Progress?

This trail side once was elm forest, graceful giants long dead and gone. Natures succession crowds about. Ash saplings galore, dogwood, grape vines, highbush cranberry, poison ivy climbing. All revel in the sunlight, carrying out natures contingency plan against disease, disaster.

The trail carries me back to all those things we humans en masse seem to demand. A brand new freeway, bandaids of sod plastering its scratches, a bare to subsoil hilltop with one lone tree, "Coming soon Maple Top Acres, 180 of the finest home sites in ——," unlabeled excavations and ditches here and yon. My heart aches to see this fair land nibbled away.

A chill wind brings me the whine of trucks climbing a grade, the buzz of a chopper blowing mulch on raw cut banks. I shiver in my coat, afraid for this lovely land. The trail along Fleming Creek gives me hope. ✹

When we built our home we figured to manage this property the way we thought it should be done. It didn't work out that way. We soon found that we were guests on our own land. The other inhabitants had certain prerogatives and insisted on exercising them.

Otters had a signpost on the riverbank near the house. They twist up little teepees of grass and bracken, leave scent on them. They roll in the grass and leave droppings all about. Otters travel a lot. Everyone that came along the river stopped at the signpost for news and to leave scent. Females with young sometimes played and rolled at length. We watched them from our balcony.

A family found our fishpond. From the far end they looked me over, discussed the matter, then continued to catch my eight-inch bass at fifty cents per serving. That we couldn't have! I paraded the dog round and round the bare pond shore. He left his scent on all their droppings. On our next visit the three otters dashed across the dam down to the river. They never came back. The signpost was abandoned. There is a new one a half-mile upstream. In winter otters come to fish in our open water. We seldom see them before freezeup.

The pond bass are long gone, winter killed. Only bullheads remain. We would welcome the otters back. I think they would tolerate us, but the dog—never. We once had our lease canceled in a fancy townhouse complex because we had a dog.

By contrast, the red squirrels welcomed us with open arms. They immediately appropriated our bird feeders; tried to defend against all comers. With endless food they flourished. In the wilds ten red squirrels per acre is peak population. We regularly saw ten to twelve in our yard. Finally they forced control. I shot an amazing number. Fire retardant in the insulation keeps them out of our reinsulated attic. My grandson shoots some every time he visits. We made one feeder squirrel proof, frighten them off the balcony when they become too obnoxious.

Red squirrels love to live with us. We like them individually, but en masse, no way. Their breeding is too unrestrained. Two litters a year and bring the kits to dinner as soon as they can climb. The crowning insult is that the feeders belong to them. As far as they are concerned our claim to the property is no more valid than those of the jays and fox squirrels that come each day to steal from them. They can't run us off, but they swear at us no end.

So, our war with the red squirrels goes on. We rely on sniper fire. They are trying to breed us into surrender. ❧

The other day I shot a grouse that had a chestnut-red neck ruff, the first I have ever seen. The red and gray color phases seem to be about evenly divided among grouse along the forty-fifth parallel where I hunt. Both colors may occur in a single brood, and the main color difference is in the tail. All that I have previously seen had black ruffs occasionally touched with brown.

The red-ruffed bird I shot brought back memories of a wonderful grouse story I read as a boy. It was entitled "Red Ruff" and described the life history of a male grouse, colored like mine, the sole survivor of his brood. That was my first contact with *Bonasa umbellus,* and I fell in love with him long before the first one thundered up before me in a New England woods.

Now, after almost fifty years I have met "Red Ruff" in the flesh. I felt a touch of regret that he could not fly off again. I make no apologies for hunting grouse. They meet me in fair contests and escape more often than not. I loved them before I saw them and learned to respect them with that first forest-shattering flush. I felt entitled to my bit of sadness over this rare specimen.

Before white men settled America, red ruffed grouse must have been more common. The center of ruffed grouse abundance was in the hardwood forests of eastern and middle America. As the fertile hardwood forest lands were cleared for farming, the grouse were eliminated or confined to marginal coniferous woodlands. About the same time our great pine forests were logged and burned. Hardwood brush came in providing ideal ruffed grouse habitat.

These are birds of the young forest, and the lush hardwood brush of the 1920s and 1930s brought grouse to their greatest historical abundance in the lakes states. Maturing trees, control of fire, and possibly competition with the deer herd is more responsible for their decline than hunting. In remote wilderness, grouse can be foolishly tame, but in contact with man they are simply not the kind of bird that can be overhunted.

Always the more northern grouse were gray and the southern, red. Recent research north of us has shown that in winters of light snow, predators got one-third more red phase than gray phase grouse. Apparently the red birds are out-of-phase with the more northern forests. Look at the gray-white colors of our birch-poplar and coniferous woods. Then go only a few miles south where the oaks predominate. The lingering oak leaves give the whole winter forest a browner ruddier look.

Is it any wonder that nature put brown birds south and gray birds north? Surely, long ago, my "Red Ruff" must have had southern relatives. ✹

Just at dark one recent drizzly evening, a barred owl sounded his contralto hoot across the swamp from where I stood. Another answered some distance to the north. They called back and forth several times before I decided to enter the discussion. With my southern accent I let go with a crudely executed "who, who, who, who cooks for you all?" Silence! I had about decided they recognized the hoax when almost over my head came a hair-raising series of answering hoots. My startled crash into a pile of dry cedar tops sent my visitor away. I saw him winging silently over the woods road beside which I stood. For a moment I had the feeling some small nocturnal mammal might get in that instant before one of these fierce hunters crushes out its life in the darkness.

No wonder owls are such subjects of superstitions and legends. That bird lit undetected, practically on top of me while I was attentively watching and listening. Surely I was justified in consigning him to the company of witches and hobgoblins. Had he sounded one of his nuptial shrieks instead of the more familiar hoots, I might well have concluded he had changed to one of those Halloween characters.

The barred owl is the most vocal of our night predators. His voice is rivaled only by the great horned owl whose bass hoots are uttered much less frequently. Both have a wide repertoire of screams, shrieks, and chuckles used mostly in the mating season. The hoots may be voiced any season, and the barred owl is readily identified by his "you all" ending of each sentence.

Nature does nothing by accident, and the owl's big head and feathered face disc are a remarkable adaptation for his nocturnal hunting. The wide head sets his ears far apart, and the face discs, made up of special little feathers, focus sounds to them like the parabolic reflectors used in sensitive tape recording. Thus equipped with binocular hearing he can zero in on his prey in total darkness. Experiments with barn owls inside a lightless room found them repeatedly pinpointing a mouse as soon as the little rodent moved. To gather what light is available the owls are further aided by large eyes placed in the front of the head. To see sideways an owl must turn his head. He can swivel it a full 180 degrees. Try it sometime to appreciate this accomplishment. To complete the adaptation the owl's feathers have downy fringes, and even the wing primaries are softer than other birds'. No whirring flight for them; not only would it warn the prey, but it might also hamper their accurate hearing aim.

Silence is the rule when hunting. No wonder our barred owl has a voice to raise the dead. If you have to be quiet to make a living, nature must surely give some compensation. 🖎

Once I visited a New York nightclub where everyone sat around eating peanuts and throwing the shells on the floor. It was fun. The grosbeaks do it everyday at our feeder with sunflower seeds. Watching the nightclub show, I tossed away shells as I emptied them. My companion built small mountains on the table, then swept them away with a grand gesture at the end of each act.

In our overpopulated, overcontainerized society, littering is stupid. Our ancestors were natural born litterers, scattering banana skins, fruit pits, and feces during millions of years of carefree roaming. It was good to have the management's blessings for a brief return to the careless ways of our simian forebearers.

Unlike many civilized containers, peanut shells and sunflower hulls are biodegradable. Problems with them stem from volume. The nightclub floor had to be cleaned daily to keep it passable. Grass below our feeder is simply smothered. We clean it several times a year to keep the bare spots within reason. The hulls make good compost.

For natural wastes nature has far better disposal systems than man has yet devised, but every system has capacity limits. Nature handles them in ingenious ways. She avoids overconcentrations. Grosbeaks eat just as many seeds in the wilds as they do at our feeder, but over a larger area. Seldom is the ecosystem overloaded. Most other birds and mammals carry seeds off to store or eat elsewhere. Where imbalance occurs, the seasons compensate.

I watched grosbeaks demolish a bumper crop of flowering crab apples. In two days the ground below was a slippery smelly mess. Then the rain of pulp was finished, snow came, and next spring the grass was greener than ever. The endless litter below our feeder snuffs out all but the lowest life-forms. They don't get time to catch up.

Bacteria and fungi are nature's ultimate waste eaters. She has many other stages. When waste rots (bacterial and fungal decomposition) it smells. One of the great odors of outdoors used to be the drying of the bar pits from the Mississippi River's annual overflow. Millions of fish died. They stank—nature's call for help. All life seemed to gravitate to the feast. Insects uncountable, snakes, turtles, rodents, possums, coons, vultures, and occasionally a bald eagle. Birds to eat the bugs, predators to catch the living that came to eat the dead. It was a wildlife wonderland if you stayed upwind. The Corps of Engineers has pretty well stopped the Mississippi's annual overflows. Nowadays few people get to learn the lessons they taught.

Nature handled pollution long before there was a man. Her systems still work, but there are rules. We must live with them or perish. That's why the nightclub owner sweeps his floor, and I haul hulls to the compost. It's a fair swap for the fun we get, and when we stick to the rules nature *always* does her part. ❧

If you want to imitate a beaver's warning signal throw a ten-pound boulder in the water. The "cachung" will alert all the wildlife within hearing. The wilds have many warnings. Deer snort, rabbits thump with their feet, squirrels bark or chatter, catbirds meow, crows and jays scream special alarm calls. All woodland creatures heed them.

It pays the hunter or nature watcher to learn these warnings. When I hear one I just stop. That first alarm has a dozen ears cocked for your next footstep. Every eye is alert for movement. Sensitive noses are testing the breeze. Why confirm their suspicions?

I think most animals have lots of curiosity, or are not too confident in other species' warnings. Like teenagers they have to find out themselves. When I stop I am in phase with the woods. Everything has stopped to look and listen. As I wait, animation slowly resumes: first the careless, the curious and the confident; then the timid and cautious. The wise wildlife takes all danger signals seriously. I never see old white-tailed deer after a warning I have caused.

The other morning my dog and I went down to the river. As I sat watching, a resounding "cachung" announced the presence of our resident bachelor beaver. He lives alone under the bank. He builds no dam, caches no food, and cuts only what brush is needed for daily meals. A real hippie of the beaver tribe. I meet him often in our stretch of the river. Always he sounds an alarm.

In a moment he was up, eyeing the dog. In the water he feared nothing but man. Still, this active red and white stranger was something new. "Cachung" again. His tail slapped the water throwing his rear up and head down for a quick dive. Soon he was up again, working ever shoreward. He floated in the lee of a log, tacked effortlessly about in the current. In spite of his pear-shaped figure he was exceeded in aquatic grace by none but the otters. Another warning slap and another. After the first splash the green young dog ignored the commotion. Finally he wandered up the shore. The beaver swam almost to my feet. Then, smooth as silk, he slipped underwater to his den—no warning here. Privacy is too important.

Last summer I sat at the same spot watching a doe and fawn cross the river. A movement of my binoculars brought a ten-pound splash from my friend. The deer left quietly, quickly. Presently I heard the doe's shrill snort from downwind. She had to know herself, but was too wise to ignore her neighbor.

Our bachelor beaver isn't a very good citizen. He shuns the busy upstream colony, yet he still sounds his warnings for all. No man is an island and neither is a hippie beaver. 🕱

Ducks really don't like those rainy good-day-for-ducks days. In spite of their waterproof feathers, they don't like to fly in the rain and don't seem very happy just sitting around in it.

Except for the big migrations ahead of fall storms, my best duck hunting has been on bright windy days. The birds spend more time feeding and seem to drop in on other flocks or decoys more confidently. Wind makes them restless and discourages settling on the big open waters.

Still, the time to go duck hunting is when you can. The drippy dawn found me up to my chest in wet cattails watching a shallow willow-grown pond. A hen mallard gave a tentative "quack-aak-aak" in the brush across the way. For once I had checked and patched my waders—no wet feet today. Rain gradually seeped through a loose seam of my rain shirt, thoroughly soaking my shoulders. I wouldn't be denied the delicious misery of duck hunting after all.

A cold drop left my hat brim, then waited for company or destruction on the end of my nose. The lightening east gradually inked in the skeletons of drowned timber. A muskrat rustled the reeds, then plowed a wrinkle across the duckweed counterpane. A bittern lumbered over and crash-landed for breakfast. How can anything so stately in flight be so awkward in landing; a half-peck of scrambled legs, wings, and neck.

I had forgotten how good it was. Scores of duck dawns came marching through my memory. Blacks whiffling unseen over the Maine tideflats; a squad of teal skidding into the blocks in Mississippi, dark little blobs rippling gray quicksilver. Their soprano quacklets helloed their wooden hosts in eager greetings. Mallards pouring overhead from Oregon wheatfields. A pair peels off the flock, swings once, then backpedals, riding a slow-speed elevator to our narrow waters. For landing control you just can't beat an old green head coming into a tight place. He spreads those orange webfoot landing flaps, pokes his head down to see the way, then comes down a wing hold at a time. It's beautiful, and the best time to watch it is just before shooting hour.

I remember the big days when you just couldn't keep 'em out of the decoys—the day my son shot his first limit—all big drake mallards, in a blinding snowstorm. All the ducks in the prairies came our way that day. They were good times.

But between dawn and sunrise is a good time too. Time to see, and hear, and feel the wetlands and shiver a bit with cold or excitement. An old drake rasped discontent, sitting in the water trying to keep dry. Others talked it up. They are getting ready to leave and still ten minutes to shooting. Wings flail the water.

Maybe they'll be back. It's really not raining very hard. ✻

If chickadees didn't announce their names so frequently, they would probably have been called some kind of titmouse. That's the name given the family in the Old World where they apparently originated. Our little blackcaps were probably the first of the family encountered by early European emigrants. They announced their name so emphatically that it stuck and has been applied to seven other similar species in North America.

Only one of these, the boreal chickadee, visits Michigan, mostly in winter. They don't say "chickadee" at all, but get their name from their more common relative.

Black-capped chickadees are the most abundant and faithful winter diners at our feeders. They desert us each spring for nesting, but June is the only month they are completely absent. Then they are scattered through the woods busy with domestic duties. The young must have a high protein diet for healthy growth. This means insects and lots of them. Chickadees may lay six or eight eggs and sometimes raise two broods. The parents work almost to death to provide an insect diet. The young continue to eat what's good for them until late in summer.

The first family group didn't show up at our feeders till mid-August. About the same time, we encountered them in the raspberry patch. Now we have scores.

Chickadees are our most tame and friendly birds. They quickly learn to feed from our hands.Even deep woods ones sometimes light on me or my gun when I'm deer watching. They are smart little birds. A friend built a feeder which dispensed one sunflower seed every time a bird lit on a certain perch. Chickadees quickly learned which of the pegs delivered the goodies. They dined royally while the frustrated sparrows left in disgust after repeated failures. Chickadees are distantly related to crows and jays. Both families get their brains from a common ancestor.

Chickadees excavate nest cavities in rotten limb knots or snags. Their bills aren't strong enough to dig sound wood. They will use an old woodpecker hole or a nest box if you cover it with bark. The nest is made of any soft material. Our Brittany spaniel provides a good supply. He is an avid hunter, but soon stopped chasing them. In May he lay for hours while chickadees gathered last winter's hair in hundreds of loads from his pen. He seemed to enjoy their presence as much as we did.

Three winters ago, we banded seventy chickadees. Of the hundred-odd here now, only two wear bands. Seventy percent annual mortality is normal in adults. It's even higher in the young. To survive, the species must have large families. Is it any wonder the parents work hard at proper feeding?

And if a short life is your destiny, surely you want your name remembered. Perhaps that's why they keep saying—"chick-a-dee-dee."

When it comes to turkeys, everyone talks about shooting them or eating them. Even in bird books the sections on turkeys talk about hunting and eating. We've become turkey watchers. A big drove has taken to roosting across the river about 300 feet from our home.

Most people see wild turkeys on the ground. Around here they feed on farm crops. In fall, back road tours through farm country should find several flocks in the fields. They look about like domesticated turkeys. To really appreciate their wildness you have to see turkeys in the air. They are real attention getters.

Turkeys in the air sail a lot. They look like a flying cross; front leg sharply pointed, rear leg broad and square. Wide rounded wings spread just behind the middle. Takeoff and landing makes lots of fuss.

We first saw turkeys on our place last fall. A pair startled one of our deer hunters when they flew down from a roost tree directly over his blind. In midwinter I flushed a flock that was budding in tall poplars. The air was full of turkeys.

This spring young broods were on several nearby farms. Two weeks ago I watched a flock chase deer away from our neighbor's apple tree. I think this is the flock that roosts with us. Logging across the river left a fringe of large maples at streamside. While making breakfast I glimpsed something big and black disappear into the grass below them. Binoculars caught a turkey in midair, then another, and more. Finally they appeared on the riverbank, worked downstream stripping seeds from the marsh grass. One was a huge long-bearded gobbler.

Next morning I looked for them early. The big tree nearest the house held seven. We counted two dozen spread a hundred yards along the river. Turkeys like to roost over water, but usually spread the roost over two or three acres. These were concentrated in the only suitable trees left by logging.

About sunrise one flew down to the lane beside our house, then another, and finally an avalanche of big birds sailed across the river. There were a few clucks from the trees at first light and more from the first to fly down. The whole flock stood around stretching, picking, and straightening out feathers needing attention. Then they strolled down the lane. Turkeys don't like heavy wet foliage. Our trails are perfect for early morning walks. We saw them later in a field almost a mile away.

Turkeys don't stick to one place to roost. After leaf fall, they will probably switch to conifers. They may range over several miles. But they are a delight to watch while they are with us. And you know, next spring, I just might apply for a hunt permit. ❧

Crawfish Cocktail
Gourmet Broiled Woodcock
Butter-Fried Stump Mushrooms
Duck Potatoes
Wild Blackberry Pie

Several times each year, my wife and I enjoy a real wild dinner. The menu above was for a meal we had last week. It was super. Half the fun is the collecting.

One of our ponds is overrun with small sunfish. In a futile effort to prevent overpopulation, we keep all we catch. A dozen provide a meal for us. The heads and trimmings go into the crayfish trap for bait. A monstrous catch of these crustaceans prompted our decision to go foraging.

The stump mushrooms were just up. Fifteen minutes filled a basket. We save cleaning time by cutting the stems as we pick. This keeps most of the trash out. If the cut stems show brown spots the caps are worm infested and should be discarded. The stumpies we gather are pale brown. The identification rule is pepper on top and a ring around the stem. They are abundant each fall in the five-year cut-over on our place. To be safe, it's best to get someone who knows to show them in the field. Some kinds of stump mushrooms aren't edible.

The dry weather has dried up the wapatoo ponds. This saved them from the muskrats, but made digging harder. Twenty minutes work yielded a full shotgun-shell box, plenty for two. The tubers are delicate lavender pink with a pointed sprout on one end. Ours were one-half to three-fourths inch in diameter. They are harder and starchier than potatoes, but can be cooked the same way, only longer. My wife says duck potatoes are good only for ducks. She slipped in a few spuds from the garden—one of the compromises of married life. I prefer wapatoo.

She also prefers grouse to woodcock, and, at the last minute, sent me out with dog and gun. What a chore! A pat in the pondside clover gave an easy chance, but not a shot. We don't kill birds we feed. A solid point in a tag alder tangle produced two birds and a clean miss. No grouse for this meal.

For Gourmet Woodcock PICK THE BIRDS. Anyone who skins woodcock can't cook them this way—too dry. Split the birds down the back and marinate in french dressing all day. Broil five or six minutes on each side, starting breast side down. Baste with the dressing. Don't overcook. Figure two birds per person, and be sure to nibble off the thighs and drumsticks. Try them once this way, and you will never skin another woodcock.

It took us an hour to shuck the crayfish. The cocktail was more like lobster than shrimp and worth the effort. When my wife got through picking over the mushrooms and cleaning the duck potatoes she said she was plum "picked out."

Me too—but it made us appreciate the industry of our pioneer ancestors. 🌾

To seriously hunt snipe it helps to be a little crazy. It also helps to have a good pair of boots or tolerance for wet feet, plenty of shells, and legs instantly adjustable to mismatched lengths. The fact that few hunters combine all these worthwhile attributes is probably the main reason the common snipe has made such a comeback in numbers.

The other day, on the way to the grouse covers, we found a real old-fashioned snipe marsh. No sane outdoorsman would pass up a grouse hunt on a bright crisp October morning, but—a quick check got permission from the farmer owner.

It was a wet meadow, recently vacated by cattle, half-overgrown with scrub willows. The grass tussocks were plenty tough enough to hold you up but often too small. Ten percent of the water-filled cattle prints were just deep enough to flood boots—lovely. The snipe were there in numbers.

Now, any experienced snipe hunter will tell you that snipe are not hard to hit. They like to flush into the wind in open country but sometimes they don't. They always fly straight sometime after they flush. The time to shoot is either before they zigzag or after they quit. Just plant your feet as on a skeet range, swing past the bird and touch her off. One pellet will bring it down.

After trekking back to the car for more shells, I determined again that all this was absolutely true. I got a shot with both feet on dry ground at a bird flying straight into the wind. The snipe weighed slightly more than the shell that downed it. We spent a wonderful morning, and finally bagged enough of these delectable morsels for one meal.

When we arrived home, wet and reeking of cow droppings, my wife's expression confirmed the opinion of less-fortunate people, that snipe hunters are insane. It's been twenty years since I had a real good snipe hunt. I had forgotten how good it could be.

Snipe love to fly. The ones we missed or failed to shoot at streaked up to flyspeck height, dived, towered, then seared the ground at grass top level, only to tower again, or plunk suddenly to earth, often not far from the point of departure. The most futile of all shotgunning exercises is trying for these flighting jack snipe. Much more profitable to marvel at their aerobatic skill and walk them up again.

In spring snipe make such flights in courtship. Then they make winnowing sounds by wind through their spread wings. The ones we hunted didn't do this, but they made every other conceivable aerial maneuver. Against the blue sky and golden poplar horizon, it was indescribable beauty.

It makes me glad I'm crazy and, like many insane people, I think everyone's nuts but us snipe hunters. ❦

I don't know why some maple leaves are yellow, some are orange, and some are red. Above our house almost all the maples are yellow. A golden river flows through a golden tunnel. Each gust of the east wind spreads gold upon the surface; nobility riding high above the populace scattering coins for lesser beings. I sit on the shore and gather my share with my eyes, and my breath, and all my being.

On another October day I sat here with a very old man as he remembered the days of his youth. Each drifting leaf was a pine log. "Plenty of 'em three feet or better through." The leaves windrow behind snags and in eddies. Some twist themselves loose and twirl slowly down the current. Vagrant breezes break up others—the river drive crew hurrying to prevent a jam.

A big raft becomes a wanigan, steaming with an almost ready meal. "It was at this very bend that the steering oar broke. A big sweeper on the far shore cleaned everything off. Put the whole shooting match in the river. Cook rented a team and drove all the way to town for grub. It was ten o'clock at night before we got a thing to eat."

Seven wood ducks skid to a landing almost at my feet. They splash my reveries aside. All are young birds. The drakes show just a promise of future splendor. Three of them plow furrows through a bright eddy cover as they swim to meet an eighth arrival. Soft twitters of greeting are barely audible above the breeze.

Two ducks climb a log with much tail wagging. Woodies are great tail shakers. They settle three feet above the golden flotillas. Do they have daydreams too? The rest of the flock drift around the bend. I spread corn there each day. They'll check the dinner table and stay till the last scrap is eaten.

One of the resting ducks bobs her head. The other bobs too. They hop in the water; drift away. I have watched suspicious ducks bobbing heads at my approach, a sure sign they are about to flush. Does this head bobbing have other meanings? Like, "Let's join the gang." "O.K., let's go." The spell of this glorious day makes me one with all the other creatures. It puts my words in their mouths.

Maple leaves bring down their stems with them. They fall stem first. Some seesaw through the air. Others slowly auger a hole toward the ground. A few spin madly down. Why do they hurry so?

I circle away from the river so as not to disturb the ducks. This is the very best time of year. For a little while let this golden tunnel with the sky blue roof be theirs to enjoy too.

For me, the best medicine comes in small doses; moments, or perhaps an hour, in the little places I love so well. Oh sure, it's good to buck the covers with the dog and a friend, huddle for hours in a duck blind, slip off boots and wiggle fatigue out of weary limbs before the fire. Good talk and good rest after a day of hunting. I don't go hunting in the little places, though I carry a gun and sometimes shoot.

Back in a patch of woods there is an old orchard, half-a-dozen trees waist-deep in sumac. One has pale green apples much esteemed by grouse. You don't have to hunt. That's where they will be. Once or twice a season I go there at sundown to flush a bird from the green windfalls. Sometimes I shoot. It's just twenty yards to safe cover. A grouse bagged is for bragging. One is enough. If I miss, there's always a pocketful of those pale apples for compensation.

There's a little pond too boggy to wade, too far to tote a boat. A family of black ducks raises there. When I had Labs, I used to shoot two blacks there every season. The dog retrieved them. Now I go alone just to check. Can't shoot unless they swing over the land. Sometimes they do. A big hunt might wipe out the family, leave the pond empty next year.

It all started when my hunting uncle picked me up after school to "go shoot a duck." We left the old Overland parked on the levee, walked half a mile across a cotton field. The pond was dried away from its fringe of button willows. Lotus pads stood two feet above green water. "It's about time. They'll come from the levee, but don't look. The sun will blind you." I hid in the willows.

Just as the sun touched the levee top, a big drake mallard swung past my uncle, collapsed on the bare bank at his shot. "Now there's a stranger." We were after wood ducks. The only migrants we might expect were blue-winged teal. Mallards would come later.

A duck swished over my head and disappeared into the lotus pads. As I poked cautiously through the pads, it flushed right at me. A desperate twist in the mud and my shot dropped him in a cloud of feathers—my very first duck. Another shot rang out from my uncle's hide as I picked up my young woodie.

"Time to go." He had a beautiful drake wood duck in addition to the mallard. As we crossed the cotton toward the black line of levee, dim shapes whistled over. "More coming," I whispered. "Leave 'em. We'll want to come back here again."

As we walked away from that stream of roost-bound wood ducks, I took my first step toward being a sportsman and to falling in love with the little places. ✺

November

It would be a better world if everyone could sit a while among hemlocks. There need not be a lot of trees, but they should be large enough to teach humility.

There is a hemlock grove on our place: a couple dozen trees sixteen to twenty inches through. The tallest may be fifty feet. It's not an easy place to visit. All around it is a tamarack-tangled bog floored in sphagnum moss, and springs that never freeze: a six-inch-high island in a long-dead pond; dry enough for the seedlings' toe holds, too small to log, too wet to burn in the fires that charred our virgin pine stumps.

Deer winter there. The yard is spider-webbed with paths of last year's droppings; rent for shelter from the winter's wind—some to feed the forest giants, some for the carpet of moss and wintergreen, some for scented mayflower throw rugs and lady's slippers just to see in spring.

There's not much here for deer to eat, yet I go there in fall to sit a little while. Sometimes deer come. I think they like the quiet as much as I do. When hunted hard they bed under the hemlocks. No man can quietly penetrate the tamarack ramparts, so the deer slip off to stand knee-deep in water till the blundering intruder departs.

Hemlocks are patient trees. They can sprout in shade and bide their time in shadows, while lesser species hurry to old age and die. Eventually they overtop their neighbors and dominate the forest. In cool moist spots they are what foresters call a climax species. Given time and freedom from catastrophe, they rule their surroundings.

I've never seen a grove of small hemlock trees. When hemlocks are small the forest is made of other trees. My hemlocks tower over a rotting birch log and fallen firs dissolved by nature's sanitarians, the insects, fungi, and bacteria. There are some pine stumps, wind shattered, and two tall white pines still remaining.

Two red squirrels prune coned twigs. They did not protest my presence. Are they tamer here, or do I sit quieter in the somber shade? Red-breasted nuthatches search, head side down the trees, while brown creepers hitch ever upward. Chickadees provide a background of "dee-dee-dees" and topsy-turvy antics.

In fall each tree has its own sound. Oaks rustle. Bare hardwoods rattle. Pines whisper or sing. Firs and spruces whine. Hemlocks murmur. They lift up their limber boughs and drop them with a sigh of tranquility.

I went there to shoot a deer. I came away before the evening. I don't want to shoot in my hemlock grove. It would be like shooting in church. 🌿

Of all the animals, beavers are most like people. They are the only wild specie I know that deliberately alters the environment to suit their needs. They build dams to provide stable water and make food trees accessible.

We admire beavers for their industry and engineering. Why shouldn't we? We Americans are industrious and the world's best engineers. Beavers belong to the establishment. Look at their dedication to growth.

Upstream from our house is a great beaver complex. A creek entering the river has at least a dozen dams. Dead trees litter the ponds. Downstream dams are in disrepair. Poplars, willows, alders, all choice beaver fodder, are gone; eaten or drowned. I explored upstream, enticed by the unfolding story of the community's history. Here was environmental exploitation rivaled only by man's—urban decay in the wilds. Finally, way in the suburbs I found an active beaver house and a happy colony working to prepare for winter. Fresh saplings had been stashed underwater. The dams and house were in good repair. At sunset two adults and three young came out to work. It fulfilled every picture I had read of beaver behavior.

Beavers are like us even more. Some are lazy and will not work at all. Their fellows drive them out. It may be they lose in competition for the females. At any rate, there are many beavers outside the usual colonies. Who knows why they flake out? Our bachelor beaver is one of these. He entertains us. He's such an individual.

The wind felled an old poplar by the boat slip. Our hippie friend topped it and stored limbs in the channel. We fretted needlessly at the obstruction. In a week they were salvaged and eaten. The peeled sticks drifted downstream. He stores nothing for winter. I don't think he believes in banks. He leaves little mud pies on the bank, patted flat and scented. The clay from the stream bottom leaves his prints so clear. I think he advertises for a mate, but not very well. By a colony the scent posts are much larger.

The otter's den is fifty yards upstream from his. Otters are said to sometimes kill beavers. These neighbors seem compatible. At any rate, our beaver has nothing to fear. He is a big fellow. His big brown teeth are as formidable as a woodsman's axe. I doubt that any Michigan predator, except a bear, could lick him.

We have a new balcony. He came to see it. He swam about and splashed repeated alarms at my wife as she worked outside. Finally, his curiosity was satisfied. We'll get no more alarms if we stay on the balcony.

We have other visitors who are curious about our house. Some of them come down the river in boats. 🐾

The other day premature winter weather gave me the blahs and my wife cabin fever. Our bad case of the downs was broken by one of the few birds capable of doing so. A pileated woodpecker visited our front yard. The delightful ten minutes we watched him examine our sick balsams perked up the whole day.

He visited several trees, tapping near the base and listening. One obviously needed attention. He returned to it several times; pried a couple of bark chips from above its root flare—the perfect diagnostician at work. I suspect the problem is carpenter ants. Several of our old firs die each year. Some are loaded with big black ants. A large colony may contain a quart or two of larvae and eggs.

A few days later he was back at the same tree, tapping and listening. A pileated operation is major surgery. It is not undertaken lightly. A huge dead elm upriver has an incision fully eight feet long and eight inches wide. During the operation last winter about two bushels of chips piled the ice below.

A big pileated may be eighteen inches long with a two-and-one-half-foot wingspread. They look black at rest, black and white in flight. The male's forehead and crest is red. He also has a red mustache. The female's only red is her crest. Small woodpeckers have pointed bills. A pileated bill is flattened vertically like an axe. He strikes with it at an angle, prying after each stroke. A skilled axeman splitting wood uses the same motion. Once a cut is well started, chips several inches long may be knocked loose. Most of their feeding holes are rectangular, parallel to the grain.

Last summer a pair of pileateds nested just across river from us. The nest was twenty-two feet up an elm snag. The hole was three and one-half inches wide, four inches high, and almost two feet deep. Nest entrances lack the beveled edges of the feeding holes and are much less conspicuous. They most always face east or south. Pileateds return to the same territory, or even the same tree, for years. Each season they dig a new cavity. It can usually be located by carefully examining the southeast side of all the likely looking trees in the territory.

The Dutch elm disease is a woodpecker boon. A few years ago I doubt there was one pair of pileateds per five miles of our river bottom. This year, in heavily timbered parts, there was a pair for almost every mile of river. It doesn't fully pay for the lost elms, but it helps.

Pileateds seldom come to suet, but when they do they become addicts. Our visitor has so far ignored our offerings, even though lesser woodpeckers feed as he watches. We appreciate his help with the ants, but we would like to get him hooked on suet. He'd make a real bragging type visitor to show off. Is that bad? 🦃

We have an injured black squirrel at our feeders. He is small enough to be a gray squirrel, but I seem to detect a few fulvous hairs in his tail. I believe he is a fox squirrel of this year's brood. He has a deep cut below and along one side at the base of his tail. It is partly healed, but he moves his tail very little. This has greatly altered his behavior.

Of the three kinds of squirrels that visit our feeders, the reds seem most aggressive, fox squirrels next, and grays least. Red squirrels maintain and defend territories. Any animals, including people, are harassed when they enter a red squirrel's territory. Fox and gray squirrels have a social hierarchy in which individuals are ranked by their dominant behavior. They fight over social status rather than territory.

Red squirrels try to chase the big squirrels from their territories. Since grays are not normally resident in our woods, they seldom stay with us long. Harassment by the reds may hasten their departure. Fox squirrels sometimes run a little from red squirrels, but generally they ignore them. The foxes are just so big there really isn't much the reds can do. The popular myth that reds castrate the big squirrels simply isn't so.

Our injured black squirrel is completely submissive. He flees from every red as they drive him from territory to territory across the yard. He feeds only in short snatches when no other squirrels are around.

A squirrel's tail is his crowning glory. Watch how they curve it over their backs, flirt it as they bark. It is essential to social status. Other fox squirrels flirt their tails at our blackie and he cringes. With a lame tail he is pushed to the bottom of the pecking order; even submissive to his little red cousins.

It is impossible to tell what injured our visitor. I suspect our resident goshawk. The cut looks like it was made by a hind talon when the hawk made his strike. Goshawks are the most effective squirrel predators in these parts. No other woods hawks are strong enough to consistently kill fox squirrels. Owls don't get many because the squirrels don't get up till owls go to sleep.

When a goshawk kills a fox squirrel, he picks it just as he would a bird, pulling off little tufts of hair until the carcass is almost denuded. He then tears off bite-size pieces. An owl usually cuts off the head, swallows it whole, then gulps down big chunks, bones, fur, and all.

But regardless of the cause, our blackie has lost his social status. If there is serious muscle damage, it may be permanent. At our feeder there is food for his survival. But without self-respect can he?
🦡

Aggravatingly beautiful, that's the first wet snowstorm. It's best when it comes at night as it did this year, with no wind. Morning finds such splendor spread about, it stirs me almost beyond bearing. I hurry to get out among it, then tarry lest I shatter the magic of this landscape.

Every twig and needle bears a cottony burden. Fence wires are massive cables, impressive, impregnable. All outdoors hangs in suspense as nature sifts down her lacy shower. How gently she places each flake. If I could touch as softly, I could build a house of cards to heaven. I pause at the doorway fearing the whole thing will tumble down.

The dog has no such sentiments. He dashes about, pushes face and shoulder to plow furrows, squirms, back down, snow bathed in luxury. His race through the weeds is a white ripple of explosion leaving a dark ditch laid out by a drunken engineer. For a moment he brings back to me the joys of early childhood.

My grasp of childish wonder is fleeting. Snow-burdened alders block the road. As I shake them free, I reprimand myself for postponing their trimming. Time was when I would have reveled in the great white shower their shaking created. The shower is the same. Only I have changed. Does it have to be that way? The first wet snow always makes me wonder.

A breeze runs a tumbling finger through the snowflakes' house of cards. Handfuls fall, stumbling from branch to branch. I can almost hear that big spruce sigh as it straightens one of its long-burdened fans. The hardwood twigs drop their loads first. Crotches hold onto little clumps. Soon the tag alder run looks like a December cotton field, but giant-sized. I remember rainy years too wet to pick cotton. Then the stalks stood leaf bare and boll heavy; white fields promising lean Christmas if we didn't get picking weather. Now machines get the cotton too fast to worry about, and I am left only with nostalgia by a snow-tufted alder run.

I follow where a deer has been. He snacked on maple tips served down to table level. Each tidbit was one bite only as the snow-loosened limbs spring back to growing height. But, there are plenty; an endless browse buffet.

Under the firs, ground pine supports its own minute snow puff landscape. Perfect in detail, tiny piles of Spanish lace on impossibly delicate green shoulders. I kneel for a closer look to marvel and enjoy.

The breeze dumps a peck of snow down my neck, blinds my bifocals, and suddenly I am old again. ❦

If they can't smell how do they know it's good to eat? This question came up when we tried peanuts in the shell at our bird feeder. A merchant friend gave us a peck of stale peanuts to feed the squirrels. We spread a few handfuls on the balcony. Thirty minutes later they were gone. Even the big fox squirrels couldn't have hauled them off so quickly. Next time we watched—blue jays.

The door was hardly closed when a jay sailed in, looked over the display, and flew off with a peanut grasped precisely at the center crease. The next jay carried his nut to a handy branch. He hacked and pried open one side, gulped the kernel, then opened the other half. An instant expert.

It is most unlikely that these birds had ever seen a peanut. Nothing edible in our part of the country resembles peanuts. Yet the jays accepted them immediately. Furthermore, we found that they cleaned up all the double-kerneled nuts before tackling the singles. When opening a nut the action was the same as used to open acorns; whack whack, pry, whack pry. The surprising thing was that the attack was always on just one kernel. The unopened end was held firmly until the first kernel was swallowed. Then the second was quickly shelled.

Blue jays belong to the Corvidae family as do crows and ravens. This family has the highest brain development of any birds. They are well known for their adaptive resourcefulness. The jays' behavior with peanuts was a perfect demonstration. Jays have insatiable curiosity. They will examine anything unusual. I would expect them to inspect the peanuts. They are plenty smart enough to pick them up at the crease, the obvious hold for easy carrying. But to find them edible, they must have a sense of smell. The olfactory lobes of most bird brains are small. The nasal passages have few of the sensory cells found in mammals' noses. Yet smell is not completely foreign to birds. The primitive kiwis of New Zealand are excellent smellers. Turkey vultures easily locate hidden carrion by its odor. I think most birds can smell a little.

A chickadee made a few tentative hacks at a peanut. Too big. I crushed several nuts. Quickly the chicks ate the crumbs. A hairy woodpecker stuffed a shelled kernel into a hole in our peanut butter feeder, hacked it to pieces, and dined. He searched the empty shells for more. A woodpecker is perfectly capable of opening a peanut. Why didn't he? Either he couldn't smell them through the shell, or was too dumb to try to open it.

The peanuts give us lots of fun and reinforce our respect for the smart jays. I wonder if the other birds will learn from them. If the nuts last, we may find out. ❦

The other day we killed an enemy. It was a satisfying experience for both my dog and me. We don't have many enemies. We war with rats, mice, rabbits, and porcupines when their numbers threaten our life-style. They are not enemies. Individually, most of them are rather appealing. It's their breeding exuberance that causes problems.

The enemy we bested was a big feral house cat. We first suspected her presence in late summer when the wildlife around the house became unexplainably skittish. Normally, small birds, rabbits, and even grouse at our feeders only retreat prudently at our approach. Suddenly they seemed in constant alarm. Grouse fed with crests alert, flushed at the slightest motion. Rabbits ate erratically, dashed about in short sprints. They even came and went in a hurry.

Small birds, particularly the ground feeders, repeatedly exploded. Peace was gone from our little community. Finally my wife identified the villain, a big wild house cat was stalking our feeders. And wild she was. A hard-hunted deer couldn't have been spookier. No way could I get a shot at her.

Domestic house cats often enter our property. They retreat at my appearance, but aren't intentionally elusive. This animal literally vanished on sight. No chance she would return home. She was at home in the woods, and our woods was her choice.

Cats are stalkers and springers. Their retractile claws equip them marvelously for snatching prey in its first dash for freedom: four built-in meat hooks on each paw. Dogs are runners, equipped for sustained speed to overtake their prey. At stalking, dogs and their fox relatives seem almost fumblers when compared to cats in that first killing leap.

Domestic cats were developed from the African and European wild cats. In North America there is no native predator that exactly duplicates them. Our bobcat and lynx are larger and are primarily night hunters. Cats have excellent night vision. They also have good sense of smell, excellent hearing, and special hairs in their ears to catch minute vibrations their other senses don't detect. Domestication has made house cats both day and night hunters. In freeing house cats, we have loosed the world's most efficient small predator on wildlife with no evolutionary experience to elude it.

The dog and I took up the hunt in earnest. Once he treed her and had a brief fight when she leaped down at my approach. Finally we located her den in an impenetrable stump pile. I decided to try trapping. Cat bait is also skunk bait. A skunk in a leg trap is a problem to set free. A live trap baited with a fish head was the answer. A week later we had her.

A .22 shot ended her snarling cage clawing. Dumped out she got a good dog shaking. He's sure he did the killing. I'm glad peace is back at Strawberry Banke. Both of us feel good. 🐾

Deer hunting has many bonuses. Knowing they come, but not knowing how or what, adds to the fun. This year while I watched, I got a bonus, a real unexpected show.

A red squirrel gathered his harvest in the grove where I sat. The ground beneath a big spruce was carpeted with fresh-cut cones. The squirrel was carrying them to a midden further in the swamp. I watched his antics, timed his three-minute round trips. From above and behind me a Cooper's hawk stooped. The squirrel's frantic dash ended in midair. Crushed to the ground, its struggle was brief. I have often seen raptors mantle over their kill. Now I got a close look at why. With wings braced against the ground, the hawk had all the leverage. Treading talons quickly finished the kill.

A mantling hawk looks terribly fierce and aggressive. They seem prepared to defend their kill against all comers. It's not defensive at all, just their fighting technique. Talons are their killing weapons. Spread wings provide the purchase for control.

The Cooper's hawk was a real thrill. The last one I saw on our place was nine years ago. These once-common hawks have all but disappeared from Michigan. Their decline came with the widespread use of DDT. They seem to be more sensitive to this poison than other accipiters.

Cooper's hawks look exactly like larger versions of a sharp-shinned. The bird I watched was a beautiful slate blue on back with darker head and wing tips. Breast and leg feathers were rufous brown. She was about twenty inches long with a wingspread of almost three feet. A male would have been much smaller, no bigger than a large sharp-shinned.

When I was a child, Cooper's hawks were very common in the South, though, like all accipiters, seldom seen. We called them blue darters or chicken hawks. They deserved both names. Chickens usually ran loose in those days. A blue darter could dash in, scoop a chick and be gone in a flash. Then all hawks were considered bad, but blue darters were the worst. Besides killing chickens, quail, and all sorts of good birds, they were so fast and sly as to be very difficult to kill.

Once in a squirrel woods, I brought down a Cooper's hawk with a quick snap shot as it chased a robin almost into my face. As I held its fierce beauty in my hands, I got a very down feeling—what a waste.

Now, fifty years later, I got another chance. The Cooper's deft flip to catch was poetry in motion. Her pose over the twitching squirrel was the essence of magnificent violence. As she carried off her prey, I got a wonderful lift. Maybe Cooper's hawks are coming back. I hope so. ✹

We have rats in our fish pond. That's one of the advantages of living in a river-side forest. It's better to have rats in the pond than in the house. In some cities rats live in houses with the people.

Ours are muskrats, about a foot long with a ten-inch tail. They prefer the water, so we aren't bothered by them in the house. So far they aren't really much trouble around the pond. They don't normally eat fish. Their only digging has been in the low shore which is flooded after every big rain. Their permanent residence seems to be underbrush covering the outlet stream.

They have made a path through the clover as they climb over the dam. To be sure of their identity we spread sand over their roadway. This morning it bore perfect prints of their five-fingered tracks. Muskrats are methodical critters. I have found no place where they entered our pond except by this narrow path. This makes them easy to trap and ready prey for many predators. It's a good thing they are so prolific.

The first litters are born in April or May. Before they are weaned the mother is pregnant again. She kicks out the young as soon as they can feed on their own. Three or four litters a year is the rule. There is no birth control for muskrats. Nature takes care of them by life control. They don't live very long. Just about everything eats them—hawks, owls, foxes, mink, snakes, pike, snapping turtles, and man. About 20 million a year are trapped for their hides. Many of them are eaten.

Try a pot full of muskrats' hind quarters roasted with vegetables. If you don't like eating rats they can be marsh hares. That's what they are called in Louisiana.

Muskrat fur is dense and waterproof underneath with long guard hairs on the outside. Probably no other animal provides more hides to cloth modern man, or rather woman. If you can't afford a mink coat a muskrat one will keep her just as warm so long as she doesn't look at the price tag.

Muskrats live in close harmony with beavers. The two don't compete directly for food. Both of these aquatic rodents use their tails to splash warnings. The muskrat's tail is flattened vertically, but he uses it just as effectively as the beaver does his flat paddle. His warning is not as loud, but it is just as universally recognized.

One spring I was watching a beaver munch willow twigs almost at my feet. A muskrat across the river saw my head above the bushes and splashed a warning. The beaver departed promptly. In the wilds when someone shouts "Danger!" no one questions him, even though he is a rat. 🌱

A flicker visited us in a drift of snowflakes. He's late, the first I've seen in over a month. In our part of the country flickers, sapsuckers, and red-headed woodpeckers migrate. Other woodpeckers stay year round.

Flickers feed on the ground more than most woodpeckers and are particularly fond of ants. That's probably the reason they migrate. They don't go far. Besides ants, they probe the lawn for grubs, catch grasshoppers, and perform aerial acrobatics chasing flying insects. They visit our feeders for corn, eat berries and acorns in fall and winter.

Woodpeckers have extensible tongues that start in front of their eyes, go over and around the cranium and to the beak. They can extend them more than twice the bill's length. Most have hard-pointed tips with back-pointing barbs. When they find a wood borer's tunnel they harpoon the grub and rake it out. Flickers don't have many barbs. Their tongues have a thick viscous mucous about like flypaper. A flicker pokes his beak into an ant's nest, runs out his tongue and brings it out loaded. The mucous is highly alkaline to offset the formic acid in the ants. That's what makes ant bites smart.

While flickers don't generally chop wood for a living, they do dig nest holes. Saw-whet and screech owls favor flicker holes. Sometimes flickers repair old nest cavities, often make the openings large enough for wood ducks. Flickers will use birdhouses—sometimes they nest in our wood duck boxes. They prefer the boxes poorly located on isolated trees. The ducks prefer more cover. If a box is consistently used by flickers, I move it to a shadier spot. One box has twice produced wood ducks followed by a late brood of flickers.

Most eastern flickers are yellow-shafted, beautiful yellow under wings and tail. We called them "yellow hammers" in the South, shot them to eat, stuck the yellow-quilled feathers in our hats. Out west flickers are red-shafted—salmon pink under wings and tails. Male eastern flickers have black mustaches, westerners have red mustaches. Where their ranges overlap, they interbreed. Sometimes a hybrid will have a mustache red on one side, black on the other. Some hybrids have orange underwings. Occasionally we see a full-fledged red-shafted flicker in the East. Ornithologists call them all one species, even including the gilded flicker that lives in the southwestern desert.

Besides three different forms, flickers probably have more nicknames than any other bird: 132 for the yellow-shafted alone. I don't recognize but one. Yellow hammer just suits him. He is bold, bright, and friendly. When he beats his mating tattoo on our T.V. aerial in spring, he can waken the dead. When I find one of his molted yellow quills, I still stick it in my hat.

And his yellow-hammering flight through the snowflakes holds off winter a little bit longer. ❧

Every hunt camp should have a stewpot. For reviving the spirits and restoring the energy of cold, wet, tired hunters, no food can compete with a steaming bowl of good camp stew.

When I was a mere slip of a kid my hunting uncle used to take me to deer camp for a week each Christmas vacation. One of my fondest memories of those adventures was the huge old soap kettle full of stew which always nestled in one corner of the big fireplace.

While the adults sat around recuperating over moonshine and branch water, I would light into a bowl or two of that steaming ambrosia. For a twelve year old, happiness was dozing before the hearth, warm inside and out, listening to the tales of bucks with rocking chair racks and infallible strike dogs that never quit on a trail. (It was, and still is, legal in Mississippi to hunt deer with dogs.) I usually had to be wakened to eat dinner. You know, I can't remember what we had for those evening meals—but that stew, man!

It was a rule in that camp that anyone who got a buck had to quit deer hunting. The lucky hunters were relegated to the pursuit of small game. This supplied a steady stream of rabbits, squirrels, quail, dove, duck, and miscellaneous critters, many of which ended up in the stewpot. Each bowl full was a new adventure in eating.

I remember my uncle telling how to start off one of those stews. Take an old dominicker rooster, four or five old squirrels, a handful of red peppers, some butter beans—and on and on. The recipe is sort of flexible, but for the modern hunt camp stew here's one way to get started. Squirrels should be the basic ingredient.

Disjoint a couple of old squirrels and put them in a pot of water with a couple of venison shanks, or you can use turkey legs if you don't have venison. Add a bay leaf and lots of red pepper flakes. Simmer for a couple of hours until the meat is ready to fall from the bones. Save the stock.

Remove the meat and debone it. This is best done with the fingers, so you can feel the small squirrel bones. Discard the bay leaf. Cover the meat with enough of the stock to keep it moist.

In a heavy pot fry out four thick slices of bacon cut in one-inch pieces until they are cooked, but not brown. In the bacon fat sauté four or five good hot onions chopped coarsely. Don't brown them. Put the remaining stock, all the meat, and the bacon back in the pot.

Drain a can each of lima beans, whole kernel corn, and tomatoes. Put these in the pot and let it simmer until it's the right consistency. Add a glass of dry vermouth or sherry. Simmer a bit to meld the flavors. Add salt to taste. Serves four. Expand as needed.

If you can ever get the hunters out of camp with this stuff on the stove, you'll find it's better the next day. But—I could never wait that long. ✹

Kinglet means little king. I think it admirably suits the two birds that bear that name. Yesterday I watched a golden-crowned kinglet from my deer blind. Next to the hummingbird he is our smallest bird and by far the smallest feathered visitor to our winter woods.

The one I watched was a male. His crown had black stripes on the sides, yellow above, then a bright orange red patch in the middle. The females lack the orange patch. This fellow thoroughly gleaned the little balsams before me. He was finding something, for his tiny bill probed in constant motion. He seemed incapable of moving without his wings. Kinglets flit about with light-speed flutters. Sometimes they hover momentarily to reach an inaccessible spot. I did not see him hop or turn upside down like a chickadee. He hovered below and reached up for the tidbits. How many ways nature has taught birds to make a living!

Some golden-crowned kinglets spend each winter with us. To stand the cold, they stay out of the wind. They knew about windchill long before the term was coined by our weather bureaus. Kinglets prefer conifers. These are always warmer than hardwoods.

Kinglets are kin to Old World warblers. They aren't closely related to the wood warblers so numerous in America. Only four of their family live in North America; the golden- and ruby-crowned kinglets and the gnatcatchers. (Now there's a name to live up to.)

We see ruby-crowned kinglets mostly in spring migration. The males have a little dab of red head top that shows sometimes. Last spring a young friend said, "Look, a hummingbird," as a ruby-crowned hovered momentarily outside her windows. It's an easy mistake to make. Kinglets are tiny and they do hover momentarily in their search for insects. They won't stay still for careful study. Their chunky shape used to cause them to be called wrens.

Both kinglets nest in the Northern lake states, but the nests are hard to find. The golden-crowned build high in conifers, up to sixty feet. The nests are of green moss lined with feathers and hair. They must be well insulated, for the hen lays eight to ten eggs in two layers. It must be a chore for such a tiny bird to keep them all warm and uniformly incubated. Can you imagine trying it for two solid weeks? Yet, they do.

These little birds are well named. Thoreau called them golden-crested wrens. My young friend said hummingbirds. In Europe they are warblers. Yet, kinglets they must be. No other name quite suited the confident sprite that searched the balsams on my winter day. The drab gray sky and gray winter woods were brightened by his presence. Only royalty could attack such dreariness so confidently.

Truly, kinglet is the right word. Miniature royalty in the wilds.

If a shrew was as big as a cat, we wouldn't be safe in the woods. These tiny, evil-smelling, hunger-driven furies will attack anything they can master and some things they cannot.

The other day, while clearing brush, I found one dead. Superficially he looked like a mouse, but his nose was more pointy, his tail shorter. His mouth, full of needle-sharp teeth, was set well back under his nose. His odor discouraged closer inspection, but I identified him as probably a masked shrew, the most common member of the family in Michigan.

Shrews, our smallest mammals, live in a superspeed miniworld, inconceivable to us humans. An earthworm is a boa constrictor, a grasshopper, a dragon. Both are grist for his mill. With 1,200 heartbeats a minute, a shrew's metabolism drives him in a constant frantic search for food. He attacks anything without fear, for his only alternative is starvation.

With such an appetite where is the time for other things? Yet, shrews breed early and often. Females may reach sexual maturity at four months. Gestation is about three weeks. They die of old age in less than two years. Here is an animal reduced to fundamentals—survival of the individual, survival of the species. Their entire existence seems devoted to these two goals.

One winter I was amazed to see what I thought was a mouse plowing through the snow to our woodpile. A stirring of sticks flushed the quarry for our dachshund, who promptly shook it to death—but not before the tiny victim fastened its teeth into the dog's lip. It was a short-tailed shrew, our only poisonous mammal. Saliva from these little devils can paralyze their prey and is extremely painful to larger animals. Our dog flung the ill-smelling varmint aside and whimpered in pain as her jaw swelled.

No mouse would have been bold enough to be about at midday in the snow. I should have recognized the shrew and left it alone. They are very beneficial, eating a multitude of insects, snails, mice, and more of our objectionable neighbors. We seldom see them, for they like damp woodsy places and are too small and quick to catch our eyes.

There are about thirty kinds of shrews in America. One of them, the water shrew, can walk on water. Long bristles on his hind feet support him in high-speed rushes over the water's surface tension. I've only seen one, but each summer some are reported by trout fishermen. A friend who saw one dive, said it glistened silver underwater from the air bubbles trapped in its hair. Who would wade our streams if these were as big as otters?

Nature, in her wisdom, has evolved everything into a place. She makes shrews small lest she decimate the world. I wonder what control she puts on man? 🦋

If you see a duck with a John Barrymore profile it's a canvasback. These big white, black, and chestnut divers arrived this fall in greater quantity than I have seen in years. Their increase is a sure sign of plentiful rain in the prairies. They nest in the most drought ridden parts of our prairie states and provinces.

I love to watch these streamlined birds feeding. They dive with a powerful thrust upwards, jackknifing under with hardly a ripple. They stay under longer than most of the other species in our refuge.

Canvasbacks are the fastest flyers of our ducks. At times they seem to literally hurtle through the air. All diving ducks have smaller wing areas than puddle ducks of the same size. This requires them to get a running start over the water to get awing. Puddle ducks leap into the air with a powerful wing thrust against the water. A mallard can fly straight up, a maneuver a canvasback would never even consider. Once in the air the divers fly with more rapid wing beats, which makes them easily distinguishable from the puddle ducks.

I will never forget my first hunting contact with canvasbacks. It was in a layout boat years ago when "cans" were much more plentiful. A small flock appeared low over the water headed right for my big decoy spread. Used to mallards in the potholes, I expected them to flare away when I sat up. I completely misjudged their speed. Suddenly I seemed the target of a dozen big black and white projectiles. They swept over, gun barrel high, with a rush of wings that actually intimidated me. Never before or since have I been so mistreated by wildfowl. My one forlorn shot charge must have been yards behind. I eventually learned to bag divers over decoys, but I never could avoid a sinking feeling when a big bunch of cans swung into the spread. It's almost like being introduced to royalty.

Canvasbacks are exclusively North American. Even strays have not been recorded elsewhere. They've been hunted since man first came to our continent. One of the earliest known decoys is a canvasback made of tightly bound reeds. It was found in a cave near one of our prehistoric lakes in the western high desert.

Watching these burly speedsters diving and flying their daily constitutional I got a wonderful feeling of well-being. They were so terribly depleted by drainage and drought in their homeland. To see them again reestablished my faith in conservation. It just has to be worthwhile. ❈

A mink can do anything he wants to do except fly, and he can do it as well as he has to. I was impressed with this the other day as I watched the little female mink that lives in our woods. She swam the river as fast as a muskrat, but with her bushy tail floating high behind. We watched her scramble over a logjam investigating every cranny. She climbed nimbly up a vertical snag, then disappeared down the shore in a hump-backed lope fast enough to overtake most any prey.

Adaptation-wise the mink falls between the weasel and the otter, both in size and ability. He climbs well enough to prey on squirrels, though he probably couldn't catch one in an all-out chase through the trees. Muskrats are easy and favorite prey. He readily catches fish and frogs. Last winter I tracked one that captured a rabbit. The big snowshoe only managed two desperate leaps. The mink's closing rush must have been lightening fast. There are better swimmers, climbers, and runners, but I know of no predator that combines all three so adequately.

We first discovered our resident female two winters ago when our Lab sent a muffled bark down a bankside hole. The odor in reply was unmistakable. Mink have musky anal glands like most of the weasel family. They can't spray like a skunk, but they are much more careless. They release their perfume at the slightest disturbance. Thank goodness it's not so foul as their striped cousins'.

That spring our mink had six kits. We saw their tracks in the June mud. She raised them alone, for we never saw the father's prints. Male mink are real rounders, though they usually settle down with the last female they mate. Ours must have been earlier in line.

Most mink I have seen seem always hunting, constantly searching about. In the snow I sometimes see their slide marks, so they must play some like otters.

One deer hunt I watched a big male come through the snowy swamp. It was bitter cold, but there was open water all about. This big fellow held a straight line. His intentness impressed me; over logs and ice, swimming and running with never even a pause to shake dry. The males are great travelers, but I wonder what errand drove him so determinedly on. It was long before mating season.

Only once have I seen a mink at rest. One spring day as I crept up to a pond, a rumbling purr caught my ear. A mink lay curled like a family cat. The purr was pure contentment. Even relaxing a mink does it exceedingly well. 🐾

The opening day for deer hunting, of bird season, duck hunting, trout opener, and pike and bass—milestones in earth's annual trek around the sun. I've spent a lifetime counting them, regretting the few I've missed, rejoicing in the others. Some of the happiest times were in getting ready for openers, and surely the sleep I lost the nights before never added one iota to fatigue.

Since arthritis slowed my hunting and fishing, I've done a lot of thinking about opening days. Except for deer, they are seldom the best days to hunt or fish. It's the anticipation. It builds and builds until for me the first day was like the gigantic "whoosh" after holding and holding my breath. Flooded trout streams, wind-swept bass lakes, leafy bird covers, and mosquito-filled duck blinds never made any difference. I haven't shot my deer on opening day since our kids got big enough to hunt. Most openers are long forgotten. It's the getting ready that sticks with me.

All hunters and fishermen are optimists. I suppose some pessimists try it, but they never become addicted. If you are not sure a deer will come down your runway, or every cover holds a bird, every pool a trout, or each weed bed a lunker bass or pike, then it's not any fun.

When I used to trout fish, getting ready started in March. For some reason my best flies were always in bad shape—moths got them, or fish slime matted them hopelessly. The new ones I tied looked delicious. I could just see that big brown behind a particular log smacking his lips. Most openers found me crawling through snow-drifted alders seeking an unflooded tributary to dunk worms in. Still, I'd had that big brown for two months in my dreams, and some day, some day, we'll meet.

Our daughters and their families and friends hunt deer with us. Since we live with the deer, my getting ready consists of checking neighboring crops and their effect on the runway usage. Our deer sleep with us and eat with the neighbors. The girls come out a day or two before the season, check the blinds, make plans.

"The best bet is the front blind. A doe and two fawns live right there; a buck's got some of those bushes all beat up. The sand ridge has some big tracks. We have killed more bucks on that stand than anywhere else. The 'hot dog stand' is all punched up. Lots of small tracks. There were six bucks in Bud's field last week. Some of them have to come by the north blind." Everyone goes to bed with a deer in their pocket.

On opening day for some it's all over in a few minutes. There are misses and sometimes just no deer. But, for everyone, there is always tomorrow and another opener and expectations that sometimes come true. That's what keeps us coming back. ❧

To really appreciate the majesty of wind I go to the lakefront in a southeast gale. My favorite place is a rocky man-made promontory thrusting a blunt nose into the foaming rollers that pile in from the big lake.

Gulls go there too. They stand in serried ranks facing direct to the wind. Let the storm shift one compass point and all will move to greet it. Each must stand so the roaring wind keeps every feather in place. The windchill glances off and hurries on to plague the landscape. I think gulls like wind.

They tolerate my presence. As I approach, they move aside reluctantly. Each has a selected spot. They side step, back and fill, but only see me corner-eyed, for bills must face the gale, compass true. They finally must go—two flaps to hoist, then tilt-winged gliding—up and down, back and forth—self-controlled puppets with the gale holding elastic strings. When I pass, invisible pulleys lower flat pink feet to the same prints. What master wisdom selected these spots to ride out the gale? They stand just off the flood brought by the big rollers. They get no wet feet, no foam-spattered plummage. With confidence they watch the awesome twelve-footers roll in and burst in white shrapnel, inches from their post.

Most are herring gulls, big gray and white veterans of our northern winters. A few brown youngsters imitate their elders. There in their midst is a stranger—small as a blue jay, yet chunky gray and white. White head and black ear spot identifies him as a Bonaparte's gull. These little gulls nest in the northern spruce forests. Each fall I see a few in wind-faced flocks of local gulls. In a storm I think they like their big cousins' company.

In spring some flocks pass our Great Lakes on their way northwest to breeding. Then they wear black heads in courtship dress. One April I watched two dozen search a Superior harbor for a proper place to light. They swept and wheeled across the waterfront till all the Audubonists in town had set up scopes and glasses to watch their flight. They lit in three-foot chop, like ballet on a stage. Next day they left for inland mating chores.

Big wind is a show of nature's strength. Sometimes it frightens me. Outside our wooded home the balsams buggy whip. The maples struggle, branch by branch. Forest birds disappear. All woodland life takes shelter. My woodland ancestors urge me to stay snug inside my architectural shell.

But I must visit the shore to dare the wind! That huge wave coming stands my hair on end! I almost flee, but stand my ground, for there the gulls face calmly windward and in their midst one small stranger—unafraid.

December

"Between the dark and the daylight" was Longfellow's "The Children's Hour." At our place, with the kids all grown-up, it's the wildlife hour. There are two of them each day: dawn and dusk. For many wild animals and birds, they are the most important times of the day. I like dawn best.

As this first shift change time approaches, the nocturnal predators step up their hunting. Often just before first light I hear our barred owl's hunting call. This is not the "who cooks———" hooting conversation. It's a loud screaming "who—ew." Always single. I think it is designed to frighten small creatures into movement. It must work, for in the still darkness it shivers me a bit. Owls often hunt till good light. No screaming then. Best not to warn the early daytime risers. In daylight, sight is a better hunting tool than sound.

Grouse like an early breakfast. They come to a little glade by the river. Its strawberry leaf pavement is choice fodder until snow. Last week the owl came there too. Scattered feathers and a smear of milk white droppings told the story.

My dog and I walk about each dawn to greet the day. He sniffs out the story of last night's happenings. Sometimes we interrupt little dramas. Last summer we found a fresh-killed robin nestling in the path. When we returned ten minutes later, it was gone. Who dropped it? Did he return, or did some other forager scoop up his prize? What a rush of unseen life goes on about us!

But, all is not violence in the wildlife hours. Chickadees are the first visitors at our feeders. Infinitesimal animated shadows in a joyous rush to the breakfast table. In winter each dawn is a new lifeline for birds. They use food at a furious rate to keep warm. In the long cold nights they get dangerously short of fuel. For small winter birds each night is potential disaster. Yet, chickadees ignore this sword of Damocles. Their only concession is to stay for seconds at supper and never be late for breakfast. Who could ask for more enthusiastic boarders?

Deer hunters see the wildlife hours at their best. On cloudy mornings the light seems not to come from east. It arrives simultaneously all around. From my "hide" suddenly I can see ghosts moving. Early deer leaving the farm fields. They dally on the way to cover. Eyes strain to hurry the laggard sun. The ghosts pause, then vanish. Some tiny sound, or perhaps a vagrant breeze gave me away.

Now, finally I can see all about. Little night creatures move to rest. Day birds appear. A fox squirrel, always sleepyhead, scampers along a limb. Another wildlife hour is past. ✹

As we ate breakfast one snowy morning we watched three common mergansers hunting theirs. They swam slowly upstream, faces submerged. Occasionally one slowed, completely submerged his head for a better look. They dived frequently. They kept out of the main current to dodge the drifting ice, explored beneath the logjams, frequently swam under the shore ice.

Despite the twelve-degree temperature, their actions reminded me of the snorkeling I once did over coral reefs on the coast of Mexico. I spent hours of one vacation floating facedown over those underwater gardens, diving occasionally for a closer look or to hand-feed fish with shrimp scrounged from the hotel cook. These mergansers were not fish feeders. They were the feedees. Most of their catch were chubs, probably the most abundant fish in our stream.

These ducks, all drakes, stayed around for several days. Once they were joined by two more, again by a single hen. We never saw them hunting downstream. They knew what I learned in Mexico. It is better to swim against the current. Going with the tide is too fast for good looking. These birds were snorkel experts.

Mergansers eat mostly fish. They catch some crayfish and occasionally a clam or snail. In spring the little hooded mergansers take grain we put out for the whistlers and puddle ducks. Our river is not a good merganser stream—too cloudy. In winter it clears. That's when the big common mergansers come to fish. They don't stay; just visit when wind keeps them off the big lake. Hundreds winter there, far out in open water. They come daily to factory outfalls to catch fish attracted by the warm water.

Common mergansers are almost identical to the European goosander which nests across northern Europe and Asia. In fact, European ornothologists call our bird "American goosander." Both species prefer to nest in tree hollows, but will use a burrow or nest on the ground. We found a nest with eighteen eggs on a Lake Huron island. It was completely masked by vegetation; would never have found it had the hen not flushed. She had sought out the nearest thing to a hollow on that little island.

Drake goosanders (I like that name) are among our most beautiful waterfowl. The impression is mostly white with black accents. The white breast is tinted salmon pink, head iridescent green, bill dark red. They are as big as mallards, but lankier. The hens are much smaller, drab gray and brown, white bellies. Young of both sexes resemble the hen. They don't complete adult plumage until the second autumn.

The beauty and skill of these fish-hunting ducks delights us. Let the winter storm blow and snow. It brings the goosanders to visit. We watch them from the luxury of thermopane and electric heat, and shiver in our comfort. 🦌

From a field-side deer stand I watched another predator doing a much better job of stand sitting. Statue still, a northern shrike sat on the tip of a bare maple commanding a view of the field. Suddenly, on flickering wings, he plunged out of sight in the grass. Minutes later he flew heavily to a nearby fence with his prey.

A sound in the brush brought me back to deer hunting, but next day I found time to examine the fence wire. A few scraps of mouse skin and bone hanging from one of the barbs identified the shrike's meal. These bloodthirsty little hunters are perching birds turned predator. They don't have strong-taloned feet like hawks and owls, and must impale their prey on a thorn or barb to hold it while they feed. This has earned them the nickname of "butcher bird."

The northern shrike which I saw, nests north of here. Some visit us every winter. Always alone, their attitude is one of arrogant self-sufficiency. A black face mask and somber gray, black, and white feathers do nothing to improve the picture. Around a bird feeder they create absolute panic; vivid testimony to their rapacious reputation.

I am more familiar with the loggerhead shrike, a slightly smaller cousin, common in the South, and a scattered nester in Michigan. A pair of these always nested in a grove of locust trees near my boyhood home. The two-inch sweet locust thorns were often festooned with grasshoppers, june bugs, and an occasional small bird or mouse. When hunting is good shrikes often store food on these natural meat hooks. With young the store is quickly used, but at other times the larder may be forgotten. This has caused an unjustified reputation for wanton killing. Where shrikes are common they are accused of impaling living victims out of plain cruelty. This is completely untrue. Their weak feet prevent them from carrying off their prey until it is quite dead.

As a child I believed butcher birds capable of any crime, and only the fearful thorns of their nesting tree protected them from my wrath. I once saw one kill a house sparrow. The shrike's aim was poor and the kill was not quick. It was a wretched bloody struggle as he pecked his victim to death. I wept bitter tears for the bloody handful of feathers from which I drove the killer. Years later I watched a more proficient shrike kill a bird with one swift blow of his hooked beak, but it did little to improve my regard for the species.

My learning tells me they are part of nature's balance, but with shrikes I still suffer from my childhood prejudices. **¥**

Color in the outdoors is a special treat in winter. We seem to be living in a gray, black, and white world. Even the evergreens look black against the pearl gray sky. This winter has been an almost endless succession of wretchedly cold, gray days. The other day my wife called me to a sight that changed the landscape.

A blue jay, evening grosbeak, and a pair of cardinals were at the feeder together. Even in summer it would have been worth seeing. Against the snow it was spectacular. These three species are our only really colorful winter birds. Some of them are with us each year. We seldom see them together.

The cardinals like to feed on the ground. The evening grosbeaks prefer our high balcony feeder. The blue jays are everywhere. This year we are overrun with blue jays. After a late jay migration, we had a normal winter population. In mid-December fifty new blue jays arrived. They stayed, and the bird feed has disappeared at an alarming rate.

Blue jays are members of a very old family. They apparently evolved in the northern hemisphere of the Old World long before flowering plants developed. They and their relatives, the crows, are among the smartest of birds and very adaptable. They will eat anything they can swallow, animal or vegetable. We marvel at the blue jays' antics and delight in their snow-framed color. Still, fifty blue jays at the feeders is too many.

The cardinals and evening grosbeaks evolved with the seed-bearing plants. They represent parallel evolution; cardinals from the New World tropics, evening grosbeaks from Eurasia. Except when feeding young, both are vegetarians. The evening grosbeaks developed to exploit seeds from large trees. I think that is the reason ours show a great preference for the high feeder.

Like most New World finches, the cardinals find most of their food near the ground. The two that stayed with us year round fed only on cracked corn we spread for the doves, grouse, and sparrows, and sunflower seed spilled below our high feeder. At Christmas another pair and an odd male cardinal arrived. The female found our high feeder and soon brought her mate. This was the couple that made up the triple color treat.

It was remarkable to have birds of such dissimilar habits side by side; high feeder, low feeder, and omnivorous. Sunflower seeds did the trick. The thing that overpowers my imagination is the miles and millenia of evolution that brought this blue, red, and yellow to our snowy window.

This miserably cold weather has almost made me homesick for Mississippi—something I thought was long since past. Those colors against the snow changed that and, once again, made the forty-fifth parallel winter worthwhile. ✹

How tall is a deer? Well, it depends on whether you are measuring or wishing. When you measure, what do you measure to? A big buck may go three feet at the withers. That's the high spot in the back between the shoulders. A real whopper might go three and one-half feet. Some deer aren't two feet tall. Sometimes that's tall enough; often it isn't.

The important height for a deer is the distance from his mouth to the ground. In winter that's one to four feet. If there is plenty of feed in that three-foot vertical spread, the deer herd will be healthy and all of them will be tall enough.

We have a big bird feeder on a front yard post. Deer come each evening to get spillings from it. Last winter some learned to stand on their hind feet and lick out the grain; a fun show, but expensive. This year we raised the feeder. One big buck can still reach it. Counting the longest tongue in the woods, he's over six feet from tip to tip. For him that's tall enough. The smaller deer just stand and watch.

When deer do much feeding on their hind legs they are in trouble. It means food in that vital three-foot-high browsing height is running short. Deer will stretch mightily for a special treat like our bird feed. They will paw through a foot of snow for one acorn. For bread and butter eating they take what's handy. Preferred food goes first, but if there is a serious overpopulation, everything in easy reach is soon eaten. Then the small deer go hungry.

I suppose Bambi would have bent down boughs for the fawns to reach. That's not the way it is in real life. Last winter we cut five acres of cedar. About thirty deer fed on the tops. Each weekend everything green was cleaned up. The little deer always missed Sunday night supper. Time after time I watched does drive their own fawns away. These deer weren't starving, but when there was the slightest bit of competition for food the smaller deer lost out. When there is serious overpopulation, Mother Nature raises the feeder just as we did. There may be plenty for the six-footers and nothing for the fawns. Then the big deer get bigger. The little deer starve; not a nice way to go.

It's a shame wishing won't make deer taller. It would help the fawns and hunters too. Last season my oldest daughter dozed in her blind. She awoke to find a beautiful buck right in front. One shot and it was all over. "If he had been eight feet tall, I would have hit him dead center."

He was so short he got away. That's tall enough. 🦌

How does the word get around? The day after the first heavy snow three doves appeared at our feeders, next day there were five, then fifteen. Who told them where the free lunch was?

These were not newly arrived migrants. Around here the southward movement of mourning doves is usually complete by mid-October. The area's winter population is already established, but widely scattered. We saw hundreds of doves feeding with the ducks in picked cornfields. When snow covered the grainfields, the ducks went south. I think most of the doves stayed. Some found our feeder. How did they do it?

Winter doves are great flockers. Like ducks, they decoy readily to members of their own kind. Most of the decoying is done on the wing. While hunting in the South I have often seen flock after flock swing to join others headed for feed or water. Migrating flocks don't decoy to each other. Like people, birds in transit seem to stick with their own group. They may follow well-defined aerial freeways, but they prefer to stay out of heavy traffic. It's at the stopping places that crowds gather. Those without prior reservations follow the locals to the shopping center.

Many birds return repeatedly to the same wintering spot. Nonmigrant chickadees, nuthatches, and woodpeckers come back to our place year after year. We check them by their band numbers. Even evening grosbeaks, great random wanderers, sometimes have favorite resorts. One banded grosbeak commuted between Sault Ste. Marie, Michigan, and Sandwich, Massachusetts, for several years, the same feeder station at both ends of the line.

Maybe doves behave the same. Last winter we fed thirty or forty of them for three months. Surely some of them survived to remember our cafe in the woods. Fall dove flocks are probably 75 percent birds of the year. A pair may nest three or four times and successfully fledge six young. Most of these youngsters don't survive to breed. This tremendous annual mortality is normal for most bird species. It is nature's way of keeping this species strong. Only one out of every three or four will live.

Last winter we watched this law at work. A goshawk fed regularly on our doves. He always caught the straggler, the panicky, the ailing. By spring the survivors were tough, wary, and super, super flyers. Evolution does not work by protecting the average. It selects the superior, but to do this, most of each year's crop must die.

Of course, no life-form dies willingly. They develop tricks to beat the rap. Flocking and decoying is one of these devices. Even a fool can survive in a crowd. These counterforces of survival are one reason evolution is so slow.

I suspect our first doves had reservations from last year. Most of the others just followed them here. It's good to have the old-timers back and the newcomers too.

Our river is the Salvador Dali of the winter landscape. Its sepia surface paints in surrealist reproduction. Cross-stream hardwoods lay snow-burdened treetops at my feet, fretted into nightmare shapes by passing water.

A breeze tumbles snow blobs from above. Images rush cross stream to meet their creators, always dead center in bull's-eyes of wavelets, drawn after splashdown, current quick erased. Quicksilver sky is bronzed by tea brown water.

I watch a tireless current bobbing drift log and fantasize of monsters surfacing to search for prey. The master artist finger-paints dimples and curls among the tree trunks. If I could freeze an instant of this animation, I would hang it to remind of sleep-hazed thoughts, days adrift in aimless contemplation—unconscious creation—watching waters.

Winter gives short time for daydreaming. Wind-loosened snow plunges down my collar to end my reveries. Shivers are natures cover tossers. They shake out hallucinations, erase reflections, and rattle treetops in cold reality. Rivers do things other than painting.

Our river is a highway past our door, a three-dimensional thoroughfare for fish and muskrats, beavers, otters, and all sorts of things that swim. The fish, the clams, crayfish, insect larva, all the mini-life-forms live in little traffic safety islands behind rocks, in eddies, by wrinkles in the bottom. Life in a river depends on how many homes it has. Left alone, water wants to wander. There are no straight rivers. They curve at pools, run straight over riffles, sort out the sediments to roughen the bottom.

Friction slows the bottom current. Surface water hurries on unhampered. This corkscrews the current, moving it ever sideways. Outside curves are cut, insides built. Gravity urges water to rush to the sea as it started from a raindrop. The laws of hydraulics bids it linger, change speed in bits and pieces, shift its freight load about. And so makes homes for little wildlife and food for bigger things.

Our river is old enough to have a floodplain, a flat valley to meander through. Each year it overflows its banks, slows as it floods and deposits silt. So it builds levees. The riverbanks get flooded most. Only a real flood reaches the floodplain shore. So the banks get most silt, building ever higher to levee in the water. Finally, some big flood beyond the levee finds a new way out. It cuts a fresh channel leaving the old one an oxbow lake to fill over the millenia.

The floodplain of our stream is full of these ancient riverbeds. Special kinds of water-loving trees live there, and animals that like muddy feet and the bounty of the river's minihomes.

A river is a nursery of life, a marvelous product of hydraulic laws. And if you dream a bit while watching, it paints surrealist pictures.

How do you fight for life? Each day we watch a small sparrow fighting the battle on the knife edge of survival.

An injured song sparrow comes to our front yard. Half its tail feathers gone, one injured wing—it flutters rather than flies. I suspect it is a near miss victim of the sharp-shinned hawk that harassed our yard at peak sparrow migration. It could not go south with its fellows, so now it must fight for life in an alien climate. Crippled, its feathers in tatters, the little mite must work very hard just to live.

Last summer a pair of song sparrows built their second nest in a small spruce a few feet from where we now scatter feed. The female built the nest in two days, then laid an egg a day for four days. One disappeared, but twelve days later three healthy youngsters hatched. In less than two weeks they were flying.

It is most unlikely that our present guest is from that brood. Still, it is interesting to see the drama of bare survival played out on the same stage where last summer we watched the theatrical performance of reproduction.

Then, while his mate brooded, the male sparrow sang endlessly. Feeding the nestlings left little time for song. Still, the two weeks after hatching were busy, lively days. There were endless trips with insects. The young literally bloomed. Every day saw a change. By fledging they overflowed the nest. Had all four eggs hatched, how could there have been room?

Earlier we had found a first nesting on the ground. Five eggs hatched. After a week we sometimes found one or more young out of the nest. We tried to help by piling them back, two deep. Somehow all five were fledged. I now suspect they may not have needed our help. Wild things are remarkably resourceful, and these wandering nestlings were never more than a few inches from home. Tree nests are much more hazardous. A fall from the site, even in our two-foot-high spruce, might have put a youngster too far from parental care. Still, freedom from ground predators must justify the risk of falling, for song sparrows almost always select a tree or bush when foliage provides concealment above ground.

Our crippled boarder roosts in a thicket of tiny firs beside the path. He can barely flutter the few feet from food to shelter. He eats the smaller bits of cracked corn. If snow covers the food he waits till the grouse arrive. They scratch away the snow. He gets the scraps they miss.

We rejoice at his daily appearance. Slowly we've learned how he does it. He fights one day at a time. Living just one day is good, even if the tail you flirt to prove it has only two bent feathers. ❦

Gulls are the garbage disposals of the bird world. They will eat anything that resembles food and some things that don't. Vultures and other carrion eaters have appetites only for meat and fish. A herring gull will eat anything from grain to a dead horse. They are as omnivorous as man and not nearly so finicky.

It seems to me that most of the herring gulls that winter in the North survive only because of our garbage dumps. When I make my weekly trip to the dump there are always ranks of them standing, face to the wind, waiting. A few restless birds sail fruitlessly over the rubbish, but mostly they just wait.

I used to think this was just a continuation of the stupid behavior of young gulls who suffer so many fatal accidents each summer. I was wrong. Gulls aren't stupid. The young are ignorant because their parents abandon them, untrained as soon as they can fly. Those that survive this rude plunge into deep water turn out to be pretty smart birds.

My plastic-bagged waste just doesn't turn them on, but let the commercial garbage trucks show up and they know dinner is served. There is no waiting then. If there were an avian Emily Post she would whirl in her grave at the behavior of gulls at a fresh-turned garbage dump.

Due to the mild fall, a few ring-billed gulls haven't migrated. They won't stay long, for in the scramble for food they stand no chance against their larger cousins. Our winter gull society is ruled strictly by the herring gulls.

They are the most abundant North American gull, possibly the most abundant worldwide—they should be. Aggressive, smart, omnivorous, and adaptable, they survive with man because they have similar characteristics. All the birds which succeed with humans have these qualities. Look at the crows, starlings, blackbirds, and house sparrows.

Herring gulls are a long time growing up. It takes four years for them to progress from the brown fledgling plumage to the pearl gray and white of an adult. This gives time for learning. They moult twice a year. Each feather change gets progressively lighter. You can pretty well gauge their age class by their color. The percentage of birds of various plumage shades gives a good idea of each year's nesting success.

Soon our herring gulls will have a new test of adaptability. Landfill dumps are obsolete. When we use them no more, we will no longer need the gulls' help in recycling. I think they will make it O.K., but they may go south with the ring-billeds.

Then I'll miss their wings against the winter sky, and their yelping will lend nostalgia even to a garbage dump. ❧

Anyone who has eaten peanut butter sandwiches would feel kinship with a chickadee eating peanut butter in warm weather. The delicious goody has a way of gumming up the eating apparatus unequaled by any other modern food.

Last year a friend presented us with a bird peanut butter feeder. It was a sixteen-inch-long, three-inch-wide cedar stick. A dozen half-inch holes were bored partway through, at random. To load it you plug the holes with peanut butter.

We filled it a few times last winter. Chickadees came to chip out the frozen nut-hard butter. Their antic clinging to the peeled stick was entertaining. Peanut butter is not a staple with us. Plenty of other bird feed was at hand, so we really didn't put our peanut butter dispenser to work.

This fall the price of sunflower seed prompted us to look for other bird feed. My wife came home with a huge jar of peanut butter. The butter stick was loaded.

Chickadees promptly attacked the holes reachable from our balcony rail. One or two pecks in the soft butter, then a strenuous chewing and licking. With glasses I tried hard to identify the motions necessary to get the gummy goody down the hatch. The action was too fast. I don't think birds lick their lips. Yet, in these little birds I could almost feel the tongue probing I did to loosen the quick-gobbled lumps of peanut butter and crackers, years ago.

Fond chuckly memories of stacks of peanut buttered crackers came flooding back. If a tongue can't loosen it, a finger finds the glob. Sometimes the chicks paused to wipe a bill against the perch, then back for more—delicious.

The peeled stick gives few footholds to reach the upper holes. Some birds hover and snatch mouthfuls from the air. A few have learned to grasp hole edges. Nuthatches also come to the butter stick. They hang head down and reach the upper larders. Some hairy and downy woodpeckers are addicted, they dig out huge gobs and haul them away.

Our peanut butter is chunk style. Nut bits are carried off in triumph. It looks almost like finding diamonds. We rejoice for the lucky diners. I think the chickadees prize these tidbits most—so small a bird with such a nugget.

Some rumor says too much peanut butter is not good for birds. To be safe we leave the butter stick empty some each week—plenty of cracked grain and sunflower seed in the feeders. We cannot hold back for long.

When I'm tying the loaded butter stick back up, the chickadees sit by my hand impatiently. They cock beady eyes and "dee-dee" back and forth—and I can taste again that wonderful after school spread of nut brown goo. ❧

"All we get at our feeder is a bunch of darn sparrows." The object of that common complaint is the house sparrow, also called English sparrow and often less printable names.

These little birds aren't sparrows at all. They are one of the weaver finches. The family contains some of the finest bird weavers in the world, most of them resident in Africa. House sparrows certainly make no effort to live up to the family name. Their nests are anything but woven, a disorderly collection of grass, string, trash, and feathers.

Where house sparrows are abundant they may usurp all available holes, seriously limiting the less aggressive native cavity nesters. If there aren't enough holes, house sparrows will stuff their trash collections into bushes, among vines, gutters, or any crack or cranny they can enter. This nonselectivity of nest sites is one reason they are so abundant.

House sparrows were first introduced from England to America in 1850 and 1852. Nicolas Pike brought some to Brooklyn, New York, to destroy cankerworms which infested the shade trees. The sparrows showed a preference for horse dung and grain. The cankerworms are still with us, and so are the sparrows.

With the decline of horses, house sparrows have decreased, but with two other imports, starlings and pigeons, they are still our most common urban birds. Many farms also have resident barnyard flocks.

In spite of their aggressive behavior, sparrows aren't all bad. My first awareness of birds was at the circus parades. The cowboys and Indians were always last. Sparrows brought up the rear picking up the droppings. I was very small, and they were the only things down at my curb-side level—my first bird love.

I remember one I shot with an air rifle. It died in my hands. I cried. I have shot thousands of birds and animals since, yet never without a touch of that universal sorrow at death.

Most literature on sparrows complains of their dirtiness. I don't think they deserve it. Any species in quantity is dirty. Look at man's litter in our city streets, and we should know better. If city sparrows are sooty it is not of their making. It comes from association with us filthy humans. Country sparrows stay bright and handsome.

If house sparrows come to your feeders, enjoy them. Seeds scattered on the ground will keep most of them out of the feeder tray. Other species will find your feeder by following the house sparrows. The fancy birds will pick out the expensive seeds, while the street gamin sparrows roistering below clean up the cheap stuff, all too abundant in some commercial bird feed.

Forget your prejudices and enjoy these urchins. Viewed objectively, their antics are fun. 🌿

Everyone should keep something on hand in case friends drop in unexpectedly for dinner. This time of year we keep venison. We do our own butchering, bone out, and defat most of the meat. For quick resurrection from freezer to table we prefer the loins. We cut out the long strips along the backbone from the rump to the neck. Professional butchering puts these into roasts or chops. We cut them into convenient lengths and label the packages "loins." Our favorite recipe is called "Thirty Second Venison."

To thaw, we put the packages in a plastic bag, and submerge in water. In a few minutes it is soft enough to slice. You don't want it thawed completely. Slice the loins across the grain one-fourth inch thick.

While the meat is thawing, mix some blue cheese with your favorite salad dressing to a soft spreadable consistency. We prefer ranch dressing, but mayonnaise is also good. We haven't tried any others.

Spread the meat on aluminum foil. Don't worry if it's still partly frozen. Stick it under the broiler for thirty seconds—NO MORE. Remove and turn it over. Spread the cheese mixture over each venison slice. Return the meat to the broiler for another thirty seconds. Serve immediately or keep on a hot platter until everything is ready. Have the dinner plates warm. Never put venison on a cold dish.

In the South we hunted deer with dogs; shot only bucks often after long runs. I think it would have taken a month's hanging to relax that adrenalin-loaded meat. My fondest memory of Mississippi venison was the delicious gravy. The meat was almost tooth-proof. I never had a good piece of venison until I moved north many years later.

In Maine any deer was fair game. The first one I shot was a doe, she was unfrightened and never knew what hit her. My hunting partner insisted on cooking the steaks rare. It was a revelation. Those steaks lived up to all the promise of the venison gravy of my childhood—and tender! My love affair with venison started right there. I've been a meat hunter ever since.

I don't think doe venison is any better than buck venison under identical conditions. During the rut, bucks lose some of their fat and ram around a lot. The meat may be a little dryer and tougher. Out west deer season opens before the rut. The mule bucks we shot were as good eating as any venison I have tasted. So, gender isn't the most important thing in good venison. A clean kill on a standing deer is important. Animals wounded and chased don't taste good. Careful dressing and quick cooling all are important. After that it's up to the cook.

My venison-cooking rules are quick and rare, or slow and gently. Either way it is delicious eating. But when you are in a hurry for gourmet food for unexpected guests, try Thirty Second Venison. On second thought, why wait for guests? ✺

If life could be sustained by bread alone there would be no need for birds to be beautiful. In my observation outdoors I find myself mostly interested in the behavior of wildlife. Occasionally I am overwhelmed by the sheer beauty of some wild creature.

The other day a Bohemian waxwing visited us. I still feel the glow of his perfection. Cedar waxwings are our common member of that family. They are handsome, friendly birds, one of my favorites. Occasionally in winter their larger western cousins visit our state. The Bohemian who called at our new home was the first I had seen in Michigan.

Waxwings are ideal for bird watchers. They are calm, cool, and collected. So many of our feathered friends seem never to be still, mere streaks of motion through the woods. Our Bohemian visitor sat and surveyed the situation, superbly confident in his proper accoutrements. Gray fawn plumage was set off by his black mask edged in white. Yellow and white wing bars, cinnamon tail coverts, and a bright yellow tail tip completed the costume. The red droplets on his wing secondaries seemed only incidental—like earrings on a beautiful woman.

Our cedar waxwings are handsome. This bird was superb, and all alone. He sat aloof while evening grosbeaks squabbled over sunflower seeds. Waxwings aren't aggressive. They prefer fruit rather than seeds. This fellow just observed, then flew to the ground, plucked a wintergreen berry, and departed.

Waxwings don't really migrate. They wander about in winter, led by the supply of small fruit. Cedar waxwings nest here every summer. Sometimes they spend the winter. Occasionally Bohemian waxwings come in from the northwest in flocks. A single bird is most unusual. They like company. Our visitor was with the evening grosbeaks, but obviously disapproved of their bad manners.

I hunted up wild grapes and viburnum missed by the grouse. Next day I scrounged mountain ash berries from my neighbors. These are draped over the shrubs and stumps. If waxwings return, the welcome mat is out.

The waxwing family is a small one—only three species. The cedar waxwing is strictly North American. The Bohemian lives in our northwest and northern Eurasia. The Japanese waxwing inhabits eastern Siberia and Japan. He has a red tail tip and lacks the waxy wing feather droplets which give the family its name. All have crests and velvety plumage that looks as soft as it really is. Few other birds can rival their sleek well-groomed appearance.

I doubt if I shall ever forget that Bohemian waxwing sitting in our fir tree. Men surround themselves with drab and shabby sights. So God made birds beautiful, and gave us hope that there is something better. 🌿

You don't look for birds in a hole in the ground, but last deer season that's exactly where I found one of our most attractive winter residents. I was runway watching in a cedar swamp and gazed idly at a mouse hole under the roots of one of the trees. The appearance of a tiny black and white face and needle sharp beak in the middle of the hole shocked me to attention. Two beady black eyes peered out intently, and in an instant their owner flitted out and to a nearby tree where he immediately started headfirst down the trunk.

His upside down stance, black eye stripe, and rusty underparts identified him as a red-breasted nuthatch, miniature cousin to the white-breasted nuthatch so familiar at most bird feeders. The red-breasted prefers conifers, particularly spruce, and generally ranges further north than his larger cousin.

The city bird feeder seldom attracts these stylish little birds, but a suburban station filled with suet or sunflower seeds near a stand of conifers is very apt to find them on hand. A hunt camp I visit has several of them regularly accepting an offering of suet. They are friendly little birds, and often appear two or three at a time, but they seldom venture far from their beloved conifer swamps.

The one I was watching proceeded down the trunk, searching every cranny for insect eggs, spiders, and other tidbits. At the base, to my surprise, he again disappeared into a mouse hole only to appear again in a moment and dart to another tree to continue his search.

He was shortly joined by two others, and I watched them fascinated as they went about their winter insect eradication. Their soprano "yank-yank" notes so held my attention that I hardly heard a twig snap on the runway I was guarding. I turned just in time to see a deer's hindquarters disappear into the cover. I never did find out if it was a buck. 🌿

The most charming and exasperating rascal in our wilds is the raccoon. These bandit-faced foragers of our woodlands live by their wits. In so doing, they display more human characteristics than any of our other native animals. These behavior similarities are probably the reason coons have been able to fare so well in the face of civilization. Certainly that's what makes them so entertaining.

Our animal fables are full of tributes to the raccoons' cleverness. In my generation every farm boy either had a pet coon or knew someone who did. These domestic associations were usually of short duration, for their ability to get into endless mischief soon exhausted the patience of the entire household. Their front feet are almost as versatile as a man's hand. They quickly learn how to open latches, doorknobs, and even refrigerators.

To really appreciate raccoons you should watch them in the wilds. They are chiefly nocturnal, but do get about some in daytime. They are so abundant in Michigan that almost anyone who spends much time in the wilds is apt to encounter one. Wooded streamsides are the best places. Late January and February are the best times. Then the breeding season keeps them abroad more in daylight.

The raccoon is probably our most successful predator, yet he certainly doesn't look the part. Watch a fox or a mink in the woods. They are the classic hunters all the time. For the coon, the wilds are a supermarket. Anything edible is theirs for the taking. I watched one recently foraging along the thin stream-side ice. Every open hole was probed, bringing up mud and an occasional tidbit. Every hollow and brush pile was investigated. His pace was sedate, and his curiosity insatiable. He resembled nothing so much as a portly house-wife on a shopping tour. I could almost see him read the labels and "squeeze the Charmin."

Due to their abundance and their preference for shoreline habitat, raccoons are one of the primary controlling factors in waterfowl nesting success. In many areas they destroy well over half the duck nests. Wood ducks are particularly vulnerable. A coon will visit a known nesting cavity nightly collecting the eggs as laid and the duck too, if she's cornered.

Nowadays coons have few natural enemies. Horned owls are the only ones of importance in our area. A coon's curiosity makes him easy to trap, but from a sporting standpoint the old-fashioned coon hunt is hard to beat. It helps keep the population in bounds, and the quarry has a bag of tricks that will tax even the most clever hunter and hounds. ❦

My wife calls them "little black and white ducks." I call them "whistlers." They are common goldeneyes. Their scientific name is *Bucephala clangula*—Greek, meaning with a broad forehead; Latin, meaning a noise, the whistle of their wings. They are one of our most common wintering waterfowl.

This year one of our boarders is crippled. His wings seem O.K. but he can't get off the water. Our daily handouts of cracked corn are proving a godsend. Whistlers dive for their food. We throw some well beyond the ice to make sure Crip gets his.

Our main aquatic boarders are black ducks. They feed from land or by tipping up in water up to eighteen inches deep. Despite their extreme wariness they occasionally wander about our front yard gleaning feeder spillings. When very hungry they will dive for food but they are not very good at it. The goldeneyes swim underwater right amongst the tipping blacks, snatching grain just like a domestic duck feeding from a pan. The blacks won't stand competition, run the little black-and-whities to deeper water, much to my wife's distress.

Of course, we do not know why our cripple is incapacitated. Goldeneyes stick to big water till freeze-up. Almost none are shot on our river. Most of the hens and young go south or east to the Atlantic Coast. One of our earliest signs of spring is the return of these migrants to join the old bull whistlers who have toughed out the cold.

Goldeneyes eat about three-fourths animal food. In winter on our stream it's mainly crayfish. The healthy divers in our flock regularly catch them over four inches long. These are swallowed whole with much shaking and gulping. Corn is not the best sick duck food. Lead-poisoned birds quickly die when corn fed. High protein helps recovery. I think our cripple is too weak to catch live food. He can dive—disappears quickly when I come to spread feed. He usually surfaces under a drift pile, safe from me but not the mink which regularly hunts our shore.

Crippled ducks always go ashore. In heavily hunted areas a man with a good retriever can often limit out by touring islands and shorelines at days end. Our ailing bird mounts the ice daily. There he preens and oils the feathers which can't be kept dry while afloat. Whistlers feet are set much further back than a black duck. They must stand straighter to maintain balance. Their waddle is much duckier. They can't run very fast.

Despite these handicaps our Crip leaves the warm thirty-two-degree water to complete his toilet. From our window my wife suffers every chill breeze that strikes him. She bleeds for his fight for life. We cheer each day of his survival. ✺

A winter sparrow with a dark spot in the center of its gray unstreaked breast is a tree sparrow. He probably won't be in a tree. If you think you heard a bird singing from the snow-covered brush, you did. It's a tree sparrow.

Most of our winter birds make sounds—few sing. My bird-counting partner has remarkable hearing. On a recent Christmas count he located kinglets in a dense conifer forest by the "noise they make." Their noise was dead silence to me. My tired old ears seldom hear winter birds. This year I got a treat.

During the deer season the woods across our stream was full of sparrows. Logging has left windrows of slash. New openings are waist high in weeds and grass—sparrow heaven. My deer watching was constantly distracted by little flitty movements. Suddenly there was a song; tinkly, canarylike—a real bird song. I couldn't believe it. Carefully I turned to look. It was a tree sparrow, the first I had ever heard sing. In a moment he was gone, but others filtered through my weed-patch hide. A few stopped near my noise-dulled ears and tinkled some song. It made the deerless morning a success.

Tree sparrows are the most common winter sparrow in the mid–United States. They summer north all the way to the Arctic Ocean. I think they sing in winter because our winters may be no worse than their springs. People who hear well say tree sparrows sing most in late winter. By the time spring migration starts they are singing as much as the song sparrows just arriving from the South. Scientifically, their winter songs may be just premature territorial announcements. That's what most birds' songs are for, but I think some birds sing for other reasons. Certainly the little songs I heard had to be fun. They just sounded like it.

I don't know how tree sparrows got their name. In their Arctic home they nest mostly on the ground. When they visit us in winter they spend little time in trees. The three that are wintering at our place never fly up to the feeders. They pick out fine bits from the cracked corn we spread for doves.

Some years ago ornithologists felt they had to justify each bird species by its benefits to man. One of them estimated that in the state of Iowa tree sparrows ate about 875 tons of weed seeds each winter. This is a remarkable and interesting statistic, even though it's no longer necessary to justify sparrows' existence. For tree sparrows their song alone is enough. 🦋

TGIF doesn't mean a thing to wildlife. Only people have weeks. Friday is just another day to the great outdoors. If weekends are different from weekdays, it is only in the greater disturbance created by the presence of people.

All life on earth moves to the rhythms of great natural units of time, the year, month, day. Only man chops time into other units. Every society has had to invent the week. Ancient Greeks split their month into three ten-day weeks. Primitive tribes use a market week varying from four to ten days. We get our week from Genesis. Its seven days has been spread through the civilized world by Christianity and Muhammadanism. A community functions more smoothly if regular recurring days are set aside for marketing, time off from the job, and worship. Wild things don't need weeks because they don't go to market, hold jobs, or have religion.

Western civilization invented the hour. Man used to eat when he was hungry. Now I get hungry at noon just because the hour says it's lunchtime. I'm not sure what system is best, but modern societies have to have smaller units of time. We invented minutes because trains must run on time, factory shifts change, appointments must be kept. I remember hurrying for my commuter train as the starter tolled, "The 5:51 ready on track 19." Now even minutes are too slow. With space travel a second is a long time. Milliseconds and microseconds are important—but not to wildlife.

But *time* is important to all things. Migrating birds navigate by the sun or the stars. They must be aware of time to allow for the varying positions of these heavenly bodies. Next spring the Kirtland's warblers will hit their jack pine patches right on the head with just the stars and their built-in time sense to guide them. To navigate as accurately as a warbler, man needs a compass, a sextant, and a chronometer.

Since the dawn of agriculture man's food supply has depended upon his awareness of the seasons—when to plow, when to plant. Wild plants have the same awareness. They must bloom and start seed growth months before autumn frosts curtail their activities. A snowshoe hare must start growing his white fur long before the first snowfall if he is to escape the winter predators. Wild things may not think about the future, but they know it's there. What they lack in intelligence they make up in instinct.

The length of daylight times the swallows' arrival at Capistrano just as it times many seasonal rhythms. Generally you can't make appointments with wildlife. They don't count time. They live it. ❧